Africana Studies

EDITED BY GRANT FARRED

Africana Studies

THEORETICAL FUTURES

TEMPLE UNIVERSITY PRESS

Philadelphia • *Rome* • *Tokyo*

TEMPLE UNIVERSITY PRESS
Philadelphia, Pennsylvania 19122
tupress.temple.edu

Library of Congress Cataloging-in-Publication Data

Names: Farred, Grant, editor.
Title: Africana studies : theoretical futures / edited by Grant Farred.
Description: Philadelphia : Temple University Press, 2022. | Includes bibliographical
   references and index. | Summary: "This book showcases new and expansive
   possibilities for Africana studies scholarship by collecting works across disciplines
   that push the boundaries of the discipline into topics both broader and more
   specific than traditionally approached: in philosophy, literature, music, political
   science, and more"—Provided by publisher.
Identifiers: LCCN 2021051888 (print) | LCCN 2021051889 (ebook) |
   ISBN 9781439923061 (cloth) | ISBN 9781439923078 (paperback) |
   ISBN 9781439923085 (pdf)
Subjects: LCSH: African Americans—Study and teaching (Higher) | Black people—
   Study and teaching (Higher) | African diaspora—Study and teaching (Higher) |
   African Americans—Intellectual life. | Black people—Intellectual life. | African
   diaspora—Intellectual life.
Classification: LCC E184.7 .A3173 2022 (print) | LCC E184.7 (ebook) |
   DDC 305.896/07300711—dc23/eng/20220214
LC record available at https://lccn.loc.gov/2021051888
LC ebook record available at https://lccn.loc.gov/2021051889

Printed in the United States of America

9 8 7 6 5 4 3 2 1

This volume is dedicated to

Ms. Renée Milligan,

Ms. Donna Pinnisi, and

Ms. Treva Levine,

*Africana Studies and Research Center
administrative staff extraordinaire;*

And to

Tẹ́júmọ́lá Ọláníyan, April 1959–November 2019:

*A scholar who embodied the Africana studies
imaginary at its very best.*

You are missed, as friend, colleague, interlocutor.

Contents

    / *Akin Adeṣọkan*   145

8   Seeing, Hearing, Breathing, *and* Witnessing from the Africana
    Center at Cornell: An Afterword / *Pierre-Philippe Fraiture*   163

    Contributors   175

    Index   177

Acknowledgments

thank all the contributors to this volume for making its publication possible. Everyone worked in good faith, for which I am grateful.

I also thank our editor at Temple University Press, Ryan Mulligan, whose diligence, perspicuity, and commitment is exemplary. I have been the beneficiary of these qualities on more than one occasion.

My thanks also to the staff at Cornell University's Africana Studies and Research Center. Treva Levine is always an enthusiastic supporter; Donna Pinnisi, notwithstanding her social reticence, can be relied upon to make everything function smoothly, and then some. Renée Milligan, truly, has no peer. My debt to her is unpayable, an imbalanced state of affairs she, I have no doubt, enjoys tremendously. Alas, such is her nature, such is her disposition.

Finally, this collection pays tribute to the memory of the late and sadly missed Tẹjúmọ́lá Ọláníyan. Tẹjú was a friend to some in this collection (and here I have Akin Adeṣọkan in mind especially), but perhaps more importantly, Teju was a scholar revered and treasured by all who came into contact with him over the course of his life. Generous and thoughtful to a fault, he made of himself a gift to all of us.

It is our hope that this collection can, in a small way, pay tribute to who it is you were and how it is you did your work.

Grant Farred, Ithaca, 2021

Africana Studies

Introduction

"Theoretical Futures"

The Creation of a Concept

GRANT FARRED

According to the Nietzschean verdict, you will know nothing
through concepts unless you have first created them—that is,
constructed them in an intuition specific to them: a field, a
plane, and a ground that must not be confused with them but
that shelters their seeds and the personae who cultivate them.
—GILLES DELEUZE *and* FÉLIX GUATTARI, *What Is Philosophy?*

Africana Studies: Theoretical Futures is, in Gilles Deleuze and Félix
Guattari's sense, a creation. It is the creation of a concept, a concept
signed "theoretical futures of Africana studies." "Theoretical" is understood here as the production of a framework within which thinking for
the becoming of Africana studies could be accommodated. That is, a thinking for that which Africana studies must become, must become as it as-
sembles a series of components. We might name these components conjec-
tures, ideas, imaginings. Regardless, in every instance this theorizing (for)
Africana studies turns, relentlessly, on the creation of components. It is
through the creation of components that thinking for the theoretical futures of Africana is undertaken. Theorizing Africana studies so as to make
it—in the course of its becoming—a creative mode for engaging those questions, difficulties, modes of being that mark, with more or less intensity,
black and diasporic life, in its broadest instantiation. (Theorizing through
this "assemblage," in Deleuze and Guattari's terms; an "assemblage," the
theoretical futures of Africana studies that is not—yet?—a body without
organs, that most tantalizing, elusive, and provocative of their concepts.[1])

Furthermore, as the plural indicates, theoretical futures is a concept that
undertakes to create a plane of immanence that can sustain—support, pro-
voke, cultivate—Africana studies as a singular yet polyvalent mode of
thinking. Thinking what it means to be black, African diasporic (as the
principal but by no means only conditions implicitly under consideration

in this volume) in our world. Thinking what it means to be immersed, fully embedded in our world, in the life of our world. To exist and remain within the (in)finite field, in the possibilities, difficulties, cruelties, intensities, desires of our world and, in so doing, to stringently oppose any inclining toward transcendence. This is how, broadly speaking, Deleuze and Guattari conceive of the plane of immanence. A conceiving that, as they recognize in *What Is Philosophy?*, must always allow for the reemergence, no matter how fleeting, of transcendence.[2] We are seemingly never done with guarding against its reemergence, thinking always in expectation of its return, a return Deleuze and Guattari seek to restrict to a temporal and conceptual minimum.

Africana Studies: Theoretical Futures marks, as such, not only the construction of a plane. It also takes as its project the posing of problems that will in any way forestall, interrupt, or delay the becoming of Africana studies' theoretical futures. However, the chapters gathered here address those problems, for the most part, implicitly rather than naming them explicitly. (And in taking up these problems—among which we might include the closed archive, certain entrenched modes of essentialism, intradiasporic tensions, and so on—we suggest that in conceiving through implication rather than direct naming a tendency toward transcendence might be discerned. Such a line of argument would, for all its Sturm and Drang, be well wide of the mark. The work of the plane of immanence, or the plateau, is to forge a series of new connections outside existing lines of flight and, in so doing, to think the problems through a different concept and through a new and different series of connections. In this way, the concept theoretical futures will be able to entangle extant problems in a set of connections that will bring different potentialities into being.) The volume is, then, in the sense offered by Deleuze and Guattari, creative rather than negative. A concept, they argue, is "never valued by reference to what it prevents: it is valued for its incomparable position and its own creation."[3] At stake in this collection is the work of "creation," of providing a terrain on which theories of Africana studies—how to think it, how to delineate the terms of its becoming, what set of problems to pose, what lines of inquiry to pursue—might be struggled over. The project is, for this reason, not in the least about preventing this or that idea from coming into being (from becoming, as it were); the project is decidedly not to predominate the discourse or to preclude the invention of new components. Au contraire. Within every concept, indeed, a priori the creation of every concept, is the necessary recognition that the concept is itself nothing other than a struggle against limit. A struggle against the limit it perceives in extant concepts and the anticipation of the struggle among the components out of which the concept is constructed. Deleuze and Guattari, as we know from their oeuvre more broadly, are fully aware of this. Hence their notions of territorialization, reterritorialization, and deterritorialization—a trio of terms for which this Introduction will shortly offer its own working definition.

The creation of a concept is a matter of no small import because, institutionally, Africana studies is a discipline of very recent standing, at most five decades old, a discipline birthed out of the intense cultural and political struggles that marked the United States in the 1960s.[4] In most institutions, even in the United States where it first found articulation, Africana studies is of a much more recent vintage. In some sites it is more or less embattled than others, a discipline whose right to institutional existence remains contested; it is subject to scrutiny, skepticism, and critique from a different array of forces, forces that have always been at work and, indeed, have emerged with fresh vigor to launch a renewed assault on black life in post-2016 America. In some institutions, however, the discipline has imbricated itself into the fabric of the university's life, and in still others (although these are too few in number), Africana studies has, for now at least, secured its place. It still awaits that moment when it can be a thriving intellectual enterprise. (Given the strange conjuncture that is our moment—the coinciding of racism, police brutality, xenophobia, the pandemic with its disproportionate effect on not only minorities but women more broadly, economic uncertainty, food insecurity, and so on—the question might be posed, if not now, when? If not now, then when will a discipline such as Africana studies or Asian American studies or gender and sexuality studies locate itself at the very core of institutional life? Now, at a conjuncture when planetary life appears to, for all political intents and purposes, have reached an unprecedented crisis? Is not now the moment for the thinking of these disciplines to constitute the first lines of flight for all institutional thinking?)

Africana Studies: Theoretical Futures is aware of this institutional history, and indeed, all the chapters (in one way or another)—although Chapters 1–4 and the sublime Afterword come readily to mind—acknowledge the import of this history and address and take up its difficulties. The concept, then, is a response to—a critique of—that mode of thinking (institutional and extrainstitutional, political, cultural, sociopolitical, as you wish) to which it is heir. And, because of what the concept has inherited, let us abbreviate it. Appending a name to it, "theoretical futures," we must decide on how it stands in relation to what it has been bequeathed.

Because of this, *Africana Studies: Theoretical Futures* is guided by a specific intuition. It takes as its project the construction of a concept in response to what it understands as the problem facing black life. ("All concepts are connected to problems without which they would have no meaning,"[5] Deleuze and Guattari remind us.) That is, how it might help black life survive, what conditions must be secured for black life to thrive, and so on. Black thinking, in its many registers: philosophically, nonphilo-sophically, in institutions of higher learning, in the sphere of popular cul-ture, within the arena of representational politics, and so forth; in a word, thinking for the dangers that threaten, daily, black life, as well as the poten-tialities immanent—in place, always already existing—to the plane of im-manence. As Deleuze and Guattari caution, while remaining hopeful of what it is the concept might yield, "a possible world, the possibility of a frightening world."⁶

The problem, we can say, demands a concept, the creation of a concept whose immanence is such that it not only accounts for a "possible world" that might very well be "frightening" (already the condition of black life, we would be well justified to rejoin) but, in seeking to eradicate those compo-nents responsible for producing the fear, might extend itself into a series of successive tomorrows that accentuate possibility, pure and simple. Possibil-ity, that is, as that affirmation of life fully cognizant of the fear it must eradicate—or if not eradicate, then keep in check at the very least. The chap-ters that constitute *Africana Studies: Theoretical Futures* represent, each in its own distinct way, components of a concept that can accommodate theo-retical futures. Components that connect with each other to form a singular line of flight, components that approach each other and then, in quick suc-cession, take their leave of each other. Components that, by turns, form entanglements and disentanglements. Components linked, as close as neighbors, distant as cousins. In Nietzsche's poetic phrasing, these compo-nents are constructed out of the language of "high winds, unrest, contradic-tion."⁷

That is, this volume has territorialized the concept that is theoretical futures so that one component of the concept may or may not extend seam-lessly into another—one mutating with little or no apparent transition into the other or one jaggedly abutting its successor, cutting across, violently, another component. In other words, the concept that is theoretical futures, a plane of immanence that, in our thinking, extends far beyond the limits of this volume, recognizes that the various components that lay claim to the theoretical futures of Africana studies are in constant struggle with not only each other but also with what, and how, the concept is becoming.

On the plane of immanence, one component can easily find itself in conflict with another because, as Deleuze and Guattari point out, "there is no concept with only one component."⁸ Because of this, it is explicable that one component will not wish to give way, does not want to cede conceptual territory. In relation to which it does not, in Deleuze and Guattari's terms, want to be de- or reterritorialized. "The concept," then, must be appre-hended as a "whole because it totalizes its components, but it is a fragmen-tary whole."⁹ With this dialectical phrasing (much as Deleuze and Guattari strongly favor multiplicity over the dialectic), containing within it the propensity for totalizing while acknowledging (if not quite celebrating) the fragmentariness of the whole, Deleuze and Guattari provide an apt and incisive description of the construction of the plane of immanence that is *Africana Studies: Theoretical Futures*. Each chapter in the collection operates in a distinct register—in disciplinary terms, race and diasporic studies (John E. Drabinski, Chapter 1; Sarah Then Bergh, Chapter 6); politics and political science, the study of the state in Africa, specifically (Radwa Saad, Chapter 3; Kasereka Kavwahirehi, Chapter 4); philosophy, or philosophical Marxism (Zeyad el Nabolsy, Chapter 2); literary theory, of the singularly poetic variety (Gregory Pardlo, Chapter 5; Pierre-Philippe Fraiture, Chapter 8); and creative nonfiction (Akin Adeṣọkan, Chapter 7).

Several of the chapters, however, do not operate in only one register. As much as anything, what the chapters share is their immanence. In their territorialization of the plane of immanence, in constructing the concept that is theoretical futures, there is, both implicitly and explicitly, a refusal of the metaphysical, even as the metaphysical lurks with the intent of manifesting itself. These chapters address what exists as the problem for, metonymically phrased, black life, the problem in its many iterations; a series of problems it would be fair to say that seem to be constantly growing. It is on this plane that these thinkings immerse themselves to address the problems that must be confronted, problems that have persisted, and thus have existed within a number (an infinite number?) of previous planes of immanence. For this reason this series of difficulties, we should insist, must be faced rather than transcended. (That which is immanent to the plane is that which is of imminent concern.) These chapters not only operate in more than one register; they also construct a plane of immanence that functions on more than one stratum; and what is more, they do so with a certain fluidity. (These strata are part of what, in Deleuze and Guattari's oeuvre, constitutes the rhizome. In their work, the rhizome can, in a necessarily insufficient word, be taken as a series of tubular rather than rooted connections. That is, a series of smooth, not striated; antiarborescent; rootless; horizontal, not vertical, connections that allows the flourishing of multiplicity. "A rhizome," they write, "ceaselessly establishes connections between semiotic chains, organizations of power, and circumstances relative to the arts, sciences, and social struggles." The rhizome is always connected to the outside, thereby multiplying itself infinitely and establishing "lines of flight" that remain distinct, despite being entangled with other lines of flight.[10])

In this regard, Deleuze and Guattari argue,

each concept will therefore be considered as the point of coincidence, condensation, or accumulation of its own components. The conceptual point constantly traverses its components, rising and falling within them. In this sense, each component is an *intensive feature*, an intensive ordinate [*ordonnée intensive*], which must be understood not as general or particular but as a pure and simple singularity—"a" possible world, "a" face, "some" words—that is particularized or generalized depending on whether it is given variable values or a constant function.[11]

That is, the chapters have multiple nodes of connection, "point[s] of coincidence, condensation, or accumulation of [their] own components," so that they, on this fluid plane of immanence, "move about" ("move up or down," "up and down"; "left and right, right and left," as it were, sometimes simultaneously operating on more than one level) between this level and that—what Deleuze and Guattari describe as "rising and falling." In so doing, the various "components," some of which have been assigned "variable values" while others perform a "constant function," create and re-create a web of connections that, in its multiplicity, opens new theoretical possibilities.[12] The web, of course, intensifies and multiplies the number of possible theoretical futures, always bespeaking not only a multiple but an infinitely mobile future or futures.

Thus, each of the chapters, individually and in their connective multiplicity, creates (enhances) the possibility that it will, at some possible future intensity, exceed (transgress) the concept that is theoretical futures as it creates or finds itself instrumental in the founding of a new plane of immanence because the problems that it takes up in theoretical futures have now spilled over into, been conscripted by, a different plane of immanence (and the difference may be one of degree or of extremity) but one that has some connection to theoretical futures. The problem raised by, say, African Marxism (Marxism in Africa; Marxist theories as they apply to Africa, and so on) or the state in Africa (again, the African state; the conflict, ever ongoing, or so it would seem, between the military and civil society; democracy in Africa) in theoretical futures will, one can with great certainty, not be resolved by theoretical futures.

However, the concept, the conceptual personae (of which the state and Marx, or cultural politics, might present the most obvious examples; not quite Nietzsche's Zarathustra or Plato's Socrates but familiar and, in all probability, recognizable) created by the concept, could be appropriated in the creation of a new concept to address a series of problems that are familiar but by no means an exact replica of what exists on the plane of immanence that is theoretical futures. If the concept does its work, it will show its creativity to be not so much sovereign—that is, faithful to theoretical futures—but generative. It will show itself as that iteration of theoretical futures that belongs, infelicitously, as it were, to futures immanent not only to this particular set of theoretical problems.

The Intensive Feature

> The concept speaks the event, not the essence or the thing.
> —DELEUZE and GUATTARI, *What Is Philosophy?*

While the volume bears the title *Africana Studies* (which we might, in this context, take as both the "thing" and the "essence"), the work of creating a plane of immanence is borne by the subtitular *Theoretical Futures*. Africana studies, as such, marks, again, both the thing and the essence (the second of which, in a related form, "essentialism,"[13] is at the core of the problematic that is Africana studies), but the concept claims for its territorialization theoretical futures. In doing so, the creation of the concept acknowledges that the discipline, Africana studies, has a history. That is, it has in the course of its becoming—coming into being, sustaining that being, institutionally—accumulated, inter alia, a set of tools, methodologies, professional practices and modes of inquiry that mark its institutional life. These accumulations have, needless to say, been subject to change over the course of the disciplinary evolution of Africana studies. All of this is to say that the discipline, thus, is recognized as the thing. (And decidedly not, as in Kant's transcendental sense, as the thing-in-itself—the proposition of which Nietzsche could not bear, in no small measure, of course, because for Nietzsche, exiled to Basel, Switzerland, to teach, Kant represented the institutional animal par excellence.)

The work of creating the concept theoretical futures thus falls to the subtitular. Or perhaps I should say, it is the work the subtitular assigns itself. The concept, then, as distinct from the discipline, or at best auxiliary or adjacent to it, not simply for its own sake; that is, not only because the concept wants to distinguish itself from the concept but because the concept responds directly to—is connected to—the set of problems it, in Deleuze and Guattari's sense, intuits.[14] Creating the plane of immanence that is theoretical futures begins with the work of ensuring multiplicity. There can, on this plane of immanence, be no one future for Africana studies. There can be only *futures*: multiple futures, operating on several stratifications, sometimes forming a complementary connection; at others, points of friction and dissonance predominate. All the while, these futures are created, unimpeded by disciplinary demands and institutional strictures, unburdened by but not impervious to disciplinary history. The lines of *becoming* that are these futures are free to interact with as many other concepts and conceptual personae as is necessary. The concept, then, always has to revivify its reason for becoming. It is necessary, that is, to follow the line of thinking (or "lines of flight," in Deleuze and Guattari's terms) that a particular problem presents while remaining cognizant of the connections (several or only a few, maybe even only one) that may emanate from following this line of flight.

Thus, *Africana Studies: Theoretical Futures* offers, in its chapters' various articulations, specific conjunctures, signal points of intersection, conflict and difference, creating a resonance among them that is by no means removed (that is, it is not far removed) from dissonance. If, that is, we attribute to dissonance the potentiality for making different—intensely different—claims on the plane of immanence, for staking out different parts of the territorialization that is the theoretical futures of Africana studies. One of the salient features of a "fragmentary whole" is precisely that it is so constituted that the whole seems, at crucial or apparently insignificant intensities, capable of dispersing into fragments. That is, the whole is at once tenaciously singular and so tenuously constructed as to risk infinite dispersion, thereby opening up into—opening itself up to—theoretical futures that, in all likelihood, will also be marked by the fragmentariness that is particular to the whole's tenuous resilience.

Despite the possibility for fragmentariness, this potentiality for resonance among chapters makes it possible that, for example, the two chapters on politics and political science not only amplify each other but also draw into their orbit, connect on their strata with, chapters that take up the difficulty that is the diasporic experience. In so doing, the ways in which the chapters contribute to the plane of immanence mean that the project as a whole not only ensures that the concept theoretical futures is brought into being but achieves, critical to Deleuze and Guattari, "consistency" and "intensity." (Furthermore, in the spirit of their attention to "sensation" in *What Is Philosophy?*, the volume concludes with Fraiture's delineation and exact naming of the senses that is, literally, organized according to the senses, as, one might say, befits the creation of a concept.) In the "Translator's Foreword" to *A Thousand Plateaus*, Brian Massumi suggests that Deleuze and Guattari's plane of consistency is best understood as a style: "The way the combination is made is an example of what Deleuze and Guattari call consistency—not in the sense of a homogeneity, but as a holding together of disparate elements (also known as a 'style')."[15]

The chapters, in their occupation of the plane of immanence, apply torque (philosophical pressure, or intensity of thought) on each other. These are, as Massumi would have it, "disparate"—but not disconnected or dissociable—"elements" that "hold[] together" on the plateau that is theoretical futures. The various critiques of the state (Kavwahirehi, Saad), say, encounter an entirely new and different set of intensities when read alongside the poetics of loss or remembrance (Adeṣọkan and Pardlo, respectively) or cultural possibility (Then Bergh; which might even be rendered as optimism), to say nothing of the philosophical contemplation of diaspora (Drabinski). In this construction of the plane of immanence, the creation of intensities thus emerges, as it should, not only from the individual chapters in themselves (obvious enough in Drabinski and El Nabolsy's contributions) but out of the "points of coincidence, condensation, or accumulation" that mark the relations among the chapters. The plane of immanence that is theoretical futures thus simultaneously or according to different intensities, randomly or in sequence, territorializes, deterritorializes, and reterritorializes the components. Consequently, every chapter is subject to these forces because they operate on the plane of immanence.

Concept/Concepts

It is not, however, only in relation to each other that the chapters exert their force and intensity. Saliently, as with all other concepts, the theoretical futures concept

> also has a *becoming* that involves its relationship with concepts situated on the same plane. Here concepts link up with each other, support one another, coordinate their contours, articulate their respective problems, and belong to the same philosophy, even if they have different histories. In fact, having a finite number of components, every concept will branch off toward other concepts that are differently composed but that constitute other regions of the same plane, answer to problems that can be connected to each other, and participate in a co-creation. A concept requires not only a problem through which it recasts or replaces earlier concepts but a junction of problems where it combines with other coexisting concepts.[16]

Every concept, then, is (potentially, at the very least) saturated with other concepts and, almost without question or exception, the components of other concepts. Every becoming is, in this way, a thinking-with—or against and with, and sometimes a thinking-for that which is not-yet—other concepts. Thus, every thinking contains within itself something other than itself, so that every thinking is already on the way to becoming something else. Because of this, every concept not only belongs to its own set of intensities but is open to being territorialized, reterritorialized, or deterritorialized by the past, present, and future. Theoretical futures thus is as much its own becoming—a coming into theoretical being, a becoming that belongs, indefatigably, to its own particular set of intensities—as it is coming out of, as acknowledged earlier, the tradition that is Africana studies. And, as it should be, theoretical futures—in which we take futures to mean the territorialization in its three manifestations—is that concept out of which other concepts will emerge. Will, not to put too fine a point on it, be able to come. (Let us, for the purposes of this Introduction, take the meaning of "territorialization" as the making of the plane of immanence; "reterritorialization" as the cutting across, remaking, through the creation of new or mutant components; and "deterritorialization" as the taking apart or uncreating of the concept.)

A territorialization, reterritorialization, and deterritorialization in which other, new, planes of immanence will emerge, in which components (that is, both the ideas that govern the individual chapters and the elements—microcomponents, shall we say) of theoretical futures will make themselves immanent, either through resonance or dissonance. Or we might say, the concept that is theoretical futures ushers in a regime of resonant-dissonance, dissonant-resonance, or both. What we think we hear—discern—in the concept is susceptible to distortion, out of which a new, dissonant-resonant unfamiliarity might emerge.

A dissonant-resonance or resonant-dissonance on the order of, say, Angelique Kidjo singing Celia Cruz. *Celia*, Kidjo's 2019 tribute to Cruz, the queen of Cuban salsa, voices two diasporic songbirds calling to each other, across an ocean filled with traumatic memory, across musical genres—the African woman from Benin, a virtuoso in lustrous soul-pop, punctuated with joy and pain, enunciates the intensity of connection wrought of deterritorialization and reterritorialization. *Celia* is the reterritorialization of a black Cuban woman's cry. What beauty, what wrenching, unforgettable beauty. How it haunts the black diaspora, how it turns the black diaspora back onto—into—itself; mangled, remade, unutterably unrecognizable. Yeatsian, with a deterritorialized twist: "A terrible beauty has been [re]born." Salsa deterritorialized. Celia Cruz, we might go so far as to suggest, territorialized in Porto-Novo (or in Quidah, Kidjo's hometown), Benin. Quidah, Porto-Novo, and Havana, Cuba, are points on a line of flight. Points that meet in the middle, if we take the middle to be that particular note on which Cruz and Kidjo conjoin, with a singular intensity, before taking their partial leave, each on her own line of flight, each line of flight "growing [multiple] offshoots." In their notes, the reorganization of an entire plane of immanence.

Or we could consider the ways in which the Afrobeat vibes of a Fẹlá Kuti track seem to turn the world upside down. Or downside up. Or in taking down the head of state in "Coffin for Head of State," Kuti offers a creative promise: rhizomatize the state, make new points of connection, create new lines of flight. Refuse the arborescent top-down model. That model runs from the head to the soles, constituted as it always is of the poor, the disenfranchised, those who can never quite get themselves off the ground; they can now forge horizontal connections with all those around them, those who are outside them. The work is to make a new plane of immanence, with neither head nor toe. Bring new "aggregates of intensities" into being.[17] How else are we to establish our relation to Kuti's music, especially—at least in this moment—as it pertains to his creation of a *Coffin for Head of State*? (Is Kuti's album, with its—eighteenth-century French class war, twentieth-century anti-colonial African struggles—revolutionary overtones and its ominous undertones for the polis, for the state, for those who stand at the head of the state that musical conception that allows us to conceive of Deleuze and Guattari's "body without organs"?) Or we could posit the following: on *Coffin for Head of State* Kuti aligns himself explicitly with the thinking of Deleuze and Guattari. Through his album title, Kuti provides an intense, reverberating soundtrack to Down with State Philosophy, the French thinkers' anthemic cry. A cry that punctuates their work, a cry especially resonant in *A Thousand Plateaus*, where they present the importance of "nomad philosophy." Fẹlá Kuti's discography, in its openness to the world (the same can be said of Kidjo and Cruz) and in its relentless demand for creativity, is what happens when you follow—musically, creatively, poetically—Deleuze and Guattari's injunction, "Don't sow, grow offshoots!"[18] Kuti's Afrobeat is how you put philosophy to music. Kuti's music is Deleuze and Guattari's "middle, . . . where things speed up."[19] Speed up in the cause of doing away entirely with the aridity that is "State philosophy." Speeding up the construction of the coffin in which the State, its rotting head (devoid of creativity, no longer able to think for the concept), and the entire carcass of State philosophy, is laid to rest. Unceremoniously. With all due haste. "Obasanjo is a liar," scream the liner notes on Fẹlá's album. In the middle, sound and fury rise to a crescendo. In the middle there is always the possibility that the crescendo can sustain itself, indefinitely. "A rhizome ceaselessly establishes connections between semiotic chains . . . and social struggles." The nomad is the enduring offshoot of the rhizome.

In this poetic way, the components out of which theoretical futures is constructed never belong, as is true of all other components that make up a plane of immanence, only to themselves—to their component self or to their plane of immanence, always capable of establishing new lines of flight, of generating (further) multiplicities, always raising the possibilities of destratification.

New Thinkings

Every plane of immanence, therefore, every construction of a theoretical future, is already the becoming of something else. Already, itself, marks the becoming of something other than itself. The concept is marked, in all probability indelibly, as much by the determination to create a new concept—

which is why it must be named "event"—as it marks the turning away from and against, as Deleuze and Guattari phrase it (and we should not be deceived by their parenthesis), "'a' possible world, 'a' face, 'some' words." To create, obviously, a new and different possible world, to mold a new face, and to conjure up a set of words that are better suited to the intensities of the concept than those, seemingly amorphous (some), but of course, this is by no means so because every one of those some words (every one of that sum of words), carries import, has impacts and effects in the world.

In this way the concept is always a straining against what it takes to be (as it must; otherwise, there would be no reason to create the concept) the insufficiencies, failures, oversights, and omissions of extant concepts. "These are," Deleuze and Guattari write, "the intensive ordinates of the Idea: a claim will be justified only through a neighborhood, a greater or lesser proximity it 'has had' in relation to the Idea, in the survey of an always necessarily anterior time."[20] *Africana Studies: Theoretical Futures*, however, much as it recognizes the particular intensities of its relationship to concepts that are au courant, those concepts that have lost their relevance (if not always their institutional standing; a resilience and continued existence, one might argue, that owes everything to their shortcomings as a concept—that is, the stubborn inability to do the work of the concept and those that belong to a "necessarily anterior time") and those concepts that retain a resonance that is more, and sometimes less, useful, is only incidentally concerned with that which it, in truth, seeks to displace. Those concepts it intends to deterritorialize, determinedly, while setting out a—and on a—new path, a distinct line of flight, for Africana studies. Having taken up occupation in the neighborhood of the Idea that is Africana studies, the work of theoretical futures is to establish its relation to said neighborhood and to, as it were, justify the claim that it is making. That is, theoretical futures has to, at once, break off relations with the neighborhood (after all, were the neighborhood sufficient in itself, there would be no need for theoretical futures; theoretical futures must, in this way, always err on the side of greater rather than lesser proximity to its neighbors) after having surveyed it, while explicating—through force, metaphorically phrased—the primacy (originality, creativity) of its particular intensive ordinates.

High Spirits

> In some it is their deprivations that philosophize; in others, their
> riches and strengths.
> —NIETZSCHE, *The Gay Science*

The work of *Africana Studies: Theoretical Futures* is, as is surely obvious by now, to create a plane of immanence composed of a series of new thinkings.

A set of thinkings that will, at the very least, be constructed out of components that will require an assiduous and creative re- or deterritorialization. The concept that allows the proliferation of infinite lines of flight. Lines of flight that are "offshoots" of an "imperceptible rupture, not [a] signifying break."[21] The concept, thus, seeks no immunity from its components, is entirely open to its (potential) multiple movements, its rearrangement of the components, its continuing creation within—on the plane of immanence of—its own creation. Such generativity is the promise of all concepts.

It is because of the flash of intensities, the individual chapters, that shoot up from the plane of immanence that is *Africana Studies: Theoretical Futures* that this collection of chapters is able to capture what the different contributors do and do not do in their individual (and yet connected) chapters. These flashes of intensities are, then, resonant and yet dissonant. On the plateau of immanence they are neighbors and yet remote. It is the flash of connection (let us name it, provisionally, reattachment, which, of course, returns us to the conjugation of territorialization)—that is, connection and "imperceptible rupture"—for which this Introduction has sought to create a concept.

A concept "written in the language of the wind that thaws ice and snow," a language that can sustain "high spirits"; indeed, a language that thrives on "unrest and contradiction," but only "contradiction" of the multiple variety.[22] More than anything, however, the plane of immanence that is theoretical futures is written in a language that is capable of, at any moment, taking off on its own, intensely singular, line of flight. That is the high-spirited language in, the restive and contradictory language out of, which each of these component chapters is written. High spirits, unrest, contradiction are the hallmarks of all the chapters in this collection because each of these components derive from a plenitude of possibility—such are their philosophical riches. These chapters all think from the position of strength. Following Deleuze and Guattari and Nietzsche, these chapters eschew the negative. They think only for creation, for the creation of the concept.

NOTES

1. Gilles Deleuze and Félix Guattari, *A Thousand Plateaus: Capitalism and Schizophrenia*, trans. Brian Massumi (Minneapolis: University of Minnesota Press, 2003). Deleuze and Guattari present their book throughout as an "assemblage," that series of intense connections that give rise to a "body without organs."

2. Gilles Deleuze and Félix Guattari, *What Is Philosophy?* trans. Hugh Tomlinson and Graham Burchell (New York: Columbia University Press, 1994).

3. Deleuze and Guattari, *What Is Philosophy?* 31. The term "assemblage" also belongs to that line of thinking that Deleuze and Guattari name a "*collective assemblages of enunciation*" (Deleuze and Guattari, *Thousand Plateaus*, 7).

4. Cornell University's Africana Studies and Research Center, where four of this volume's contributors are located, was founded in 1969. It was the first of its kind. Africana studies is, in this way, distinct but not entirely disconnected from the area studies programs birthed across the United States and the world during the Cold War, American studies being the most notable of these Cold War undertakings.

5. *Africana Studies: Theoretical Futures* undertakes the work of creating a concept—theoretical futures—because it understands itself as the necessary response to "problems which are thought to be badly understood or badly posed (pedagogy of the concept)" (Deleuze and Guattari, *What Is Philosophy?* 16). That is, the future/theoretical futures of Africana studies can be entrusted only to the concept of theoretical futures because, pedagogically speaking, only through creating its singular plane of immanence, by rejecting any inclination to transcendence (that is, through fidelity to the particular, to what is immanent), can the conditions for it to become the territory out of which futures can emerge be ensured. That is, "theoretical futures" is both a stay and a hedge. It is a stay against what we might name tradition, that which Africana studies understands itself to have been, its first articulation (that which sustained it, the ground in which it grew), that which inclined, decidedly, in the direction of transcendence (incorporating and making a claim on vast territories and many aspects of black and diasporic life; what in some quarters is named racial essentialism). It is a hedge against any such future transcendent inclinations. This collection also proffers the concept of theoretical futures as the creation of a plane of immanence where what exists, and because it exists, is thought in its multivalence and prized open to give full life to the various components that make up the concept. Out of one concept, many futures.

6. Deleuze and Guattari, *What Is Philosophy?* 17.

7. Friedrich Nietzsche, *The Gay Science*, trans. Walter Kaufman (New York: Vintage Books, 1974), 32.

8. Deleuze and Guattari, *What Is Philosophy?* 15.

9. Deleuze and Guattari, *What Is Philosophy?* 16.

10. Deleuze and Guattari, *Thousand Plateaus*, 7, 4.

11. Deleuze and Guattari, *What Is Philosophy?* 20.

12. Deleuze and Guattari, *What Is Philosophy?* 20.

13. "Essentialism," particularly when rendered as "racial essentialism," has been a core term within the discipline. That is, the term intends to designate a certain, to coin a phrase, absolute knowledge, an epistemological certainty about what it means, especially, to be black (what set of apparatuses and functions attend to being black, as such; what modes of being in the world, what modes of representation—modes of address, aesthetic self-representation, and so on—are permissible or are deemed to be sufficiently transgressive). Racial essentialism, of course, is not what Deleuze and Guattari are invoking when they speak of essence. However, because of how I deploy *What Is Philosophy?* in this chapter, it would be remiss for me not to acknowledge the effects and resonances of their invocation.

14. "Intuition," then, not in its mystical colloquial sense as something that comes to one, often out nowhere, without being able to account for its arrival, for why it produces or demands a response, but rather as an immediate or quick perception or cognition of truth (*philos*) or the direct perception of truth—or in this case, a difficulty for thinking—without its reason being immediately discernible. Or a knowledge that is inferred without prior training. All in all, a fine line, one acknowledges, but a difference critical for thinking as derived, in some instances, from intuition—both within this context and more broadly.

15. Brian Massumi, "Translator's Foreword," in Deleuze and Guattari, *A Thousand Plateaus*, xiv.

16. Deleuze and Guattari, *What Is Philosophy?* 18.

17. Deleuze and Guattari, *Thousand Plateaus*, 15.

18. Deleuze and Guattari, *Thousand Plateaus*, 24.

19. Deleuze and Guattari, *Thousand Plateaus*, 25.

20. Deleuze and Guattari, *What Is Philosophy?* 30.

21. Deleuze and Guattari, *Thousand Plateaus*, 24.

22. Nietzsche, *The Gay Science*, 32.

On the Fecundity of Small Places

John E. Drabinski

Thinking thought usually amounts to a withdrawing into a
dimensionless place in which the idea of thought alone persists.
But thought in reality spaces itself out into the world. It
informs the imaginary of peoples, their varied poetics, which it
then transforms, meaning, in them its risk becomes realized.
—**Glissant**, *Poetics of Relation*

Patrick Chamoiseau's *Chemin-d'école* (*School Days*) tells a long story about the persistence of colonial models of education in the postcolonial state, a story told with the kind of charm and anarchy you get with a child as protagonist. His depiction of Caribbean childhood is its own matter, but what always strikes me about *Chemin-d'école* is how the playfulness of the boy and his antagonist-compatriot Big BellyButton is interrupted at the beginning of the novel with an evocation of deepest violence. The boy learns French, which means he learns to speak and write French but, more importantly, to conceive his *name* in French. A name is a special thing. Our names attach to our singularity, denoting the substance of our bodies and ephemera of the intellect with a unique marker that also inflates the sign with existential, memorial, and historical meaning. To inherit a family name, to create a name, to embed a name in cultural history—naming introduces us to a world while also carving out a space that is ours and ours alone.

So when the boy learns his name in French, which means he renames himself *out of* Creole and *into* French, he learns something about the condition of his own nameability. And therefore, the necessity of writing his Creole name. Everything is at stake in the intersection of writing and the name. "He saw himself there, captured whole within a chalk mark," Chamoiseau writes. The boy "began to copy out his first name a thousand times, in order to proliferate and avoid genocide. . . . Discovery: he held the chalk with his entire hand (either one), *like a dagger*."[1] Everything is at stake in writing, everything is at stake in the name. It is the condition of fecundity. In fecundity, there may be reproduction of hegemony. Or there may be its reversal in revolutionary action. But there is also fecundity as the alleviation of hegemony *as such*. This fecundity, I argue below, comprises a movement to small places and away from the spectral power of the world as *the whole world*, movement toward and toward again *this world of ours*. The small place shines. The small place needs writing. Writing like a dagger—an instrument of carving deep signs, as well as an instrument of defense.

One of the more provocative aspects of Frantz Fanon's work comes in the early pages of the opening chapter of *Black Skin, White Masks* in which he theorizes the interlacing of language, thought, and colonial power.[2] In terms of its life in the political sphere, but also in scholarship on his work, Fanon's legacy has largely been tied to his descriptions and prescriptions in *The Wretched of the Earth*.[3] We can think here of the links drawn in that text between violence, pathology, liberation, nation making and unmaking and the future as a "new humanism" and how Fanon's notion resonated across the rapidly decolonizing global south (and still does). But the opening pages of *Black Skin, White Masks* take on a different philosophical task. Fanon there articulates the problem of language in ways that seem irrevocably pessimistic. To speak, he argues, is to adopt the colonizer's language, and to adopt that language is, further, to adopt an entire world. Language is thought, thought is self. To colonize subjugated subjects, the colonizer installs the colonial language in thinking, being, and knowing. A total project. This is Fanon's enduringly profound insight into the intimacy of colonial, racialized violence.

Now, on the one hand, Fanon is merely picking up on trends in midcentury European thought—namely, Martin Heidegger and the horizon of existential hermeneutics he puts into motion—and with some modifications of register and repurposing that trend to illuminate a sense of anti-colonial situatedness. Language and world are inseparable, and this has profound consequences for the oppressed and the colonized. On the other hand, Fanon is completely rewriting that hermeneutics of language and world under the rubric of what has come to be called Afropessimism, except that, rather than speculations about libidinal economies of race and vague gestures toward ontology, he routes desire, embodiment, being, and knowing through the inextricable link between word and thought. An entire ontology, epistemology, and aesthetics flow from this simple claim concerning the intimacy of language and thought to colonial domination, but it also remains the unanswered question at the heart of Fanon's work: How does one write against colonialism inside the language of the colonizer? That is, how does Fanon answer himself? The suffocating character of Fanon's epistemology and ontology, which also informs his early aesthetics and cultural theory, makes it hard to breathe as a thinker. That lack of breath is the condition of revolutionary consciousness and praxis in *The Wretched of the Earth*. But it is also the condition of his apocalyptic thinking. Is there a robust and legitimate form of life at work *in the midst of* colonial domination? And where does that life find voice and perform the labor of self-expression and collective expression? For surely the dominated live. Social death is never total. Or is it?

There is no real answer in Fanon's early texts. But that is not my point here. Rather, I begin with this Fanonian motif because it underscores an important theme that emerges out of the post-Fanon black Atlantic intellectual tradition: how writing is an act against genocide, how we can see negotiations over vernacular culture and language, precolonial practices, and transformative approaches to a broken world confront Fanon's problematic and chart a path (or paths) out. The total project of colonial domination—siting that domination in language, thought, and its possibilities—poses the terms of liberation, and therefore a robust and vibrant site for the study of Black life, in ways Fanon never could have expected. His aversion and outright hostility to vernacular forms of life and culture conceal intensive kinds of being in the very same location as kinds of social death and other fatal anti-Black practices.

I

Are the socially dead devoid of life? Or, what is the social of social death?

Let me restart my reflections here with three moments in the Black intellectual tradition. First, an early essay by W.E.B. Du Bois titled "The Conservation of Races"; second, the closing remark to Aimé Césaire's essay "Culture and Colonization"; and third, the closing moment and logic of Fanon's final work *The Wretched of the Earth*. These three moments underscore the key role played by what I call, following Césaire, the world stage and its cultural and political significance in thinking Black liberation. Further, too, this notion of the world stage is crucial for conceiving the inspirations, aspirations, and imperatives of the study of Black life—that is, of theorizing theory in Africana theory.

Du Bois's 1897 essay "The Conservation of Races" is an important precursor to his more familiar works. Written barely three decades after emancipation and just a handful of years before *Souls of Black Folk*,[4] Du Bois's essay holds two key questions in view: what is meant by "race" and what ought "the Negro race" imagine as a future? These are of course questions that dominate Du Bois's work across his long career, but "The Conservation of Races" is particularly direct, programmatic, and declarative, proceeding from the simple observation that slavery and colonialism have stunted racial cultural growth and political progress. But neither cultural growth nor political progress are instantly restored at the moment of emancipation, and the task of growth and progress lies not in the inversion of white consciousness but in the expansion of Black cultural production and effort. This is also not a matter of community or diasporic concern alone. Rather, Du Bois claims, one needs to configure the future of the race in relation to the progress and achievements of companion racial groups. He writes that "some of the great races of today—particularly the Negro race—have not as yet given to civilization the full spiritual message which they are capable of giving" and that "the fact remains that the full, complete Negro message of the whole Negro race has not as yet been given to the world."[5] History's trajectory has built this deficiency into the Black work, on Du Bois's account, and his argument turns in part on a late nineteenth-century conception of race that is at once biological and cultural. The *cultural* element of racial formation is what drives Du Bois's argument with real urgency. Black people suffer not just the law and the lash but also, and perhaps foremost, stunted cultural growth. Black people, he argues, must "rise above the pressing, but smaller questions of separate schools and cars, wage-discrimination and lynch law, to survey the whole question of race in human philosophy and to lay, on a basis of broad knowledge and careful insight, those large lines of policy and higher ideals."[6] Black humanity is restored and expanded through cultural labor. And so,

> we cannot reverse history; we are subject to the same natural laws as other races, and if the Negro is ever to be a factor in the world's history—if among the gaily-colored banners that deck the broad ramparts of civilization is to hang one uncompromising black, then it must be placed there by black hands, fashioned by black heads and hallowed by the travail of 200,000,000 black hearts beating in one glad song of jubilee.[7]

Du Bois's characteristically flowery language indicates something of the grandeur of the question. The world stage, the "broad ramparts of civilization," *lacks* Black presence, which simultaneously demeans Black people and demeans the stage itself. The early language of diaspora here, in the evocation of two hundred million Black hearts, is crucial, not simply because it draws on a long-debunked and deeply problematic essentialism about race but because, more importantly here, it stages the question of the world stage so precisely. If the world is composed of races, the stage of culture is racially coded and linked. Du Bois's proposal for the American

Negro Academy is therefore the American contribution to an Atlantic world racial project. The Academy "aims at once to be the epitome and expression of the intellect of the black-blooded people of America" and "the exponent of the race ideals of one of the world's great races."[8] Diasporic labor restores racial content, expands it, and places it alongside extant forms of cultural expression across the world. The small place is surmounted by a concern for wider racial consciousness and meaning, in the interest of comparative intellectual space and common measure. The *stage* of the world stage.

We see this same sort of logic deployed over a half century later in Césaire's essay "Culture and Colonization." Written on the occasion of the 1956 Paris Congress of Black Writers and Artists, a gathering of black Atlantic thinkers, most of whom argued for forms of unity in the diaspora at a key moment in global decolonization, the essay's leading distinction between culture (local formations) and civilization (animating spirits that bind culture differences in a single identity) structures Césaire's inquiry. The distinction allows Césaire to walk a difficult fault line between cultural difference and racial unity, which translates my language here of the small place and the world stage. It is important that Césaire is not trying to Africanize the black Americas. He, instead, is working toward a theory of how the small places in the diaspora *appear* to be different but in reality, at the level of civilization as a creative spirit, are the same. The scattering of seeds, after all, presupposes a common tree and root. That common tree, the civilizational spirit of Africa, orders the chaos of small places spread across the Atlantic world. And so Césaire closes his essay with an argument for diasporic identity and the kind of voice it brings to the "stage of history." He writes:

> Today we are in cultural chaos. Our role is to say: free the demiurge that alone can organize this chaos into a new synthesis, a synthesis that will deserve the name of culture, a synthesis that will be the reconciliation and surpassing of old and new. We are here to say and to demand: Let the peoples speak. Let the black peoples come onto the great stage of history.[9]

Césaire's argument for the unity of diaspora aims at this very conclusion, a conclusion that depends on the legitimacy of the language of civilization and spirit—remnants of French vitalist life philosophy, to which so much of Césaire's (as well as Léopold Senghor's) theoretical work turns for justification.[10] It is also the endgame of Négritude—namely, to energize anti-colonial agitation with a view toward cultural and existential transformation. Existential transformation through art and ideas is crucial for decolonization, and this atavistic and essentialist work is committed to the cultivation of

Black civilizational and cultural expression. Expressive life is cultural transformation at the level of the individual and the collective, which in turn
inserts the life of Black peoples into the story of History. Excessive and as-
pirational Black modernism, perhaps. The small place is the illness. The cure
is identification, then expansion, of the elevated spirit of what *appears* as
small. Redemption, cure. This is the work of Négritude and the curative
function of the world stage of history, culture, and racial self-expression and
collective expression.

Fanon's work, however, charts a very different path with regard to race
and racial identification. For Fanon, Blackness is a construct of the white
gaze and, per his formulation in the introduction to *Black Skin, White
Masks*, racial categories of "white" and "black" lock consciousness down
and stunt creativity itself. So, between Du Bois or Césaire and Fanon, these
initially seem to be disconnected moments. Indeed, Fanon in no way appears influenced by Du Bois (theoretical convergences around notions of
double consciousness notwithstanding), and the latter's adherence to conventional, largely biological notions of race in the "Conservation of Races"
stands in stark contrast to the former's repudiation of notions of race altogether. Du Bois's essentialism stands as a theoretical counterpoint to Fanon's
existential phenomenology and its commitment to description and critical
account of the relationship between ontology and social dynamics of power.
Fanon's critique of Négritude (and thus Césaire) is well known, following
the same logic: without a robust conception of race, there is nothing legitimate to anchor talk of collective identity outside shared political struggle.
But, at the same time, all three are deeply committed to notions of the global
and the world stage, reflecting the influence of Hegel's philosophy of history,
to be sure, but also a sense of what the liberation of Black folk looks like.
Liberation work is intellectual labor that transforms the place of Black people or the colonized—the damned and the wretched—in a world context,
rebuilding what that context, that stage, looks like, how it functions, and
therefore what it means for long-standing anti-Black violence and domination.

The movement toward liberation as entry onto the world stage might
proceed differently in terms of race, but Fanon shares with Du Bois and
Césaire a certain contempt for the present landscape. The present, informed
by the past of enslavement and colonialism, is a landscape of social death.
Nothing that comes *from* that landscape, that cultural and political space,
can articulate or promise liberation. Du Bois phrases this in terms of the
deficiency of Black cultural life, Césaire in terms of the torpor of colonized
places. For Fanon, it is the same question and answer: if colonized, anti-
Black space and landscape generates expression, that is an expression tied
to death, to the white gaze, and therefore to the impossibility of cultural

production as world making. This is particularly clear when Fanon reflects on blues music in his "Racism and Culture" essay from 1956, tying the expressive life of African American vernacular culture to the oppressor's gaze. Fanon writes:

> Thus the blues—"the black slave lament"—was offered up for the admiration of the oppressors. This modicum of stylized oppression is the exploiter's and the racist's rightful due. Without oppression and without racism you have no blues. The end of racism would sound the knell of great Negro music.[11]

This is an important passage for understanding the prerogative of Fanonian thinking. That is, rather than a problematic or limited understanding of musical culture in the United States, this passage links Fanon's Afropessimism—a claim that anti-Blackness (colonialism) is a total project that leaves no aspect of life untouched—to cultural formation under enslavement and segregation. *Everything produced under an anti-Black regime is an expression of anti-Blackness.* And so the blues, rather than an expression of life, is an expression of spiritual death, something "offered up" to the oppressors because, Fanon believes, the oppressed have no sense of life and its complexity outside that gaze.

The answer to this pessimism, which *Black Skin, White Masks* for the most part leaves as utterly dispiriting, is the apocalyptic vision of cultural and political transformation in *The Wretched of the Earth*. It is interesting how that book details so many pathologies, forms of backwardness and colonial hangover, and related matters in largely institutional terms but is bookended by emphatic and bombastic ontological claims about violence and the new. Violence, the theme of the most famous chapter, the first, in *The Wretched of the Earth*, is redeemed by the emergence—always promised, always in a wholly open future—of a new humanism, an unprecedented sense of relation to self and other. Violence destroys, the future begins again, wholly anew. This binary shift—it is *either* recurrence of the same *or* a complete break with history and memory—reinscribes Fanon's work on the mythic world stage: *after* the apocalypse, there is the new messiah of humanism and the world it creates. For everyone. Political violence aims at global, not just local, transformation. Fanon, hero of the global south. Fanon, transformer of the entire world. A new stage that hosts a new world stage.

Whatever their differences, Du Bois, Césaire, and Fanon share this demand that Black liberation be tied to an entrance into global cultural and political life. Interracial, always, even if that interracial functions only as formal comparative space. Small places, the local and the vernacular, gain meaning only in the moment the small names itself as part of a whole—culture subsumed under civilization. And that whole is that cultural formation that makes the stage a stage for the world, rather than the vernacular left to itself, which risks, inevitably, condemnation as opaque and illegitimate. The specter of measure.

In this sense, the notion of a world stage and the imperatives it implies or gathers to it is a quiet remnant of the very colonialism that critical Africana theory putatively seeks to displace or upend. Very much like humanism, the notion of the world stage performs two fundamentally incompatible functions: to clear the space for comparative work and creation *and* to establish a set of measures of communicability that serve to exclude, demean, and further the work of domination. The question for the world stage is very much the question Césaire posed in *Discourse on Colonialism*: should we remake and rewrite the stage "to the measure of the world," paralleling what Césaire wanted to do with humanism?[12] Or is it better to imagine a new model of cultural production, meaning, and significance?

This problematic is brought into particularly clear focus when we consider the place of the vernacular in cultural production and meaning and the sorts of fecundity borne by that mode of production and meaning making. At the intersection of theorizing the world stage and the apocalyptic vision of Black futures lies a strange and estranged sense of fecundity. The orientation toward a future that elevates, or creates for the first time, Black cultural production in relation to a global measure turns on a vision of the past and present in which the landscape of Black life is characterized by torpor, loss, and melancholy. Afropessimism, in a word. Fecundity is always something to come, something postponed, but in no way related to the melancholic, pessimistic space of loss and violence. In other words, a sense of futurity without deconstructive interruption. A pure future. An invented future. A future without the present and its past.

And yet, in that melancholic space of loss and torpor, there is also the obstinacy of life. Senses of the interstitial that lie outside the construction of anti-Black sociality, culture, and politics. What kind of fecundity emerges in that space? What kind of fecundity works in small places rather than world stages and their demands? Or, what becomes of the margin without center?

II

Édouard Glissant's work as a poet, novelist, and critical theorist spans a fascinating time period in Caribbean thought. He was Aimé Césaire's student, attended the 1956 Congress of Black Writers and Artists, and labored initially in the horizon of Négritude, Caribbean surrealism, and Fanon's rewriting of existentialism in a black Atlantic register. But he was never to be that kind of thinker and poet. Glissant's early poetry and exploratory essays take up a very different sense of relation to place—that intersection of space or landscape and the time of historical memory—in the Caribbean, then later globalized and globalizing, context.

For Glissant, the Middle Passage and the Plantation mark a massive shift in paradigm for thinking about identity, culture, world making, and intellectual production—the very terms of Africana theory. The Middle Passage, he argues, comprises three intertwined notions of the abyss: the abyss of forced departure from the continent, the abyss of the belly of the slave ship, and the abyss of arrival on the shoreline. *Poetics of Relation* opens with evocation of each sense toward a single end: the unicity of beginning for Africans in the New World.[13] The threefold abyss severs roots to the continent; beginning in the New World means beginning with fragments that do not reassemble into originals. *The Afropostmodern in the birth of European modernity.* Beginning without atavism and its fantasies means reassembly with difference, differentiation, and chaotic mixture, or what Glissant calls creolization. Creolized production—cultural, social, political—is a phenomenon derived from the Plantation. Plantation functions as a historical place but, more, as a critical concept in Glissant's work, describing the conditions for the possibility of life without atavism and in the swirl of difference that comes from mixtures of Africa's cultural variety, European incursion and violence, and remnants of indigeneity that survived conquest and genocide. Enslavers wanted the Plantation to eliminate life, to produce radical and irrevocable social death through strict borders and control. But plantation life was not only resilient but porous, producing mixture and opening unexpected, unprecedented horizons of language, thought, and world in the very same space that produced immeasurable pain and death. In other words, the plantation produces Relation and, in Relation, the plantation becomes the critical concept Plantation. Glissant writes:

> The Plantation is one of the focal points for the development of present-day modes of Relation. Within this universe of domination and oppression, of silent or professed dehumanization, forms of humanity stubbornly persisted.[14]

Affirmation of the humanity of the enslaved, and therefore the kinds of cultural and political habitus, or everydayness, that persists after emancipation, is both a simple and a complex conceptual move. It is simple because life goes on. The future is obstinate. Life asserts itself. Radical dehumanization has limits. But this is a complex claim precisely because the cultural and political work done by the enslaved, working with fragments in the sense Glissant describes as *djobbers* of the New World, does not reconcile itself with larger narratives about Blackness or Africa or even strong senses of diaspora. Rather, the *djobber* works inside the small place for the sake of *that* life, not a wider sense of racial life and its spirit or a pan-African vision of restored identity. Contra Césaire, Glissant's teacher and great poet predecessor, the *djobber*'s indulgence of vernacular life reflects the everydayness of the people in *this place* without reference to other places, ancestral elsewhere, or sites and citations of domination.

Across his poetics, Glissant develops this sensibility and its link to vernaculars of the small place as a form of cultural or poetic *marronage*. Flight, here, is not from the plantation to the remote mountainside as a historical act but instead a demand that creation reinvent the norms of cultural production in the word and world of the small place. Glissant has plenty critical to say about their deeper commitments, but this is one moment in which he praises the work of Chamoiseau, Raphael Confiant, and Jean Bernabé in *Éloge de la créolité*—the stubborn refusal to move away from the opacity of small places and instead lean into the fact that Creole (language, culture, sociality) has words for all the parts of the world.[15] Not translatable words, and so not words ready-made for the world stage, but instead words specific to the entire world of the small place. Kamau Brathwaite calls this simply, and with a mix of appropriate irony and grandeur, "nation language." Brathwaite writes:

> Language does really have a role to play here, certainly in the Caribbean. But it is an English that is not the standard, imported, educated English, but that of the submerged, surrealist experience and sensibility, which has always been there and which is now increasingly coming to the surface and influencing the perception of contemporary Caribbean people. It is what I call, as I say, *nation language*. I use the term in contrast to *dialect*. . . . Dialect is the language when you want to make fun of someone. . . . Nation language, on the other hand, is the submerged area of that dialect that is much more closely allied to the African aspect of experience in the Caribbean. It may be in English, but often it is in an English which is like a howl, or a shout, or a machine-gun, or the wind, or a wave. It is also like the blues.[16]

Like the blues, like Africa in the Caribbean—the language of the *djobber* now becomes the linguist and the grammarian. If small places distinguish themselves in language and language is thought and being—Fanon's insight, put to work as a form of Afropessimism—and small places reserve the right to name themselves whole unto themselves, then Brathwaite's phrase is entirely appropriate. Vernacularity is world making, world sustains a people, a people make a nation in language. Small places are fecund.

We see this in a number of other thinkers and emerging critical black Atlantic debates and dissents, including figures like Ngũgĩ wa Thiong'o, Ralph Ellison, Zora Neale Hurston, and Albert Murray. I am thinking in particular of the argument in Ngũgĩ's *Decolonizing the Mind* for Kikuyu language theater written for and performed in particular places: the village, evoking its life, sounded in its vernacular, without prioritizing or foregrounding the possibility of translation.[17] Or Hurston's peculiar blend of anthropology and fiction writing that draws on her aesthetic theory in the 1934 "Characteristics of Negro Expression," an essay that documents the sounds and rhythms of African American life for the sake of articulating a world, rather than eliding the opacity of those sounds and rhythms.[18] The blues aesthetic that structures a novel like *Invisible Man* and gives life to the lower frequencies or that informs the cultural politics of Murray, Baldwin, and even aspects of Richard Wright's work. Each in their own way moves into opaque worlds without the imperative of translation and translatability, opting instead for the world *as it already functions as a space of life.* That movement speaks against the command to make general, to make a part of a global stage and its standards for comparison. These sorts of debates and emerging critical responses to large-picture inquiries, imperatives, and aspirations return us to the motif I noted at the outset, Chamoiseau's notion of writing to avoid genocide. What is at stake in that writing? What form does genocide take? And what or how can writing be undertaken that says yes to life, that makes life fecund *without* appeal to the world stage and its cognates?

Glissant's appeal to opacity, both as necessity and as an epistemological feature of small places, is an important critical frame. Opacity defends, as a right and as critical theory, the radical particularity and specificity of the small place, underscoring the fecundity of one's here that is always another's elsewhere. Opacity describes what is already there; it is no invention or supervening ethico-political structure. And opacity refuses the compulsion to translate, to comprehend—something that Glissant notes, playing on the French verb *comprendre*, is always linked to forms of seizing and taking as one's own (*prendre*). The small place, then, when understood as a critical site of cultural production and world making, has its own kind of double session. In the very same gesture that produces culture and world, setting roots (rhizomatic, always), there is the return of that specificity and radical singularity to the fantasies of the world stage and metanarrative of comparative space. If the metanarrative of comparative space sets particular achievements and expressive traditions in relation to a measure, then we can see the radical collective singularity of small places, asserting their rights to opacity, as a supplement and interruption of the world stage. That is, the small place performs deconstructive work against hegemony, not as an alternative story or companion narrative, but as a story against the idea of story—a mixed place that does not resolve. A history that is not History. A story that is not a global epic. One can think here of Derek Walcott's Nobel lecture "The Antilles: Fragments of Epic Memory," in which the poet argues *for* the reality of place and its idiosyncrasies—Felicity and its sigh—and against any and all ideas of History.[19] Such an argument affirms the opacity of New World formations, removing the very idea of measure, which in turn neutralizes the sort of melancholy that haunts the work of Césaire, Fanon, and most emphatically V. S. Naipaul (if we stay in a Caribbean register). Without melancholy, there is the pleasure and depth of *this place*, a place that refers to no other place beyond itself, not only satisfied with but ecstatic within the rhizomatic swirl of making worlds, making place, and making subjects of that world and place. As Ellison and Murray remind us, always, the blues is not mourning or supplication. The blues is music for fighting, fucking, drinking, courtship, rage, romance, laughter, and every other affect that attends to being human in the small place that makes you.

What would it mean, then, to adopt this sort of thinking about space, time, place, and world as a kind of first philosophy? First philosophy, that is, as a foundational set of ethics, politics, and aesthetics that sees, rather than explains away, the ontology and epistemology made in vernacular cultural traditions, modes of expression, Being and knowing as creolized, as becoming. Against being and Being, in the name of a radical becoming in what Glissant calls Relation, in what Walcott calls the long-drawn sigh, and in what Chamoiseau dramatizes as writing against genocide. For the world stage and its sense of measure, the comparative space it glamorizes and makes into its own kind of first philosophy, compelling the subaltern to *aspire* and *desire* participation in such a space, is a kind of genocidal threat. The threat takes the form of the demand and compulsion: *explain yourself and make yourself transparent to others. The prendre* in *comprendre.* Refusing that in the name of creolization, opacity, and vernacularity is survival and revolution. It is also deconstructive, supplementing empire to the end of empire's demise, in the name of life itself, the refusal to die and the refusal of apocalypse. *We are already enough.* Thus begins an appreciation of the end of the world that has already happened. There is no pure future. Or at least we do not need it. We need, instead, the small place and its opaque epistemology and ontology without exoticism. Fecundity of the small place as the future of Black study.

III

One of the more aggressive critiques of the institutionalization of Black studies, or what has come to be called, more commonly, Africana studies, is that making a department, field of study, and therefore institutional academic presence neutralizes and neuters the study of Black life. Institutions are not radical. Institutions are, like the state in Louis Althusser's famous "Ideology and Ideological State Apparatuses" essay, largely dedicated to reproducing themselves.[20] And in that reproduction, an emerging field, like any established field, draws on the principles and values of a given milieu of production and reproduction: neoliberal in funding, conciliatory in situating itself in relation to extant disciplines, structures, and forms of knowledge production.

I am less interested here in funding and relationships to long-time disciplines and area studies; it strikes me that there are as many stories about those relations as there are scholars in the field. What interests me is how disputes within Africana studies reproduce or interrupt the antechamber of conventional kinds of knowledge production. How does the larger stage of inquiry, whether Du Bois's modernist estimation of the future of "the Negro" or the politically radical, culturally innovative (or conservative) iterations of Pan-Africanism, Afrocentrism, and the like, reproduce a sense of what *counts* and what *ought to be valued* as the outcome of a field or mode of inquiry? That is, how are differences in content, in the end, really just varieties of one and the same form of producing legitimate knowledge— establishing, then deploying and policing such boundaries—rather than radical interventions in how we conceive knowing, being, and sociality? Something very important is at stake for Africana theory in these questions.

Let me turn to a canonical work to spell out a series of decisions one makes as a reader and how those decisions presuppose, then reproduce, specific norms of knowledge production. Du Bois's *Souls of Black Folk* is a cornerstone of African American thought, a piece without which the tradition is all but unimaginable. Whereas for most it is a text defined by either his dispute with Booker T. Washington, spelled out across its most important pages, or the central figures of the veil, double consciousness, and the color line, I argue that the closing chapter on the Spirituals is what establishes *Souls* as a foundation piece of the *African American* intellectual tradition. This is not to dispute the profundity of Du Bois's insights; he is, after all, an utterly singular thinker in the tradition. But how we frame and theorize the text is paramount. Conventional debates about labor and intellectual life, where we ought to place our priority in thinking the conditions of social and political progress, or the role of education in narratives of uplift, or the dialectics of self-world relation—these are the standard features of *Souls* and embed the text within larger European and white American debates about selfhood, political ethics, and class relations. Du Bois is an important thinker for this reason, because of how he shifts standard European debates into the register of racial prejudice and its effects and affects. However, if we begin with the closing chapter, we reframe the trajectory of the book with the specificity of the experience of the enslaved, the particularities of their expressive life, and how that specificity and particularity has formed a sense of culture and life in and on the interstices of an anti-Black world. In other words, we can propose a reading of *Souls* as a book about small places rather than a twist on broader themes in European theory.

Such an interpretative move, a hermeneutic practice that draws from small places rather than drawing back from them, opens up dimensions of the text that create a sense of tradition. The Spirituals are the birthplace, or what Glissant called, in the Caribbean context, the "womb abyss," of the small places that comprise African American memory and history.[21] Spirituals become the sound of what Baldwin calls "black English," tracing sound, figure, and gesture to "the auction block" and the pain of living amid such violence.[22] And the sound of blues, that sonic testimony to place and its memories. Working from this insight and its orientation, Albert Murray writes:

> What a case of the blues represents is chaos, entropy, futility, depression, defeat, contention—all of that. Now, to survive you got to have an affirmative attitude toward your possibilities rather than an attitude of defeatism and lamentation . . . the juke joint is a temple where this rite takes place.[23]

The character of the blues as rite, a Dionysian and fertility one through and through, underscores the fecundity of suffering not only in the hands of the musical artist but in the world that artist produces, reproduces, and participates in as a form of life. Ellison extends this insight when he writes that the blues aesthetic, in the person of Bessie Smith, is a religious principle. He writes:

> There are levels of time and function involved here, and the blues which might be used in one place as entertainment (as gospel music is now being used in night clubs and on theater stages) might be put to a ritual use in another. Bessie Smith might have been a "blues queen" to the society at large, but within the tighter Negro community where the blues were part of a total way of life, and a major expression of an attitude toward life, she was a priestess, a celebrant who affirmed the values of the group and man's ability to deal with chaos.[24]

The ability to deal with chaos, this closing formulation, is utterly crucial for understanding the condition of the study of Black life in the Americas, as well as, perhaps, colonial and postcolonial Africa. But chaos takes on specific forms, and community or small-place responses to that chaos is what gives the study of Black life real substance and complexity.

African American studies, a subset of Africana theory, is itself a fragmented and varied site of theorization. From the Spirituals to the blues and on, to late twentieth- and twenty-first-century hip-hop, then, the blues aesthetic describes an arc of cultural formation and identity that is inseparable from the particularities of place: the space of the American South, the time of slavery and its long shadow, and the creation of expressive life and language that turns on a subtle yet overwhelming vernacular character. Each iteration of expressive life points to place, sometimes broad, but often to subtle small places with nuance, detail, and differing forms of opacity. The subtlety of vernacular lies, again, in the particularities of the situation of the thinker-maker, of the world making effort of art and artist and community, in the (determinative) sense in which the enslaved, then emancipated but subjugated and precarious, live alongside their oppressor. Double entendre, lower frequencies, the cracks and fissures in which life is made. The vernacular forms of life are nevertheless overwhelming, surmounting centuries of effort to erase, silence, obscure, and otherwise lock out African Americans from fully vibrant forms of life. Entropy, yes, and also chaos with the contention against depression and futility. Making life in a small place that overwhelms the possibilities of the one who subjugates and proliferates genocide. This sort of work against the putative center, life that is interstitial and yet entirely life and possibility. It needs no relation to a center. It is rather what Baldwin calls "the relation Negroes bear to one another," a formulation he employs to describe the unicity of the African American tradition *outside the white gaze*.[25]

The turn to small places and the fecundity of their conditions—creolism, vernacularity, the blues aesthetic, just to name a few—draws attention to the facts of Black cultural life in the Americas, emphasizing the limitations or even violence of deficiency models of analysis. The deficiency model imagines Black life under conditions of oppression and unimaginable, transgenerational violence as just that: structured entirely from the inside by the abjection projected by white violence. We see this in so much social science, as well as the anecdote-critic inclusion of Black texts and thinkers as part of the diversification of curricula and research programs. We also see this in the pessimist strain of the black Atlantic tradition, which has turned the literary nihilism of a Richard Wright and speculations of an early Fanon into thumbnail sketches of an ontology and libidinal economy under the rubric of *Afropessimism*. In these cases, though, the deficiency model is strangely colonized by notions of the common, of Being as such, and therefore iterations of what used to be called the world stage. The turn to small places and the fecundity of their conditions upends that mode of analysis in a shift from fundamental ontology (the common, the world, the *Umwelt* of anti-Blackness) to regional ontological concerns that generate languages, beliefs, practices, and theorizations that mobilize Black life outside the white gaze—Baldwin's phrase, "the relation Negroes bear to one another." In that bearing are the components of world making. In a world made outside the white gaze, small places emerge as not only forms of resistance, disruption, and the unassimilable (they are surely that) but also, and most emphatically, entire worlds of meaning, significance, and *life*.

It would be enough to leave it at that. But there is a short, final bit to say.

Small places are fecund and speak back to empire and imperial notions with the assertion of *place*—the particularity and peculiarity of time, memory, and space. "The land of our forefathers' exile had been made, by that travail, our home," as Baldwin puts it in "Princes and Powers."[26] In this quick, even offhand, yet transformative statement, Baldwin restarts a conversation about identity that effectively decenters and destructures the work of empire—even on questions of diaspora. The travail that makes home, that work and existential effort that reconfigures space across memorial and historical time, speaks back to empire by asking what sort of work empire has done to make land into home, a conventional, though always radical, insight drawn from the lordship and bondage chapter of Hegel's *Phenomenology of Spirit*: through his work, the bondsman captures a sense of identity that the lord cannot claim.[27] Namely, a connection to place.

The decolonizing work here is worth noting. In theorizing the function of small places in cultural formation and the labors of identity making and world making, we move away from the long shadow of empire in languages of domination (Eurocentrism, white nationalism, white identity and politics) and languages of liberation (diaspora, remnants of racial essentialism, nationalisms of all sorts), not to establish a new center or cluster of centers— the fantasy of reversed and inverted forms of nationalism, but to contest the idea of center itself. Small places do not refer to anything other than themselves. This is the ethical and epistemological work of opacity. In that particular form of *kath auto*, as it were, every place is revealed to be a small place, and the very notion of a center or a pure culture is self-aggrandizing, chauvinistic mythmaking. We here arrive at one of Antonio Benítez-Rojo's great insights from *The Repeating Island*—namely, that every culture is syncretic, there are no single roots, and what makes cultural production interesting is the dynamic of response to the component parts of syncretic work.[28] And so in the wake of the decolonizing work of decentering, uprooting the explicit and implicit work of empire, we are returned again to the question of influence. Small places are not atomistic sites or cultural entities. Rather, every site and cultural entity emerges from syncretic work in the past that, when calibrated for identity and nation formation, becomes singular, unique, and to some extent unifying. So how do we think about the dynamics of influence and confluence in a decolonizing register? Again, Glissant: the thought of *tout-monde*. Perhaps in a twist on his phrasing, recalling Derrida's refrain *tout autre est tout autre*, we can say it: *tout monde est tout-monde*.

NOTES

1. Patrick Chamoiseau, *School Days*, trans. Linda Coverdale (Lincoln: University of Nebraska Press, 1997), 21; my emphasis.
2. Frantz Fanon, *Black Skin, White Masks*, trans. Richard Philcox (New York: Grove Press: 2006).
3. Frantz Fanon, *The Wretched of the Earth*, trans. Richard Philcox (New York: Grove Press, 2005).
4. W.E.B. Du Bois, *The Souls of Black Folk*, ed. David W. Blight and Robert Gooding-Williams (Boston: Bedford Books, 1997).
5. W.E.B. Du Bois, "The Conservation of Races," in *W.E.B Du Bois: A Reader*, ed. David Levering Lewis (New York: Henry Holt, 1995), 23.
6. Du Bois, "The Conservation of Races," 20.
7. Du Bois, "The Conservation of Races," 23.
8. Du Bois, "The Conservation of Races," 25.
9. Aimé Césaire, "Culture and Colonization," *Social Text* 28, no. 2 (103; June 2010): 142.
10. On life philosophy and vitalism in the Négritude movement, see Donna V. Jones's excellent work in *The Racial Discourses of Life Philosophy* (New York: Columbia University Press, 2010).
11. Fanon, "Racism and Culture," in *Toward the African Revolution*, trans. Haakon Chevalier (New York: Grove Press, 1994), 29–44.
12. Aimé Césaire, *Discourse on Colonialism*, trans. Joan Pinkham (New York: Monthly Review Press, 2001).
13. Édouard Glissant, *Poetics of Relation*, trans. Betsy Wing (Ann Arbor: University of Michigan Press, 1999).
14. Glissant, 65.
15. Patrick Chamoiseau, Raphael Confiant, and Jean Bernabé, *Éloge de la créolité* (Paris: Gallimard, 1993).
16. Kamau Brathwaite, *Roots* (Ann Arbor: University of Michigan Press, 1993), 266.
17. Ngũgĩ wa Thiong'o, *Decolonizing the Mind* (Portsmouth, NH: Heinemann, 2011).
18. Zora Neale Hurston, "Characteristics of Negro Expression," in *Zora Neale Hurston: Folklore, Memoirs, and Other Writings* (New York: Library of America, 1995), 830–846.
19. Derek Walcott. "The Antilles: Fragments of Epic Memory," in *What the Twilight Says* (New York: Farrar, Straus and Giroux, 1999), 65–86.
20. Louis Althusser, "Ideology and Ideological State Apparatuses," in *Lenin and Philosophy* (New York: Monthly Review Press, 2001), 127–186.
21. Glissant, *Poetics of Relation*, 6–8.
22. James Baldwin, "Black English: A Dishonest Argument," in *The Cross of Redemption* (New York: Pantheon Books, 2010), 125–130.

23. Albert Murray, "Interview: An All-Purpose, All-American Literary Intellectual," in *Albert Murray: Collected Essays and Memoirs* (New York: Library of America, 2016), 867.

24. Ralph Ellison, "Blues People," in *Shadow and Act* (New York: Vintage, 1995), 251.

25. James Baldwin, "Many Thousands Gone," in *The Price of the Ticket* (New York: St. Martin's Press, 1985), 72.

26. Baldwin, "Princes and Powers," in *The Price of the Ticket*, 45.

27. G.W.F. Hegel, *Phenomenology of Spirit*, trans. A. V. Miller (Oxford: Oxford University Press, 1977), part B, section 4.

28. Antonio Benítez-Rojo, *The Repeating Island*, trans. James Maraniss (Durham, NC: Duke University Press, 2015).

Paulin J. Hountondji on Philosophy, Science, and Technology

From Husserl and Althusser to a Synthesis of the Hessen-Grossmann Thesis and Dependency Theory

Zeyad el Nabolsy

To explain Paulin J. Hountondji's intellectual trajectory, I offer a critical account of his conception of the relationship between science and philosophy. Mapping the shift from his well-known critical writings on ethnophilosophy to his later work on scientific dependency is possible only if we recognize that Hountondji conceives of philosophy as essentially a theory of science (*Wissenschaftslehre*). Adequately characterizing Hountondji's metaphilosophical orientation, however, requires greater specificity. The two most influential philosophers on Hountondji's conception of the relationship between science and philosophy, Edmund Husserl and Louis Althusser, would both have assented to the claim that philosophy is fundamentally a *Wissenschaftslehre*. However, they each adhered to different (and indeed contradictory) understandings of this claim. While Hountondji explicitly recognizes the dual influence of Husserl and Althusser on his conception of philosophy as a theory of science, he does not attempt to resolve the contradictions between Husserl's understanding of the relationship between philosophy and science and Althusser's conception of that relationship. In fact, Anglophone scholarly work on Hountondji's writings, produced in the 2010s, does not explicitly attempt to resolve this tension.

By examining Hountondji's relatively neglected later writings on scientific dependency, it becomes clear that his emphasis on the significance of the history and sociology of science points toward an Althusserian conception of philosophy qua theory of science rather than a Husserlian conception of what it is for philosophy to be a *Wissenschaftslehre*. However, Hountondji is mistaken in his reliance on Althusser's arguments for the claim that philosophy is essentially a second-order discourse that is parasitic on first-order scientific discourse. Althusser, in analyzing the mutual historical interactions between the sciences and philosophy in order to provide evidence for his claim, merely gestures toward such connections without engaging in any rigorous examination of the history of science in relation to the history of philosophy. Unfortunately, Hountondji, through his excessive reliance on Althusser, falls into the same error. Nonetheless, this chapter provides evidentiary support for Althusser's claims (and therefore for Hountondji's) about the relationship between science and philosophy by drawing on the work of contemporary historians of philosophy, historians of science, and historians of philosophy of science. I show how Hountondji's later work on scientific dependency can be situated in the context of a transnational tradition of Marxist scientific philosophy, through the reconstruction of his claims about the relationship among philosophy, science, and technology, as a version of the Hessen-Grossmann thesis in the context of his embrace of a version of dependency theory. (According to the Hessen-Grossmann thesis, technology was developed to facilitate capitalist economic development, and early modern science was able to make the advances that it did by studying the technology that was developed to facilitate capitalist economic development.)

Hountondji's Critique of Ethnophilosophy's Metaphysics of Difference

Because Hountondji is best known for his critique of ethnophilosophy, as well as for his concern with the development of African philosophy as an academic discipline, it is important to recognize the connections between his early work on the limits of ethnophilosophy qua African philosophy and his later work on scientific dependency on the African continent. Hountondji criticizes attempts at reconstructing a philosophical system through the ethnographic study of the worldview of a specific African people—for example, Placide Tempels's *Bantu Philosophy* (2021).[1] Hountondji argues that such projects are ill conceived for several reasons. First, the researcher almost always projects "a philosophical discourse on to products of language which expressly offer themselves as something other than philosophy" (Hountondji 1996, 43). Second, this ethnographic approach to "discovering" African philosophies presupposes the "myth of primitive unanimity," as Hountondji terms it, "with its suggestion that in 'primitive' societies—that is to say, non-Western societies—everybody always agrees with everybody else. It follows that in such societies there can never be individual beliefs or philosophies but only collective systems of belief" (60).[2] Hountondji argues that this approach underemphasizes the existence of conflicts in such societies, because according to him there are no societies in which everybody agrees with everyone else (165).[3]

Nobody would think of engaging in an ethnographic study of, say, the English conception of time (in a way that discounts the differentiation brought about by social stratification, regional differences, specific individual histories, etc.) and then attempt to pass off the results as philosophy, but it was not uncommon for ethnophilosophers to speak about the Yoruba conception of time or the Bantu philosophy of time, and so on.[4]

The third reason that Hountondji finds ethnophilosophy to be inadequate is that this discourse involves implicitly (and sometimes explicitly) a search for originality and distinctiveness that reaffirms the positing of an essential difference in kind between African peoples and Western peoples: "the generally tacit thesis that non-Western societies are absolutely specific, the silent postulate of a difference in *nature* (and not merely in the *evolutionary stage* attained with regard to particular types of achievement), of a difference in *quality* (not merely in quantity or *scale*) between so-called 'primitive' societies and developed ones" (Hountondji 1996, 61).[5] Hountondji is referring to what Olúfẹ́mi Táíwò (2013) has described as the "metaphysics of difference," or the thesis that there is an essential *difference in kind* between Black African peoples and other peoples.[6] According to Táíwò, the metaphysics of difference was used to justify colonialism. In fact, as Mahmood Mamdani has pointed out, colonial rule, specifically the doctrine of indirect rule "aimed at the reproduction of difference as custom" (2013, 44). The anthropological discourse of "custom" led to the dehistoricization of differences in social structures and their representation as unchanging reified differences (in existence since "time immemorial").[7] The reification of difference was central to the colonial discourse of tribalism (53). We can therefore understand Hountondji's suspicion of any discourse that takes reified differences between Africans and non-Africans for granted.[8]

The fourth criticism that Hountondji levels at ethnophilosophy is perhaps the most important in relation to explaining his later turn to the sociology of scientific knowledge in the peripheries. Hountondji argues that the most debilitating limitation of ethnophilosophy is that it is fundamentally directed toward a non-African audience: "African philosophy, inasmuch as it remains an ethnophilosophy, has been built up essentially *for a European public*. The African ethnophilosopher's discourse is not intended for Africans. It has not been produced for their benefit, and its authors understood that it would be challenged, if at all, not by Africans but by Europe alone" (1996, 45). For Hountondji, ethnophilosophy is essentially a performance produced to satisfy an Other who occupies a position of power vis-à-vis the performers. Hountondji thinks that the other faults of ethnophilosophy essentially stem from this extraversion (the structural fact of being directed toward an external audience). For example, according to Hountondji, extraversion is what explains the overemphasis on African originality: "The quest for originality is always bound up with a desire to show off. It has meaning only in relation to the Other, from whom one wishes to distinguish oneself at all costs. This is an ambiguous relationship, inasmuch as the assertion of one's difference goes hand in hand with a passionate urge to have it recognized by the Other" (44).[9] According to Hountondji, this assertion of difference was even encouraged by the Other (former colonizing powers), especially when the assertion of cultural difference was used to mask political and economic dependency (159).[10]

Indeed, Hountondji even argues that "ethnophilosophy appears as a by-product of underdevelopment" (1996, xxiv). He thus posits a causal connection between a certain kind of intellectual discourse and equivalent socioeconomic structures. Ethnophilosophy is the by-product of a weak postcolonial petty bourgeoisie incapable of carrying out an economic and political struggle for real independence and that therefore seeks to transform the struggle for real independence into an exclusively cultural struggle centered on assertions of cultural authenticity and difference. This is what Hountondji means in writing, "Hypertrophy of cultural nationalism generally serves to compensate for the hypotrophy of political nationalism" (159). Convergence occurs between Hountondji's analysis of the socioeconomic roots of ethnophilosophy and Dani Nabudere's analysis of the socioeconomic roots of discourse around cultural uniqueness. The claim to cultural uniqueness was not in fact unique at all; it obtained all across those parts of the world dominated by neocolonialism. As Nabudere points out, the valorization of cultural uniqueness is the product of underdevelopment in the neocolonial world, which leads the ruling petty bourgeoisie to abandon the arena of political and economic struggle against imperialism and to struggle exclusively in the cultural field: "Neocolonial culture as expressed in the writings of the neocolonial intellectual reflected this depressed culture. Appeal to the past instead of the future dominated so-called 'Black culture,' 'Arab culture' or 'Asian culture.' This reflected generally backward conditions in the neocolony" (Nabudere 1979, 86). Thus, underlying the claims to uniqueness was a more or less uniform condition of underdevelopment and domination by finance capital. Hountondji's suspicion of any discourse of cultural authenticity was reinforced by his experiences in Mobutu Sese Seko's Zaire (Dübgen and Skupien 2019, 90).

The causal connection between economic structures and philosophical discourse, however, is not direct and unmediated. As we see later, for Hountondji this causal connection is mediated by science and technology. To this extent Hountondji adopts a version of historical materialism in his critique of ethnophilosophy (offering both an argument against ethnophilosophy qua philosophy and an explanation that ties its development to certain economic, social, and political conditions). Hountondji is quite explicit about this: "In the pure domain of thought every mutation or revolution, every *event* in the strong sense, refers to some event in the material world and owes its own occurrence as an event to this relation" (1996, 91). He firmly locates his approach to the study of the history of philosophy within the context of the problematic of historical materialist modes of the study of the history of philosophy. According to this approach, the history of philosophy "is not autonomous and does not draw from itself the law of its own development, which is determined in the last analysis by the historical production of material goods and that of the social relations of production" (1996, 93).[11]

This approach is a "problematic" because Hountondji does not pretend that it provides indubitable answers to key questions arising in the historiography of philosophy. Instead, he emphasizes that its significance lies in developing a set of distinct research questions. For Hountondji the central questions are, "What, outside philosophy, determines the transitions which are the stuff of history? How, by what mediations, is philosophical practice finally determined by material practices?" (1996, 97). While Hountondji does not offer definitive answers to these questions, he does propose some hypotheses.

Hountondji's Conception of Philosophy as a Theory of Science and the Future of African Philosophy

According to Hountondji, philosophy is essentially a second-order discourse that is parasitic on first-order scientific discourse—that is, the theories and practices that constitute the natural sciences, along with mathematics. Hountondji takes Galileo's mechanics as the paradigmatic exemplar of science. Philosophy, in this view, is essentially a theory of science. As he puts it, "[Philosophy] is no more than reflection on the aims of science" (Hountondji 1996, 73). Hountondji explicitly draws on Althusser's conception of the relationship between science and philosophy to argue that "the great philosophical revolutions are always the sequel of great scientific revolutions, so that philosophy is organically linked, in its growth and evolution, with the birth and development of the sciences" (97). In his essay "Lenin and Philosophy," Althusser supports Hegel's claim that philosophy is parasitic on science: "Hegel was not wrong to say that philosophy takes wing at *dusk*: when science, born at dawn, has already lived the time of a long day. Philosophy is thus always a long day behind the science which induces the birth of its first form and the rebirths of its revolutions, a long day which may last years, decades, a half-century or a century" (Althusser 1971a, 41). Thus, for Althusser, philosophy's development is tied up with the development of science (to which, of course, it can sometimes contribute by clarifying certain conceptual issues that may block further scientific progress): "If philosophy is to be born, or reborn, one or more sciences must exist. Perhaps this is why philosophy in the strict sense only began with Plato, its birth induced by the existence of Greek Mathematics; was overhauled by Descartes, its modern revolution induced by Galilean physics; was recast by Kant under the influence of Newton's discovery; and was remodelled by Husserl under the impetus of the first axiomatics, etc." (41). This view does not imply, however, that philosophy cannot in principle contribute to the development of the sciences. For example, Althusser thought that Cartesianism offered a new conception of causality that further contributed to the development of Galilean physics, which had run into epistemological obstacles in relation to the deployment of the Aristotelean conception of causality: "But it is also true that in certain cases (to be precise, Plato, Descartes) what is called philosophy also serves as a theoretical laboratory in which the new categories required by the concepts of the new science are brought into focus. For example, was it not in Cartesianism that a new category of causality was worked out for Galilean physics, which had run up against Aristotelean cause as an 'epistemological obstacle'?" (Althusser 1971a, 42).[12] Moreover, from the study of the history of science, we know that philosophical commitments often motivate scientists to develop new scientific theories (DeWitt 2010, 132).[13] Strictly speaking, to claim that philosophy draws its problems from the first-order discourses of the sciences does not imply that philosophy cannot shape the sciences by aiding (or even hindering) their progress.[14] Hountondji, in adhering to the claim that philosophy is a second-order discourse that is parasitic on first-order scientific discourse, need not logically commit himself to the claim that philosophy is somehow causally inert vis-à-vis the sciences.

However, Hountondji's reliance on Althusser is problematic because Althusser, by his own admission, did not study the history of philosophy or the history of science in any rigorous or systematic fashion (Fraser 1976, 458). Speaking of his knowledge of the history of philosophy in 1962, Althusser makes the following confession: "I felt I had to get involved in philosophy for political and ideological reasons and therefore 'accepted it' as it was with the knowledge I had: a little Hegel, a lot of Descartes, not much Kant, a fair amount of Malebranche, a bit of Bachelard (*Le Nouvel Esprit scientifique*), a great deal of Pascal, a little Rousseau, Spinoza, and Bergson, and my bedside book, Bréhier's *L'Histoire de la philosophie*" (Althusser 1993, 182). In 1965, the situation was not much better: "But then I became obsessed with the terrifying thought that these texts [*Pour Marx* and *Lire 'le Capital'*] would expose me completely to the public at large as I really was, namely a trickster and a deceiver and nothing more, a philosopher who knew almost nothing about the history of philosophy or about Marx (though I had certainly made a close study of his early work, I had only seriously studied Book I of *Capital* in 1964 when I took a seminar which resulted in *Lire 'le Capital'*)" (148). Fortunately, despite Hountondji relying uncritically on Althusser and not offering independent evidence to support his claim, one need not rely on Althusser's rather dubious knowledge of the history of science and philosophy to find evidentiary support for the claim that the development of the empirical sciences provided philosophy with both its problematic (i.e., the questions that it raised) and the tools by means of which philosophers have attempted to answer those questions. The thesis that the scientific revolution was a necessary condition for the development of modern philosophy is not unique to Althusser, and it was advanced by others whose historical knowledge was more reliable. For example, Hegel, who essentially founded the history of philosophy as a subdiscipline of academic philosophy in the modern research university (Collingwood 1994, 126; Hösle 2003, 186; Kaufmann 1972, 21; Lukács 1975, 265), claims that "without the working out of the empirical sciences on their own account, philosophy could not have reached further than with the ancients" (ohne die Ausbildung der Erfahrungwissenschaften für sich hätte die Philosophie nicht weiter kommen können als bei den Alten) (Hegel 1995, 176). In other words, without the modern scientific revolution, modern philosophy would have been impossible.[15] Other thinkers who put forward the claim that the problematic of modern philosophy is derived from the development of modern science include Otto Bauer. Speaking of Kant, Bauer claims that "in order for Kant to have accomplished his works, much had to precede it. The emergence of modern science: without a Newton, no Kant" (Bauer 2015, 301). Kant took Hume's problem of induction to constitute a challenge to Newton's mechanics, precisely because it undermined the epistemic warrant for attributing necessity to Newton's three laws of motion. This was the primary motivation behind Kant's attempt at deriving the three laws of motion, in his *Metaphysical Foundations of Natural Science* (1786), in such a way as to demonstrate their necessity.[16]

Alexandre Koyré is another key thinker who throughout his career attempted to emphasize the intimate connection that existed between developments in modern science (specifically, modern Galilean physics) and modern philosophy. Koyré contends that the history of scientific thought and the history of philosophy in the fifteenth and sixteenth centuries cannot be separated from one another (Koyré 1957, 2).[17] One can also point to contemporary scholarship using methodological approaches to the history of early modern philosophy that recognize the importance of taking into account early modern science when attempting to understand early modern philosophy (Klein 2013, 157; J. Smith 2013, 42–43).

We also know that Thomas Hobbes set out to reconstruct philosophy not on the basis of Aristotle's categories but rather on the basis of categories derived from Galileo's new science, hence his attempt to reduce the concept of being to one of matter in motion (Foisneau 2011, 802). Furthermore, a key metaphor in early modern philosophical discourse, that of the universe as a clock (and later as a watch), clearly cannot be explained without an account of the development of late medieval and early modern mechanical technology.[18] Moving on to the nineteenth century, one can also point toward the manner in which Charles Sanders Peirce's philosophy was deeply influenced by his reflection on Darwin's theory of evolution (El Nabolsy 2020a).

The point is that, while Hountondji weakens his argument through his reliance on Althusser's rather dubious account of the history of philosophy and the history of science, the thesis that he adopts from Althusser gains independent support from the work of historians of philosophy and science who are more reliable than Althusser. Hountondji does not devote much space to an account that supports this thesis; however, the account provided above reflects his own self-understanding: "Nothing or not much is understood of Plato if you don't realize the development of Greek mathematics during his era. You don't understand at all Descartes if you do not see in his philosophy, as Judith Miller put it, a 'metaphysic of Galilean physics.' You underrate the stakes of Kantianism if you ignore Kant's admiration of Newton and the deep fascination exerted on his thinking by the new physics" (Hountondji 2011, 92). Given this claim, it is reasonable to believe that Hountondji would sympathize with the reconstruction of his views that is presented above.

Hountondji also draws on Edmund Husserl, whom he studied rigorously in the course of his philosophical formation (Hountondji 2002b, 3–25), in his formulation of the relationship between philosophy and science in general (and African philosophy and African science in particular). For Husserl, "philosophy in general is first of all reflection on science" (Hountondji 2002b, 31). Indeed, for Husserl, science is both the object of philosophical discourse and a model for philosophical thought. In this sense, Husserl belongs to what some philosophers and historians of the philosophy of science have referred to as the tradition of scientific philosophy. According to Alan Richardson (1997), "scientific philosophy" refers to a set of methodological and metaphilosophical theses that were held by philosophers from the 1860s to the 1930s who diverged widely in terms of their attitudes toward substantial philosophical questions (or first-order philosophical questions). The list of scientific philosophers includes Bertrand

Russell, Edmund Husserl, the members of the Vienna Circle, Richard Avenarius, and Alois Riehl. What unites this set of disparate philosophers is their emphasis on science as the subject matter of philosophy and on the need to model philosophy on the structure of modern science.

While all the philosophers who belong to the movement that historians of philosophy of science label scientific philosophy can be said to take the empirical sciences seriously, scientific philosophers differ among themselves as to the exact nature of the relationship between philosophy and the natural sciences. For example, Avenarius thinks that philosophy should deal with only an empirically given subject matter if it is to become scientific and if it is to make any kind of progress (Richardson 1997, 428). According to Avenarius, this subject matter is composed of the empirically given scientific disciplines, and philosophy is understood to be a general science of the sciences. By a general science of the science, Avenarius means that the aim of philosophy is to provide a methodology of the sciences by means of which it can demonstrate the unity of the different sciences (428). For Avenarius, philosophy qua general science of the sciences is itself an empirical science, since all it does is organize the different empirically given (at a certain historical moment) scientific disciplines in a manner that brings out their unity.

Husserl, in contrast, thinks that the subject matter of scientific philosophy (which in his case is identical with phenomenology) is pure consciousness, as opposed to empirical consciousness, which is the object of psychology (Richardson 1997, 433). Husserl does not think that philosophy is only a second-order discourse on existing empirical sciences. Instead, he conceives of it as justifying the empirical sciences. The empirical sciences cannot provide answers for epistemological questions, such as "How can experience as consciousness give or contact an object? How can experiences be mutually legitimated or corrected by means of each other, and not merely replace each other or confirm each other subjectively?" (Husserl 1965b, 87). Husserl is clear that philosophy cannot be based on the empirical sciences: "If certain riddles, are generally speaking, inherent in principle in natural science, then it is self-evident that the solution of these riddles according to premises and conclusion in principle transcends natural science [otherwise there would be a vicious circularity]" (88).[19] For Husserl the natural sciences cannot serve as a foundation for philosophy because they are methodologically naive insofar as they proceed by assuming the existence of their objects and our epistemic access to them: "All natural science is naïve in regard to its point of departure. The nature that it will investigate is for it simply there" (85). For Husserl the natural sciences are epistemically naive insofar as they simply assume that they can grasp their objects. Indeed, for him the empirical sciences require epistemic justification from philosophy since it is only philosophy that can validate their methods (Lauer 1965, 44). Husserl's understanding of philosophy as a "strict science" (*als strenge Wissenschaft*) is thus not continuous with that of the more naturalistically inclined philosophers (who did not think that the task of philosophy is to justify the procedures of the empirical sciences).

That Husserl describes philosophy as a *Wissenschaft* does not by itself imply that he conceived of philosophy as an intellectual enterprise that is continuous with the natural sciences; the German word *Wissenschaft* can be used to refer to organized bodies of knowledge in general (Beiser 2011, 6). That is, it does not necessarily carry the connotations of a body of knowledge that deals with natural phenomena and that seeks to describe them in terms of quantitative relations (which I take to be the connotations of the English word "science" today). In fact, for Husserl, philosophy is more scientific than the natural sciences because it is able to attain the classical ideal of science: a system of necessary truths derived from self-evident first principles (Hardy 2014). The self-evident first principles are to function as axioms (the classical ideal being instantiated in Euclidean geometry). The empirical sciences cannot attain this classical ideal (although according to Husserl they strive to attain it), because the laws of the empirical sciences are only contingent and cannot be known to be certainly true. Husserl clearly thinks that, whatever ultimate reality is (presumably the intuitively given reality that phenomenology is supposed to study), it is not revealed by the natural sciences: "The natural sciences have not in a single instance unraveled for us actual reality, the reality in which we live, move, and are" (Husserl 1965b, 140). Moreover, while Hountondji notes that for Husserl "philosophy in general is first of all reflection on science" (Hountondji 2002b, 31), we should recognize that, for Husserl, phenomenology qua eidetic science that dealt with idealities is not dependent on any sciences that deal with factual existence (Kusch 1995, 183). In fact, it is an a priori science that would provide the foundation for all the other sciences (Friedman 2000, 44).

This leads us to an important problem for Hountondji—namely, the incompatibility between the concept of philosophy as theory of science as it is found in Althusser and the conception of philosophy as theory of science as it is found in Husserl. For Althusser, philosophy is dependent on the empirical sciences, on sciences that deal with factual existence. According to Althusser, philosophy can contribute to organizing the empirical sciences, but it does not aim at justifying them (N. Smith 1980, 67). We may, then, say that the empirical sciences are epistemically self-sufficient for Althusser (Schwartzman 1975, 323). Hountondji himself adopts this interpretation; he writes that Althusser abandons "philosophy's earlier and bizarre pretensions to 'founding' science" and limits his conception of philosophy "only to recognizing and identifying retrospectively [empirical science's] real procedures in order to give them conceptual clarity" (Hountondji 2002b, 11).[20] Now it is clear that this conception of philosophy as a theory of science is radically different from Husserl's conception of philosophy as a theory of science. Hountondji himself acknowledges "the enormous distance separating the author of *Formal and Transcendental Logic* from that of *For Marx*" (11). However, to speak of an "enormous distance" is to understate the problem, for they hold *logically contradictory* conceptions of philosophy as a theory of science (to uphold both the claim that the empirical sciences do not require epistemic justification from philosophy and the claim that philosophy is tasked with providing the empirical sciences with epistemic justification is to fall into contradiction). In their book on Hountondji, Franziska Dübgen and Stefan Skupien register the dual influence of Althusser and Husserl on Hountondji's conception of philosophy as science (Dübgen and Skupien 2019, 33). However, they do not recognize that, strictly speaking, Althusser and Husserl hold contradictory conceptions of philosophy as science, and Dübgen and Skupien do not point this out as a problem for interpreters of Hountondji (El Nabolsy 2020c). This problem is not recognized in Sanya Osha's engagement with Dübgen and Skupien's book (Osha 2019). Hountondji himself is aware that those two thinkers cannot be easily reconciled. On the basis of Hountondji's later work, it seems that, regarding the sociology of scientific knowledge, the influence of Althusser prevailed on this point (even though Althusser did not really devote himself to the study of the empirical sciences), because Husserl's understanding of philosophy as a theory of science does not seem to imply that a philosopher should study the history of science and the actual development of the different empirical sciences under different social conditions (Hardy 2014).

This is not to suggest that Hountondji's work is unmarked by his formative engagement with Husserl. It is clear that Husserl's strict distinction between philosophy proper as a strict science (in the aforementioned sense) and pseudophilosophy (philosophy as mere wisdom or a worldview [*Weltanschauung*]; Husserl 1965b, 143–144), influenced Hountondji's rejection of ethnophilosophy (which equated a given people's worldview with philosophy proper).[21] Husserl's paradigm of the science on which philosophy should reflect is the modern mathematical physics associated with Galileo: "With regard to the knowledge of external nature, the decisive step from naïve to scientific experience, from vague everyday concepts to scientific concepts in full clarity, was, as is known, first realized by Galileo" (Husserl 1965b, 100). Hountondji agrees with Husserl. Galileo represents to Hountondji a "turning point in the history of thought in Italy and in Europe" (Hountondji 2002a, 27). The emphasis on the significance of Galileo's mathematical physics is also evident in a comment he made on a paper presented by

Albert Bienvenu Akoha in which Hountondji refers to Joseph Needham's work on Chinese science and asks, "According to Needham, until the seventeenth century at least, Chinese science was considerably more advanced than Western science and technology ['Western' has only a geographic referent in this context]. . . . What happened, then, in the sixteenth and seventeenth centuries? The new development is Galileo's science" (Akoha 1997, 335). Modern science is characterized, according to Hountondji, by an underlying hypothesis—namely, that "reality could be hypothetically structured as a mathematical model" (Akoha 1997, 335).[22] When Hountondji speaks of philosophy as a theory of science, the paradigmatic science that he has in mind is modern mathematical physics. This represents a point of contrast with Althusser. While Althusser speaks of philosophy as a theory of science, the sciences that he has in mind include not only geometry and Galilean physics but also historical materialism qua science of history. Althusser is primarily concerned with developing a Marxist philosophy that would be the product of a reflection on the Marxist science of history: "Historical materialism thus means: science of history. If the birth of something like a Marxist philosophy is ever to be possible, it would seem that it must be from the very gestation of this science . . . after the long interval which always divides a philosophical reorganization from the scientific revolution which induced it" (Althusser 1971a, 40–41). Hountondji does not explicitly deny that the science that philosophy should be a theory of need not be natural science, he simply shows very little interest in that discussion.[23] Instead he focuses on modern mathematical physics as the paradigm of science, and in this we can detect the influence of Husserl.

Husserl's modernist attitude in relation to the relentless demand for rational justification and the suspicion of whatever is inherited from the past is carried forward (toward an emancipative project) in Hountondji's own work. Hountondji would doubtless agree with Husserl that "most essential to the theoretical attitude of philosophical man is the characteristic universality of the critical standpoint, which [is] its determination not to accept without question any pregiven opinion, any tradition, and thus to seek out, with regard to the entire universe handed down in tradition, the true in itself" (Husserl 1965a, 174). In other words, philosophy proper presupposes individual autonomy. This Cartesian aspect of Husserl's project appeals to Hountondji, who is above all concerned with establishing the necessity of the individual autonomy of the thinker. Hountondji seeks to demonstrate that anybody who wishes to see African philosophy flourish must also work toward the institutionalization of guarantees for individual autonomy. Only a fully autonomous subject can dare to "raze everything to the ground and begin again from the original foundations" (Descartes 1998, 59). Hountondji is very clear about the political stakes in his critique of ethnophilosophy: "In relation to this intellectual responsibility [of the autonomous subject], it was easy to see 'the political danger of ethnophilosophy': 'speaking through it is the ideology of group supremacy'" (Hountondji 2002b, 188–189).

Despite this, we cannot say that Hountondji's research program for a sociology of scientific knowledge in the peripheries can be located in a Husserlian paradigm.[24] Husserl's analysis of modern science (with Galileo as spokesman for modern science) almost completely neglects the technological underpinnings of modern science. Husserl's account of Galileo proceeds without any mention of the importance of the telescope for Galileo's discoveries (Ihde 2016, 50). In contrast to Husserl, Hountondji emphasizes the importance of the interactions between technology and science.

It is possible to object that Hountondji's definition of philosophy is too narrow, because to define philosophy as a theory of science is to constrain philosophy by leaving out the axiological subfields of philosophy (ethics, political philosophy, and aesthetics), which cannot be adequately understood as reflections on science.[25] In response to criticism by Lansana Keita to this effect, Hountondji seems to have acknowledged that his definition of philosophy is restrictive, conceding that philosophy is not exclusively a theory of science, but he still maintains that the *core of philosophy* is a theory of science: "While science theory [i.e., theory of science] is not all what philosophy is about, it remains an essential component and in some way the hardest nucleus, the specific concern of a genuine philosophical thinking as distinguished from the other forms of discourse" (Hountondji 2011, 92). He thus recognizes the limitations of his conception of philosophy, but he does not recant. Since my aim is to reconstruct his turn to the sociology of scientific knowledge through an analysis of his metaphilosophical views, I am primarily concerned with providing an interpretation of those views rather than defending them (which would require a much longer discussion).

We are now well placed to make sense of Hountondji's transition from a critique of ethnophilosophy to the sociology of scientific knowledge in the peripheries (especially on the African continent). If philosophy is dependent on science, it follows that philosophy "will not really take off in Africa until the other disciplines have done so. In any case, it seems to [Hountondji] a serious mistake to consider the problem of philosophy separately from the more general problem of science" (Hountondji 1996, 155). If philosophical discourse is parasitic on scientific discourse, it follows that "it is not philosophy but science that Africa needs first" (98). For if a robust tradition of modern scientific discourse does not exist on the continent, then African philosophy, insofar as it must reflect on science to generate problems (just like any other philosophical discourse), will replicate the primary failing of ethnophilosophy, its "extraversion" (its orientation to an intellectual discourse that primarily takes place outside the continent and that does not reflect the interests of Africans). Strictly speaking, the claim that philosophy is parasitic on the sciences, in that they provide it with its subject matter, does not imply that African philosophy cannot exist and develop without the existence of an institutionalized modern scientific discourse on the continent. Presumably, African philosophy can proceed by reflecting on modern scientific discourse that takes place elsewhere in the world. However, Hountondji is concerned not only with the existence of African philosophy; he is interested in identifying the conditions that would allow for the flourishing of African philosophy as a nonextraverted discourse on the African continent.

A Synthesis between the Hessen-Grossmann Thesis and Dependency Theory

For Hountondji, science and technology are the mediating links in the causal nexus that connects philosophical discourse with economic structures. Following Althusser, Hountondji claims that philosophical revolutions are dependent on scientific revolutions. Such scientific revolutions are in turn dependent on experimental breakthroughs that in turn depend on technological advances, which are ultimately a function of the level of development of the productive forces of a given society: "These breaks [i.e., scientific revolutions] are not, of course, in themselves purely discursive events but rather theoretical effects in the field of discourse, of experimental practices which inform science throughout, practices organically linked to human material practices as a whole, employing various technical processes and hence dependent on the development of technology and therefore of the productive forces" (Hountondji 1996, 98). It is important to preempt the objection that Hountondji is somehow engaged in a reductivist economistic project here. Hountondji does not claim anything like a one-to-one correspondence between specific kinds of philosophical discourse and specific kinds of economic structures. Nor is he arguing that science develops to meet demands for technological improvement that are put forward by those who own the means of production. Instead, it seems quite reasonable to interpret Hountondji as adhering to a version of the thesis advanced by Boris Hessen and Henryk Grossmann as reconstructed by Gideon Freudenthal and Peter McLaughlin. According to this thesis, technology was developed to facilitate economic development, and early modern (seventeenth century) science was able to make the advances that it did by studying that technology (Freudenthal and McLaughlin 2009, 4). Further, the purpose of early modern science was *not* the development of technology per se (let alone contributing to economic development) but rather the analysis of idealized structures (16).[26] Early modern physics dealt with idealized structures by relying on models that abstracted from reality—for example, modeling canon balls as point masses and assuming that projectiles were launched in a vacuum and not in a medium that offers resistance (air). Early modern science was not developed with immediate application in mind: "Scientific knowledge developed only when it was not required to give immediate solutions to existing problems" (17).

Hessen advanced two more specific theses. The first is that theoretical mechanics developed through the study of existing machine technology during the seventeenth century. The point here is that, according to Hessen, a study of the relationship between technology and science in the seventeenth century shows that existing technology was not developed by way of the application of theoretical mechanics (the common view being that technology was applied science). Hessen argues instead that theoretical mechanics developed through the study of existing technology (Freudenthal and McLaughlin 2009, 11). He points out that if one looks at, for example, mining, the ventilation and draining of the mines were accomplished by air and water pumps. Those air and water pumps were not the products of technology conceived of as an application of a preexisting theoretical science; rather, historically speaking, aerostatics and hydrostatics developed as fields of research through the study of existing air and water pumps (4). Even historians of science who are hostile to the Hessen-Grossmann approach to the study of early modern science admit that the study of ballistics led to the development of Galileo's mechanics, albeit via an indirect path (Pyenson and Sheets-Pyenson 1999, 306). A key point made by Hessen and Grossmann is that the abstract idea of motion, which was central to the development of mechanics, was derived from the study of actual machines that transform rectilinear motion into circular motion and vice versa (Freudenthal and McLaughlin 2009, 21).

The second thesis is that we can refer to technology (or its lack) to explain why a science of heat and its transformation into mechanical forms of energy did not develop in the seventeenth century (Freudenthal and McLaughlin 2009, 20). In short, Hessen argues that because steam technology was underdeveloped in the seventeenth century, a science of heat and its relation to other forms of energy could not be developed (22). It is well known that the science of thermodynamics emerged from the study of the steam engine and the internal combustion engine and not the other way around: "Thermodynamics not only received an impetus to its development from the steam engine, but in fact developed from the study of that engine" (Hessen 2009, 79). As the historians of science Lewis Pyenson and Susan Sheets-Pyenson (1999, 269) put it, "The steam engine did more for science than science did for the steam engine."[27] Thinking of technology as merely applied science (with science developing independently) is far too simplistic and ahistorical. As the philosopher of technology Barry Allen (2008, 120) notes, "A characteristic of an advanced technoscientific economy is that problems arising at the technological frontier prime the research agenda of the sciences."[28]

Hountondji does not explicitly refer to the Hessen-Grossmann thesis; however, he is drawing on a tradition of thought in which it is embedded, Marxist theorizing of the relationship among technology, science, and capitalism inflected through Althusser's influence.[29] Hountondji presents the preceding formulation (which is essentially a recapitulation of the Hessen-Grossmann thesis) as a hypothesis that requires further empirical historical research.[30] Specifically, he notes that it would involve answering some difficult questions, such as the possibility of discovering an experimental basis for calculus. Freudenthal and McLaughlin recognize the centrality of this question. They claim that "it can be shown at least for some cases that the conceptualization of the infinitesimal in mathematics and of the mathematical concept of motion in mechanics were developed in one and the same argument and were dependent on the same experience with mechanical devices" (Freudenthal and McLaughlin 2009, 20). With respect to the infinitesimal calculus, its conceptualization in terms of motions, or "fluxions" (20), points to how the development of the mechanical notion of motion (which in turn was derived from the study of existing machines) was key to mathematical progress.

Key here is that Hountondji thinks that the development of technology is a necessary condition for the development of modern science. Modern science is in turn, according to Hountondji, a necessary condition for the development of modern philosophy. The question becomes, is it possible to formulate a thesis that would, in general terms, describe the causal relations between technology and capitalism as a mode of production? Hountondji's answer, and that of other African theorists who were influenced by dependency theory and helped develop it as a research paradigm, is no. For them, there is an important distinction between capitalism in the metropolitan countries and capitalism in the colonies (and ex-colonies). This is not to say that two different capitalisms are in operation here. Rather, in the world-capitalist system, the effects of capitalism on social formations in the metropole are quantitatively and even qualitatively different from the effects of capitalism on social formations in the periphery and semiperiphery. Thus, it is not possible to speak of the relationship between capitalism and technology in general; one must further specify the question. One must pose two questions: one about the causal relationship between capitalism and technology in the metropolitan countries, and another about the relationship between capitalism and technology in the peripheries. According to Hountondji, the form of capitalism that was introduced in the colonies (and specifically in African colonies) was a stunted form of capitalism that lacked the inner dynamism of capitalism as it existed in the metropolitan countries: "The capitalist mode of production was basically new with respect to the traditional one, but it was deprived of the industrial activity, the sense of initiative, the propensity to incur risk, that made this form of economic organization productive in the colonizer's own country" (Hountondji 1990, 9).[31] For Hountondji the form of capitalism introduced in the peripheries (and specifically in African countries) was a dependent form that lacked any internal dynamism and that slowed down the rate of development of the productive forces. Hountondji argues that the scientific dependency that characterizes African countries today is essentially "a side-effect of economic domination, of forced integration into the world capitalist market, but within a subordinate sphere" (9).[32] Hountondji presents his claim as an application of Samir Amin's work on dependency to the sociology of scientific knowledge, as he admits in an interview with Franziska Dübgen and Stefan Skupien (2019, 175): "All my reflection and writings on scientific dependence owe much to my reading of Samir Amin."

Marx and Engels may have been right in thinking that capitalism, at a certain stage of its development, massively contributed to the development of the productive forces of metropolitan societies and therefore to the development of science insofar as its development is dependent on the growth of the productive forces. But they were mistaken in thinking that this was a global phenomenon. For example, in their ode to the marvelous creative powers of the capitalist mode of production, *The Communist Manifesto*, they claim that the "bourgeoisie during its rule of scarce one hundred years has created more massive and more colossal productive forces than have all preceding generations together" (Marx and Engels 1948, 13–14). They also argue that the bourgeoisie in its incessant search for markets, cheap labor power, and raw materials essentially "creates a world after its own image" (13).[33] For Hountondji, as well as Claude Ake (1978) and Amílcar Cabral (1979), this is not exactly correct, because what are created in the peripheries are extraverted economies, as opposed to internally cohesive economies (such as those that were created in the metropolitan countries), or what might be described as disarticulated economies.[34] This caused African economies in the colonial period to be responsive to external demands but not to internal needs. African economies are export oriented and internally disarticulated. They lack complementarity between different sectors of their national economies—for example, agricultural production does not serve the needs of industrial development in most African countries because agricultural production remains oriented toward the cultivation of cash crops for export: "Our economies are rendered always responsive only to what the Western world is prepared to buy and sell, and hardly responsive to our internal development needs" (Babu 2002, 5). This pattern characterizes not only the colonial period but also the neocolonial period. For example, in postindependence East African countries, the agriculture sector, geared as it was toward the production of crops that could be exported, was articulated with the industrial sectors of Europe, the United States, and Japan and not with local industrial sectors (Nabudere 1981, 129).

The form of capitalism introduced to the African colonies not only provided little incentive for technological development; it led to deindustrialization in some instances.[35] Alexis B. A. Adande (1997, 71) has argued that the collapse of primary metallurgy in West Africa can be attributed to both the Atlantic slave trade, which led to the decline of iron metallurgy on the coast of Benin between the seventeenth and eighteenth centuries, and explicit colonial policies under formal colonialism.[36] The suppression of *sodabi*, an alcoholic drink made in Benin by distilling palm wine, by French colonial authorities during the 1930s is documented by Goudjinou P. Metinhoue (1997, 60). To substantiate Hountondji's more general claim, of course, one needs to provide more empirical evidence, and while I cannot provide an account of deindustrialization across the African continent during the colonial period in this chapter, I can point to a very well-studied example of the deindustrialization of an African country—the deindustrialization of Egypt during the nineteenth century (Al Sherbiny 2007, 28; Amin 1978, 31; 1984; 2016; Al-Dāly 2007; Ayubi 1995, 99–108; Batou 1993; Clawson 1981; Marlowe 1974, 81). After the British invasion of 1882, Sir Evelyn Baring (who later became Lord Cromer) made it very clear that British policy would be focused on ensuring that Egypt would be deindustrialized and maintained as an agricultural country: "The policy of the government may be summed up thus: 1) export of cotton to Europe subject to 1 percent export duty; 2) imports of textile products manufactured abroad subject to 8 percent import duty; nothing else enters into the government's intentions, *nor will it protect the Egyptian cotton industry*, because of the danger and evils that arise from such measures. . . . *Since Egypt is by nature an agricultural country, it follows logically that industrial training could lead only to the neglect of agriculture while diverting the Egyptian from the land, and both these things would be disasters for the nation*" (Abdel-Malek 1968, 7–8; emphasis added).

Combining the Hessen-Grossmann thesis with dependency theory allows for the reconstruction of Hountondji's argument regarding the relationship between science, technology, capitalism, and colonialism on the African continent. First, there is the premise, derived from the Hessen-Grossmann thesis, that social forms that impede the development of productive forces impede the development of science. As Hessen puts it, "science develops out of production, and those social forms that become fetters upon the productive forces likewise become fetters upon science" (Hessen 2009, 87). The second premise is that the form of capitalism that was introduced in African social formations through colonialism impeded the development of productive forces (and in some cases led to deindustrialization). This premise is derived from some versions of dependency theory. From these two premises we arrive at the conclusion that colonialism was a social form that fettered the development of science. This synthesis of the Hessen-Grossmann thesis and dependency theory while not explicitly identified as such by Hountondji is an adequate reconstruction of his argument. Drawing on the Hessen-Grossmann thesis allows for a response to critiques (often not well placed) of dependency theory that say it has no theoretical account of superstructural elements such as science.[37]

Finally, I preempt one possible misinterpretation. One must distinguish between two claims. The first claim is that colonialism, by slowing down the rate of development of the productive forces in African societies, contributed to the technological and scientific gap between Western countries and African countries. The second claim, which is much stronger than the first, is that colonialism is *sufficient* to explain the technological and scientific gap between Western countries and African countries.[38] Hountondji is arguing for the first claim; there is nothing in his writings that compels us to think that he is arguing for the second claim. Logically, no contradiction is involved in holding that colonialism contributed to the widening of the technological and scientific gap between Western countries and African countries and affirming that colonialism alone cannot account for this technological and scientific gap. For instance, adherents of the first claim might also recognize that the technological basis of agricultural production in most African societies was different from that in European societies (and Eurasian societies more generally). The plow formed the technological basis of agricultural production in the latter (from the Bronze Age onward), and the technological basis of agricultural production was the hoe in the former (specifically in African societies south of the Sudan, with the exception of Ethiopia) (Goody 1971, 25–27).[39] Jack Goody also points to a technological gap in military equipment by the fifteenth century (28). The point is that one can concede all this and still maintain the claim that colonialism contributed to the widening of the technological and scientific gap between Western countries and African countries.

NOTES

Acknowledgments: I gratefully acknowledge the helpful comments provided by Jessica R. Ratcliff, Olúfẹ́mi Táíwò, Siba Grovogui, Angela Roothaan, and Salah M. Hassan on earlier versions of this chapter. I am especially grateful for Grant Farred's detailed engagement with this text. I am also grateful for Dhruv Jain's helpful editorial suggestions and for Sascha Freyberg's encouragement to think of these issues in the context of debates in philosophy of culture. Portions of this chapter were presented at the Science Studies Reading Group at Cornell University in December 2020 and at the Canadian Society for History and Philosophy of Science in June 2021. I thank the audiences at these two talks. I am especially grateful to Jason Ludwig, Owen Marshall, Gordon McOuat, Spencer Hayden, Alan Richardson, Bianca Crewe, Alex Bryant, and Georg Borg for their helpful and encouraging comments. I also thank Max Ajl for teaching me how to talk about dependency theory without sounding too silly. All errors are my own.

1. Tempels's significance lies in explicitly rejecting prior ethnophilosophical theories that depicted Africans, qua "primitive peoples," as unable to engage in theoretical thinking: "to declare on *a priori* grounds that primitive peoples have no ideas on the nature of beings, that they have no ontology and that they are completely lacking in logic, is simply to turn one's back on reality" (Tempels 2021, 22). However, for Hountondji, Tempels initiated a pernicious trend insofar as he presented worldviews as philosophical systems. Of course, the Belgian missionary is not the only target of Hountondji's critique of ethnophilosophy. For a list of African philosophers who engaged in ethnophilosophy and who are the targets of Hountondji's criticism, see Hountondji 1996, 44.

2. Hountondji later conceded that he did not pay sufficient attention to the critical thrust of Placide Tempels's writings (which eventually led to clashes with the Belgian colonial authorities), but Hountondji still maintained that despite Tempels's intentions, Tempels's essentialist attitude is evident in his contempt for the *évolués*, whom he considered to be "inauthentic" (Dübgen and Skupien 2019, 17; Hountondji 2002b, 214). Tempels was worried about "deracinated Africans" who could potentially revolt against colonial rule: "one runs the risk, while believing that one is 'civilizing' the individual, of in fact corrupting him, working to increase the numbers of the deracinated and to become the architects of revolt" (Tempels 2021, 22). This places Tempels in a line of colonial thinking that pathologized "detribalized" Africans, e.g., the Belgian colonial officials' well-documented contempt for *évolués* (Bouwer 2010, 59–60), H. L. Gordon's claim that only Africans who received a European education exhibited schizophrenia (Tilley 2011, 236), and the manner in which Western-educated Africans were often referred to as "half-educated" to denigrate them (Fyfe 1972, 94).

3. We can find literary illustrations of Hountondji's point in Chinua Achebe's *Things Fall Apart* and *Arrow of God* (Achebe 2009, 2010). In both novels internal conflicts and disagreements are primary plot movers.

4. Hountondji's critique cannot be leveled at attempts that do not presuppose unanimity. For example, Kwasi Wiredu explicitly distances himself from the myth of unanimity: "In talking of Akan traditional thought I do not mean to imply that there is a monolithic corpus of ideas entertained by all traditional Akans" (1995, 126). Wiredu points to internal differentiation in Akan thought—e.g., several solutions to the problem of evil (2006, 323–326). Wiredu also stresses the importance of attributing philosophical positions to individual thinkers (1996, 116).

5. Not all the philosophers who are identified by Hountondji as adherents to ethnophilosophy as a research program adhered to the goal of searching for African uniqueness, however. For example, William Abraham is quite explicit in his rejection of this pursuit: "The question of the existence of an African philosophy is not a 'uniqueness' question. There is no reason why, in order that there should be an African

philosophy, it has to be different from every other philosophy" (1962, 104). Abraham makes a distinction between the claim that there is a unity to African cultures and the claim that African cultures are unique. He adheres to the former but not to the latter claim: "When one speaks of the unity of African cultures, one does not thereby imply any uniqueness" (115). In light of this, to what extent can we even speak of Abraham as an ethnophilosopher in Hountondji's sense? First, while Abraham sometimes explicitly denies that he thinks of all members of Akan society as adhering to the same set of beliefs, he nevertheless proceeds in his analysis by speaking of an undifferentiated "Akan mind" (48), an error that Wiredu, for example, is careful to avoid. Second, there is also the manner in which he allows Akan culture to stand in as a paradigm for all African cultures (49). Third, there is a marked lacked of historicization in his account of Akan society, in the sense that in his structuralist discussion of Akan culture we hardly encounter any dates; instead we are presented with a thoroughly synchronic picture of Akan culture even though, for example, gender relations among the Asante were transformed dramatically after 1900.The relative independence that characterized the position of married women in Asante in relation to their husbands was increasingly undermined after 1900 (Tashjian and Allman 2002, 237).

6. This point was also raised in the 1950s by the historian Thomas Lionel Hodgkin: "There is some advantage in ceasing to regard Africa, as it has sometimes been regarded in the past, as a kind of 'thing-in-itself,' the private preserve of *Africanistes*" (1957, 16).

7. Although Tempels did recognize that Bantu customs changed over time: "The Bantu among whom we live are not completely primitive people. They have evolved. It is certain that their religion, especially, has done so. Their customs, habits, and behaviour must also have developed" (Tempels 2021, 34). To this extent Hountondji's characterization of Tempels is perhaps unfair. Moreover, Tempels was also concerned with showing that Bantu philosophy is fundamentally compatible with Christianity: "That which for rationalistic Western science remains just a hypothesis, an unproved theory, to wit, the internal and intrinsic growth of being, in the way in which the Bantu teach it, is precisely what is taught by the Christian doctrine of Grace, founded on the assured rock of Revelation" (Tempels 2021, 185). Hence, strictly speaking, it is inaccurate to say that Tempels was concerned with emphasizing difference. However, Hountondji is correct insofar as Tempels strives to show that the Bantu of whom he speaks are fundamentally different from modern, secular Europeans (even if they are not essentially different from Catholic Europeans) and that they do not need a secularized morality: "They are not yet so civilized as to lend a new lease of life to our dead-alive rationalism of 'lay morality'" (Tempels 2021, 116). Hence, Tempels does indeed construct Bantu philosophy as the essential other of modern secular philosophy. The positive axiological judgment that he passes on it is irrelevant for Hountondji's critique.

8. In colonial legal systems the fundamental distinction was not between colonizers and colonized but rather between those who were deemed native and those who were deemed non-native: "*Non-natives* were tagged as *races*, whereas *natives* were said to belong to *tribes*. *Races* were said to comprise all those officially categorized as not indigenous to Africa, whether they were indisputably foreign (Europeans, Asians) or whether their foreignness was the result of an official designation (Arabs, Colored, Tutsi). *Tribes*, in contrast, were all those defined as indigenous in origin" (Mamdani 2013, 47).

9. Hountondji is essentially asking, for whom does the African philosopher write? And for whom should the African philosopher write?

10. Hountondji's thinking converged with African Marxists who criticized African socialism as an attempt to sidestep the issue of economic and political dependency by way of redefining the struggle between formerly colonized and former colonizing countries as a cultural struggle. Abdelrahman Mohammed Babu implicitly argued that by claiming that the trajectory of African history was so completely different from the history of all other societies and thus that it was not possible to study African societies using the conceptual tools developed to study other societies, the proponents of African socialism were essentially adopting a version of the metaphysics of difference and therefore reinforcing colonial misperceptions about African societies and African history. Babu does not deny the existence of strong bonds of solidarity in many African societies at various points in African history. However, he argues that such bonds of solidarity were a characteristic of *all human societies that were at a similar level with respect to the development of their productive forces*: "The qualities which our petty-bourgeois intellectuals describe as essentially African are really *human* qualities which find expression when a community is at a certain level of productive capacity. When a community does not have the capacity to produce *social surplus*, there is simply no means of becoming unequal" (1981, 57). For instance, the claim advanced by some African socialists to the effect that rule through consensus was a unique feature of many African societies neglects rule through consensus (as opposed to majority rule) also being characteristic of many indigenous societies in North America (Dunbar-Ortiz 2014, 25). With respect to communal solidarity, Babu claims that the emergence of individuals capable of asserting themselves in relation to their communities in a manner that can undermine communal ties of solidarity is contingent on the existence of sufficient levels of surplus that would allow for the emergence of inequality. Babu's point is that when we adopt a historical materialist approach to the study of African history, we do not need to rely on the metaphysics of difference to explain African realities.

11. To deny full autonomy to the history of philosophy (or the history of science for that matter) is not the same thing as denying the relative autonomy thesis (even if it has been notoriously difficult to spell out this thesis in a convincing manner). According to the relative autonomy thesis, while the social relations of production exercise a causally determining effect on intellectual discourses (science, religion, philosophy, etc.), those discourses also have their own internal logics that cannot be ignored when attempting to understand, for example, the relationship between science and capitalism. The most well-known formulation of the relative autonomy thesis was made by Engels in a letter to Conrad Schmidt dated October 27, 1890 (Engels 1934, 81).

12. We do not need to rely on Althusser's judgment in relation to this point. We can point to recent work on the history of philosophy of science. Thus, for example, Schelling's *Naturphilosophie* has generally had a poor reputation, but Michael Friedman has attempted to show its influence on Hans Christian Oersted's discovery of electromagnetism (Friedman 2006).

13. For example, Copernicus was influenced by Plato and the Pythagoreans (at least as he thought he understood them) in his formulation of his heliocentric astronomical system (Koyré 1957, 29).

14. Hindering is a possible outcome because philosophers have sometimes expressed opposition to new scientific discoveries, e.g., the Aristotelean philosophers who opposed Galileo (Drake 1977). However, this incident must not be depicted simplistically, for there were also significant problems with Galileo's arguments; Galileo had no optical theory that could explain his telescope's magnifying properties (Chalmers 2013, 91).

15. A common misconception is that Hegel essentially knew nothing about the empirical sciences and their history. But his competence in the empirical sciences of his day has been established by many Hegel scholars (Burbidge 1996, 2006; Engelhardt 1984, 1993; Pinkard 2005; Posch 2011; Wandschneider 2013, 105; Westphal 2008, 284; Zuckert 2017). During his so-called Jena period (1801–1806), Hegel was actively involved in scientific research himself: he did research in botany, chemistry, optics, medicine, and geology (Ferrini 2009, 94). Hegel was deeply committed to ensuring that the contents of philosophy do not contradict the results obtained through empirical sciences. In the philosophy of nature section of the *Encyclopaedia* he writes, "It is not only that philosophy must accord with the experience nature gives rise to; in its formation and in its development, philosophic science presupposes and is conditioned by empirical physics" (Hegel 1970, 197). Thus, Althusser is entirely wrong to claim that "for Hegel, science, meaning the science of the scientists (which remains in the Intellect [*Verstand*]), has no primacy; since in Hegel it is subject to the primacy of Religion and Philosophy, which is the Truth of Religion" (Althusser 1971b, 119–120).

16. Kant thought that the concept of laws of nature implies necessity: "The word nature already carries with it the concept of laws, and the latter carries with it the concept of the *necessity* of all determinations of a thing belonging to its existence" (Kant 2004, 4).

17. Some scholars argue that, unlike Marxist historians of science, Koyré does not emphasize the technological or experimental underpinnings of scientific developments (Cohen and Clagett 1966, 160). While it is true that Koyré does not highlight the technological or experimental underpinnings of scientific developments to the same extent as Marxist historians of science, he also does not neglect them. He underlines the decisive importance of Galileo's telescope: "From now on [the development of astronomy] became so closely linked together with that of its instruments that every progress of the one implies and involved the progress of the other. One could even say that not only astronomy, but science as such, began, with Galileo's invention, a new phase of its development, the phase that we might call the instrumental one" (Koyré 1957, 90).

18. The first philosopher to use the clockwork metaphor as a description of the heavens was Nicholas Oresme during the fourteenth century (Casey 1996, 221). Note, however, that Oresme did not think of clocks as machines in the modern sense, and he was not propounding a mechanical philosophy (Wootton 2015, 436).

19. Heidegger criticizes Husserl's "pure consciousness" for essentially being exclusively concerned with ideal essences and therefore unable to bridge the gap between the ideal and concrete existence, i.e., reproducing the epistemological problems that Husserl identified as inherent in natural science (Friedman 2000, 46). Thus, Heidegger's analysis does not depart from pure consciousness but rather from *Dasein* qua concrete historical subject.

20. Here I also note the existence of a significant metaphilosophical disagreement between Hountondji and Tempels. Tempels, qua Catholic philosopher, thinks of philosophy as entirely independent of the natural sciences: "natural sciences can no more refute a system of philosophy than they can create one. Our elders used to possess a systematized philosophy which the most advanced modern sciences have not broken down" (Tempels 2021, 78). It is clear that Hountondji disagrees with this conception of philosophy.

21. Tempels is clear that this is what he is doing: "We have set down only the popular wisdom of the common man" (Tempels 2021, 76).

22. The common characterization of Galileo as a thinker who bracketed our immediate sensory experience is also found in Husserl. Husserl is critical of this abstraction, however, or at least of interpretations of it that deny our lifeworld. Husserl claims that, while the Copernican worldview involves a denial of our experience (nobody experiences earth as a body), the viewpoint of phenomenology, a viewpoint that does not deny our experience in this manner, is more fundamental than the viewpoint of the natural sciences (Himanka 2005, 640–641). Hountondji, as far as I know, does not comment on Husserl's critique of Galilean science.

Furthermore, Hountondji, in the passages quoted above, does not emphasize the other feature that is also distinctive of modern science, the institutionalization of an emphasis on experimentation (Pyenson and Sheets-Pyenson 1999, 74). This is especially startling given his professed commitment to the technological and instrumental basis of scientific discovery. This may be explained by those passages being transcriptions of extemporaneous comments.

23. Neither does Hountondji, despite employing historical materialism, explicitly define himself as a Marxist (Hountondji 2002b, 183). I suspect that this is because of the connotations of the word "Marxist" in Benin during the time in which he was writing, especially the connotations implying dogmatism. For his analysis and critique of the Dahomey Communist Party, see Hountondji 2002b, 181–184.

24. Neglect of Hountondji's work on the sociology of scientific knowledge is evident in Omedi Ochieng's account of Hountondji's philosophy. Ochieng overemphasizes Hountondji's commitment to individualistic epistemological orientations (specifically, Cartesian and Husserlian orientations) because he completely neglects Hountondji's writings on the sociology of knowledge (Ochieng 2010, 28).

25. Dübgen and Skupien (2019, 54) point out that Hountondji's definition of philosophy excludes several canonical texts that we would consider to be philosophy.

26. Misinterpretations of the Hessen-Grossmann thesis on this specific point are quite common (see, e.g., Pyenson and Sheets-Pyenson 1999, 89).

27. Nor should we discount the fact that many of the experimenters of the eighteenth century would not have been able to carry out their experiments or make their observations without the artisans who provided them with the necessary instruments. Without polishing and grinding techniques developed by artisans, the natural philosophers would not have been able to use their telescopes (Werrett 2019, 90).

28. The role of technology in the development of science has been discounted in some discussions of the place of science and technology on the African continent (see, e.g., Táíwò 2014, 80–90). Táíwò is of course correct in saying that theoretical inquiry has a different aim than technology (i.e., a physicist need not be concerned with producing anything at all). However, he does not seem to recognize the manner in which technology in many cases served as a necessary condition for the development of theoretical scientific enterprises.

29. This approach is also more subtle than thinking of science as a branch of the productive forces in a social formation that is dominated by the capitalist mode of production; such a view has been ascribed to Marx by some interpreters (Rose and Rose 1976).

30. It is unclear whether Hountondji ever read the work of Hessen or Grossmann. As far as I know, he never explicitly cites them. He may have learned of their work through Althusser or through direct contact with French Marxist historians and philosophers of science.

31. Under colonial French rule in West Africa, for example, a local African bour-geoisie was not allowed to develop. Entrepreneurial functions were instead allocated to Lebanese and Syrian immigrants (Arrighi 2002).

32. Some critics of Hountondji completely neglect his engagement with dependency theory while implicitly drawing on it in formulating their critiques of him (e.g., Ochieng 2010, 33–35).

33. For a counter to the charge of Eurocentrism that has been leveled at Marx by ex-cavating his relatively unknown writings on the non-Western world, see Anderson 2010. For an attempt that focuses on Marx's scattered references to the African continent, see Kalmring and Nowak 2017.

34. For a critique of disarticulation being unique to colonial economies, see the work of Sandra Halperin (2004, 2013). Halperin's basic contention is that all the features that dependency theorists have identified as unique to the disarticulated economies of the peripheries obtained in the metropolitan core areas until the post–World War II period. Halperin's model, however, underemphasizes the significance of imperialism (El Nabolsy 2020b).

35. This was especially true of the large concession companies of the Congo, which accumulated through systematic pillage: "Abir, the largest rubber concession company in the Congo Free State founded with Belgian and British capital, created no long-lasting entrepreneurial structures, introduced no new technology, no new market relations, no new indigenous elite" (Mavhunga 2013, 13).

36. In other parts of the continent the decline of metallurgy was due to internal processes—for example, the decline of metallurgy in Kordofan in Sudan by the eigh-teenth century (Spaulding 2016, 204).

37. An example of such a critique is found in Nabudere (2011, 34). I think that most such critiques are misplaced. They assume a monolithic entity is their referent in depen-dency theory, but dependency theorists display tremendous diversity. Often, critiques like those of Nabudere are really just references to Andre Gunder Frank's work (Frank 1994), which is then assumed (without argument) to stand for all dependency theory. Furthermore, the superstructure's role in contributing to social revolutionary trans-formations held much interest for many dependency theorists, and they were deeply influenced by Maoist China's Cultural Revolution. These points were brought to my attention by Max Ajl.

38. An example of somebody who has this view is Albert Mosley, who argues that "instead of science making possible Europe's exploitation of other cultures, it is equally plausible that Europe's exploitation of non-Western cultures allowed [Europeans] to de-velop the technological base we now attribute to science" (Mosley 2000, 29).

39. Jack Goody argues that this technological difference led to different forms of land tenure, which implies that it is not appropriate to use the concept of feudalism in analyzing African history (Goody 1971, 73).

WORKS CITED

Abdel-Malek, Anouar. 1968. *Egypt: Military Society: The Army Regime, the Left, and Social Change under Nasser*, translated by Charles Lam Markmann. New York: Random House.

Abraham, William E. 1962. *The Mind of Africa*. Chicago: University of Chicago Press.

Achebe, Chinua. 2009. *Things Fall Apart*. Toronto: Anchor Canada.

————. 2010. *Arrow of God*. London: Penguin.

Adande, Alexis B. A. 1997. "'Traditional' Iron Metallurgy in West Africa." In *Endogenous Knowledge: Research Trails*, edited by Paulin J. Hountondji, 63–81. Dakar: CODESRIA.

Ake, Claude. 1978. *Revolutionary Pressures in Africa*. London: Zed Press.

Akoha, Albert Bienvenu. 1997. "Graphic Representational Systems in Postcolonial Africa." In *Endogenous Knowledge: Research Trails*, edited by Paulin J. Hountondji, 281–308. Dakar: CODESRIA.

Al-Dāly, Muḥammad Ṣabry. 2007. "Jadal al-siyāsa wa al-iqtiṣād fi'azma Mehmed Ali Pasha bal sham: derāsa fi mawqif'ingilterā 1831–1838" [The dialectic of politics and economy in the crisis of Mehmed Ali Pasha in the Levant: A study of the position of England 1831–1838]. *Miṣr al-ḥadītha* [Modern Egypt] 6:19–68.

Allen, Barry. 2008. *Artifice and Design: Art and Technology in Human Experience*. Ithaca, NY: Cornell University Press.

Al-Sherbiny, Aḥmad. 2007. *Al-iqtiṣād al-miṣrī: bayn al-tab'aīa wa al-istiqlāl* [The Egyptian economy: Between dependency and independence]. Cairo: Dar El Shorouk.

Althusser, Louis. 1971a. "Lenin and Philosophy." In *Lenin and Philosophy and Other Essays*, translated by Ben Brewster, 23–70. New York: Monthly Review Press.

————. 1971b. "Lenin before Hegel." In *Lenin and Philosophy and Other Essays*, 107–125.

————. 1993. *The Future Lasts Forever: A Memoir*. Edited by Oliver Corpet and Yann Moulier Boutang. Translated by Richard Veasey. New York: New Press.

Amin, Samir. 1978. *The Arab Nation: Nationalism and Class Struggle*. Translated by Michael Pallis. London: Zed Press.

————. 1984. "Contradictions in the Capitalist Development of Egypt: A Review Essay." *Monthly Review* 36 (4): 13–21.

————. 2016. "Egypt: Failed Emergence, Conniving Capitalism, Fall of the Muslim Brothers—A Possible Popular Alternative." In *Development Challenges and Solutions after the Arab Spring*, edited by Ali Kadri, 19–38. London: Palgrave Macmillan.

Anderson, Kevin B. 2010. *Marx at the Margins: On Nationalism, Ethnicity, and Non-Western Societies*. Chicago: University of Chicago Press.

Arrighi, Giovanni. 2002. "The African Crisis: World Systemic and Regional Aspects." *New Left Review* 15:5–36.

Ayubi, Nazih N. 1995. *Over-stating the Arab State: Politics and Society in the Middle East*. London: I. B. Tauris.

Babu, A. M. 1981. *African Socialism or Socialist Africa?* London: Zed Press.

————. 2002. "Postscript to *How Europe Underdeveloped Africa*." In *The Future That Works: Selected Writings of A.M. Babu*, edited by Salma Babu and Amrit Wilson, 3–9. Asmara, Eritrea: Africa World Press.

Batou, Jean. 1993. "Nineteenth-Century Attempted Escapes from the Periphery: The Cases of Egypt and Paraguay." *Review (Ferdinand Braudel Center)* 16 (3): 279–318.

Bauer, Otto. 2015. "Marxism and Ethics." In *Austro-Marxism: The Ideology of Unity*. Vol. 1, *Austro-Marxist Theory and Strategy*, edited by Mark E. Blum and William Smaldone, 295–314. Leiden, Netherlands: Brill Academic.

Beiser, Fredrick. 2011. *The German Historicist Tradition*. Oxford: Oxford University Press.

Bouwer, Karen. 2010. *Gender and Decolonization in the Congo: The Legacy of Patrice Lumumba*. London: Palgrave Macmillan.

Burbidge, John. 1993. "Chemistry and Hegel's Logic." In *Hegel and Newtonianism*, edited by Michael J. Petry, 609–617. Dordrecht, Netherlands: Kluwer Academic.

———. 2006. "New Directions in Hegel's Philosophy of Nature." In *Hegel: New Directions*, edited by Katerina Deligiorgi, 177–192. Montreal: McGill-Queen's University Press.

Cabral, Amílcar. 1979. "The Weapon of Theory." In *Unity and Struggle: Speeches and Writings of Amilcar*, translated by Michael Wolfers, 119–137. New York: Monthly Review Press.

Casey, Timothy. 1996. "Medieval Technology and the Husserlian Critique of Galilean Science." *Proceedings of the American Catholic Philosophical Association* 70:219–227.

Chalmers, A. F. 2013. *What Is This Thing Called Science?* 4th ed. Indianapolis, IN: Hackett.

Clawson, Patrick. 1981. "The Development of Capitalism in Egypt." *Khamsin* 9:77–116.

Cohen, I. Bernard, and Marshall Clagett. 1966. "Alexandre Koyré (1892–1964): Commemoration." *Isis* 57 (2): 157–166.

Collingwood, R. G. 1994. *The Idea of History*. Revised edition with lectures 1926–1928, edited by Jan Van Der Dussen. Oxford: Oxford University Press.

Descartes, René. 1998. "Meditations on First Philosophy." In *Discourse on Method and Meditations on First Philosophy*, edited and translated by Donald A. Cress, 47–103. Indianapolis, IN: Hackett.

DeWitt, Richard. 2010. *Worldviews: An Introduction to the History and Philosophy of Science*. 2nd ed. Hoboken, NJ: Wiley-Blackwell.

Drake, Stillman. 1977. "Galileo and the Career of Philosophy." *Journal of the History of Ideas* 38 (1): 19–32.

Dübgen, Franziska, and Stefan Skupien. 2019. *Paulin Hountondji: African Philosophy as Critical Universalism*. London: Palgrave Macmillan.

Dunbar-Ortiz, Roxanne. 2014. *An Indigenous Peoples' History of the United States*. Boston: Beacon Press.

El Nabolsy, Zeyad. 2020a. "Freedom Giving Birth to Order: Philosophical Reflections on Peirce's Evolutionary Cosmology and Its Contemporary Resurrections." *Cosmos and History: Journal of Natural and Social Philosophy* 16 (1): 1–23.

———. 2020b. "Is the World of the Elites Really Flat? The View from Egypt: Critical Remarks on Sandra Halperin's *Re-Envisioning Global Development*." *Jadaliyya*. https://www.jadaliyya.com/Details/40763.

———. 2020c. "Review of *Paulin Hountondji: African Philosophy as Critical Universalism* by Franziska Dübgen and Stefan Skupien." *Marx and Philosophy Review of Books*. https://marxandphilosophy.org.uk/reviews/18110_paulin-hountondji-african-philosophy-as-critical-universalism-by-franziska-dubgen-and-stefan-skupien-reviewed-by-zeyad-el-nabolsy/.

Engelhardt, Dietrich von. 1984. "The Chemical System of Substances, Forces and Processes in Hegel's Philosophy of Nature and the Science of His Time." In *Hegel and the Sciences*, edited by Robert S. Cohen and Marx Wartofsky, 41–54. Dordrecht, Netherlands: D. Reidel.

———. 1993. "Hegel on Chemistry and the Organic Sciences." In *Hegel and Newtonianism*, edited by Michael J. Petry, 657–665. Dordrecht, Netherlands: Kluwer Academic.

Engels, Friedrich. 1934. "Four Letters on Historical Materialism." *New International* 1 (3): 81–85. https://www.marxists.org/history/etol/newspape/ni/vol01/no03/engels.htm.

Ferrini, Cinzia. 2009. "Reason Observing Nature." In *The Blackwell Guide to Hegel's Phenomenology of Spirit*, edited by Kenneth Westphal, 92–135. Oxford: Blackwell.

Foisneau, Luc. 2011. "Hobbes's First Philosophy and Galilean Science." *British Journal for the History of Philosophy* 19 (4): 795–809.

Frank, Andre Gunder. 1994. "The Development of Underdevelopment." In *Paradigms in Economic Development*, edited by Rajani Kanth, 149–159. Armonk, NY: M. E. Sharpe.

Fraser, John. 1976. "Louis Althusser on Science, Marxism and Politics." *Science and Society* 40 (4): 438–464.

Freudenthal, Gideon, and Peter McLaughlin. 2009. "Classical Marxist Historiography of Science: The Hessen-Grossmann-Thesis." In *The Social and Economic Roots of the Scientific Revolution: Texts by Boris Hessen and Henryk Grossmann*, edited by Gideon Freudenthal and Peter McLaughlin, 1–40. Berlin: Springer.

Friedman, Michael. 2000. *A Parting of the Ways: Carnap, Cassirer, and Heidegger*. Chicago: Open Court.

———. 2006. "Kant—*Naturphilosophie*—Electromagnetism." In *The Kantian Legacy in Nineteenth-Century Science*, edited by Michael Friedman and Alfred Nordmann, 51–80. Cambridge, MA: MIT Press.

Fyfe, Christopher. 1972. *Africanus Horton, 1835–1883: West African Scientist and Patriot*. New York: Oxford University Press.

Goody, Jack. 1971. *Technology, Tradition and the State in Africa*. New York: Cambridge University Press.

Halperin, Sandra. 2004. *War and Social Change in Modern Europe: The Great Transformation Revisited*. Cambridge: Cambridge University Press.

———. 2013. *Re-Envisioning Global Development: A Horizontal Perspective*. London: Routledge.

Hardy, Lee. 2014. *Nature's Suit: Husserl's Phenomenological Philosophy of the Physical Sciences*. Athens: Ohio University Press.

Hegel, G.W.F. 1970. *Philosophy of Nature*. Vol. 1. Edited and translated by Michael John Petry. London: George Allen and Unwin.

———. 1995. *Lectures on the History of Philosophy*. Vol. 3, *Medieval and Modern Philosophy*. Translated by E. S. Haldane and Frances H. Simson. Lincoln: University of Nebraska Press.

Hessen, Boris. 2009. "The Social and Economic Roots of Newton's *Principia*." In *The Social and Economic Roots of the Scientific Revolution: Texts by Boris Hessen and Henryk Grossmann*, edited by Gideon Freudenthal and Peter McLaughlin, 41–102. Berlin: Springer.

Himanka, Juha. 2005. "Husserl's Argumentation for the Pre-Copernican View of the Earth." *Review of Metaphysics* 58 (3): 621–644.

Hodgkin, Thomas L. 1957. *Nationalism in Colonial Africa*. New York: New York University Press.

Hösle, Vittorio. 2003. "Is There Progress in the History of Philosophy?" *Hegel's History of Philosophy: New Interpretations*, edited by David A. Duquette, 185–204. Albany, NY: SUNY Press.

Hountondji, Paulin J. 1990. "Scientific Dependence in Africa Today." *Research in African Literatures* 21 (3): 5–15.

———. 1996. *African Philosophy: Myth and Reality*. 2nd ed. Translated by Henri Evans with the collaboration of Jonathan Rée. Bloomington: Indiana University Press.

———. 2002a. "Knowledge Appropriation in a Post-Colonial Context." In *Indigenous Knowledge and the Integration of Knowledge Systems: Towards a Philosophy of Articulation*, edited by Catherine A. Odora Hoppers, 23–38. Cape Town: New Africa Education.

———. 2002b. *The Struggle for Meaning: Reflections on Philosophy, Culture, and Democracy in Africa*. Translated by John Conteh-Morgan. Athens: Ohio University Press.

———. 2011. "Dialogue with Lansana Keita: Reflections on African Development." In *Philosophy and African Development: Theory and Practice*, edited by Lansana Keita, 87–96. Dakar: CODESRIA.

Husserl, Edmund. 1965a. "Philosophy and the Crisis of European Man." In *Phenomenology and the Crisis of Philosophy*, translated by Quentin Lauer, 149–192. New York: Harper and Row.

———. 1965b. "Philosophy as Rigorous Science." In *Phenomenology and the Crisis of Philosophy*, translated by Quentin Lauer, 71–147. New York: Harper and Row.

Ihde, Don. 2016. *Husserl's Missing Technologies*. New York: Fordham University Press.

Kalmring, Stefan, and Andreas Nowak. 2017. "Viewing Africa with Marx: Remarks on Marx's Fragmented Engagement with the African Continent." *Science and Society* 81 (3): 331–347.

Kant, Immanuel. 2004. *Metaphysical Foundations of Natural Science*. Translated and edited by Michael Friedman. Cambridge: Cambridge University Press.

Kaufmann, Walter. 1972. "The Hegel Myth and Its Method." In *Hegel: A Collection of Critical Essays*, edited by Alasdair MacIntyre, 21–60. Garden City, NY: Doubleday.

Klein, Julie R. 2013. "Philosophizing Historically/Historicizing Philosophy: Some Spinozistic Reflections." In *Philosophy and Its History: Aims and Methods in the Study of Early Modern Philosophy*, edited by Mogens Laerke, Justin E. H. Smith, and Eric Schliesser, 134–158. Oxford: Oxford University Press.

Koyré, Alexandre. 1957. *From the Closed World to the Infinite Universe*. Baltimore: Johns Hopkins University Press.

Kusch, Martin. 1995. *Psychologism: A Case Study in the Sociology of Philosophical Knowledge*. London: Routledge.

Lauer, Quentin. 1965. Introduction to *Phenomenology and the Crisis of Philosophy*, by Edmund Husserl. Translated by Quentin Lauer, 1–68. New York: Harper and Row.

Lukács, Georg. 1975. *The Young Hegel: Studies in the Relations between Dialectics and Economics*. Translated by Rodney Livingstone. London: Merlin Press.

Mamdani, Mahmood. 2013. *Define and Rule: Native as Political Identity*. Kampala: Makerere Institute of Social Research.

Marlowe, John. 1974. *Spoiling the Egyptians*. London: Andre Deutsch.

Marx, Karl, and Frederick Engels. 1948. *The Communist Manifesto*. New York: International Publishers.

Mavhunga, Clapperton Chakanetsa. 2013. "Introduction: What Do Science, Technology, and Innovation Mean from Africa?" In *What Do Science, Technology, and Innovation Mean from Africa?* edited by Clapperton Chakanetsa Mavhunga, 1–27. Cambridge, MA: MIT Press.

Metinhoue, Goudjinou P. 1997. "Methodological Issues in the Study of 'Traditional' Techniques and Know-How." In *Endogenous Knowledge: Research Trails*, edited by Paulin J. Hountondji, 43–62. Dakar: CODESRIA.

Mosley, Albert. 2000. "Science, Technology and Tradition in Contemporary African Philosophy." *African Philosophy* 13 (1): 25–32.

Nabudere, Dani. 1979. *Essays on the Theory and Practice of Imperialism*. London: Onyx Press.

———. 1981. *Imperialism in East Africa*. Vol. 1, *Imperialism and Exploitation*. London: Zed Press.

———. 2011. *Archie Mafeje: Scholar, Activist and Thinker*. Pretoria: Africa Institute of South Africa.

Ochieng, Omedi. 2010. "The African Intellectual: Hountondji and After." *Radical Philosophy* 164: 25–37.

Osha, Sanya. 2019. "Critical Universalism." *Radical Philosophy* 206: 105–107.

Pinkard, Terry. 2005. "Speculative *Naturphilosophie* and the Development of the Empirical Sciences: Hegel's Perspective." In *Continental Philosophy of Science*, edited by Gary Gutting, 19–34. Oxford: Blackwell.

Posch, Thomas. 2011. "Hegel and the Sciences." In *A Companion to Hegel*, edited by Stephen Houlgate and Michael Baur, 177–202. Oxford: Blackwell.

Pyenson, Lewis, and Susan Sheets-Pyenson. 1999. *Servants of Nature: A History of Scientific Institutions, Enterprises and Sensibilities*. New York: W. W. Norton.

Richardson, Alan. 1997. "Toward a History of Scientific Philosophy." *Perspectives on Science* 5 (3): 418–451.

Rose, Hilary, and Stephen Rose. 1976. "The Problematic Inheritance: Marx and Engels on the Natural Sciences." In *The Political Economy of Science: Ideology of/in the Natural Sciences*, edited by Hilary Rose and Stephen Rose, 1–13. London: Macmillan.

Schwartzman, Daniel W. 1975. "Althusser, Dialectical Materialism and the Philosophy of Science." *Science and Society* 39 (3): 318–330.

Smith, Justin E. H. 2013. "The History of Philosophy as Past and as Process." In *Philosophy and Its History: Aims and Methods in the Study of Early Modern Philosophy*, edited by Mogens Laerke, Justin E. H. Smith, and Eric Schliesser, 30–49. Oxford: Oxford University Press.

Smith, Neil. 1980. "Symptomatic Silence in Althusser: The Concept of Nature and the Unity of Science." *Science and Society* 44 (1): 58–81.

Spaulding, Jay. 2016. "Iron Metallurgy in Ancient Sudan." In *African Indigenous Knowledge and the Sciences*, edited by Gloria Emeagwali and Edward Shizha, 199–206. Boston: Brill.

Táíwò, Olúfẹ́mi. 2013. "Cabral, Culture, Progress, and the Metaphysics of Difference." In *Claim No Easy Victories: The Legacy of Amílcar Cabral*, edited by Firoze Manji and Bill Fletcher Jr., 355–364. Dakar: CODESRIA and Daraja Press.

———. 2014. *Africa Must Be Modern: A Manifesto*. Bloomington: Indiana University Press.

Tashjian, Victoria B., and Jean Allman. 2002. "Marrying and Marriage on a Shifting Terrain: Reconfigurations of Power and Authority in Early Colonial Asante." In *Women in African Colonial Histories*, edited by Jean Allman, Susan Geiger, and Nakanyike Musisi, 237–259. Bloomington: Indiana University Press.

Tempels, Placide. 2021. *Bantu Philosophy*. Orlando, FL: HBC Publishing.

Tilley, Helen. 2011. *Africa as a Living Laboratory: Empire, Development, and the Problem of Scientific Knowledge, 1870–1950*. Chicago: University of Chicago Press.

Wandschneider, Dieter. 2013. "Philosophy of Nature." In *The Bloomsbury Companion to Hegel*, edited by Allegrade Laurentiis and Jeffrey Edwards, 103–126. London: Bloomsbury.

Werrett, Simon. 2019. *Thrifty Science: Making the Most of Materials in the History of Experiment*. Chicago: University of Chicago Press.

Westphal, Kenneth. 2008. "Philosophizing about Nature: Hegel's Philosophical Project." In *The Cambridge Companion to Hegel and Nineteenth-Century Philosophy*, edited by Frederick Beiser, 281–310. Cambridge: Cambridge University Press.

Wiredu, Kwasi. 1995. "The Concept of Mind with Particular Reference to the Language and Thought of the Akan." In *Readings in African Philosophy: An Akan Collection*, edited by Safro Kwame, 123–150. Lanham, MD: University of America Press.

———. 1996. *Cultural Universals and Particulars: An African Perspective*. Bloomington: Indiana University Press.

———. 2006. "Toward Decolonizing African Philosophy and Religion." In *Inculturation and Postcolonial Discourse in African Theology*, edited by Edward P. Antonio, 291–331. New York: Peter Lang.

Wootton, David. 2015. *The Invention of Science: A New History of the Scientific Revolution*. New York: Harper.

Zuckert, Rachel. 2017. "Organism and System in German Idealism." In *The Cambridge Companion to German Philosophy*. 2nd ed., edited by Karl Ameriks, 271–291. Cambridge: Cambridge University Press.

3

The State of Crisis and the Crisis of the State in the Twenty-First Century

RADWA SAAD

For nearly three centuries, the Westphalian nation-state model has been the foundation of modern political life. This model has slowly but surely obscured our ability to conceive of an alternative form of political organization. "If the State did not exist," argues Haskell Fain, "man would find it necessary to invent it."[1] The state, according to Hegel, is the "divine idea as it exists on Earth."[2] At the same time, the irrefutably violent origins of state building and the myriad crimes authorized in the name of state power make it one of history's most reproached political arrangements. In all its types and sociopolitical formations, the state is, according to Michael Bakunin, the "negation of humanity."[3] Within these age-old debates, the state's omnipotence in the modern world is nonetheless treated as an undisputed reality, one disguising the historical truth that it is a contingent historical development, not a permanent feature of human society. The human species as we know it today has existed for at least two hundred thousand years. The modern state only surfaced less than six thousand years ago. And yet, despite its relatively short existence, few can imagine human society without it.[4]

Part of the reason why few can conceive of a world beyond the state is the state's ability to reinvent itself and assume a multiplicity of functions throughout space and time. Indeed, history has witnessed many types of states ranging from city-states, feudal states, imperial states, and more recently, nation-states. Nation-states, this chapter's object of analysis, are indisputably the most supreme entities governing contemporary political affairs. However, their quintessential characteristics are easier to observe than they are to define. The concept of a state is reasonably straightforward. Its two main ingredients can be reduced to territorial sovereignty and a central government.[5] The state radiates authoritatively outward from a center but halts at defined territorial boundaries. As Michael Mann notes, "The state is, indeed, a [mere] *place*—both a central place and a unified territorial reach."[6]

The concept of a nation, however, has proved more elusive. The inescapable paradox of nationalism in the modern world is its incontrovertible political saliency vis-à-vis its "philosophical poverty and even incoherence."[7] Unlike most other isms and ideologies, notes Benedict Anderson, "nationalism has never produced its own grand thinkers: no Hobbeses, Tocquevilles, Marxes, or Webers." Its scholars are therefore constrained by its conceptual emptiness.[8] The reason for this paucity of thinkers, according to Anderson, is that the nation is a social construct, an imagined political community embedded in a set of symbols, myths, and other cultural artifacts that foster a sense of collectivity.[9] Political mythology, historical revisionism, and the use of fiction are indispensable mechanisms in the imagining of a nation and its genesis. The nation-*state* arises when a group moves from mythical accounts pertaining to the birth of a nation and its attendant calls to territory, ethnicity, language, and the like, to claims of statehood. State-building processes may lend credence to the imagined concept of a nation through not only references to bloodshed in battles but also the succeeding formation of tangible constitutions, institutions, doctrines, and legal codes that grant the state legitimacy and meaning. Nations can exist without states, true, but there cannot be a state without a nation or, at the very least, the pursuit, imagining, or quest for it. This marriage between the nation and the state or the interplay between myth and reality is the sanctified dialectic that constitutes the modern political landscape as we know it.

This chapter examines how this sanctioned dialectic simultaneously enhances the state's vulnerability and reinforces its saliency. I argue that the survival of the nation-state throughout the twentieth century was contingent on a delicate balance of material truths and fictitious narratives that has come under threat by the rise of neoliberal capitalism and paradigms. First, I establish the centrality of political fiction and mythology in the making of nation-states, a tool that distinguishes it from other historical forms of political organization. Second, I demonstrate how neoliberalism's attack on the "collective" and the "social" challenge the nation-state's monopoly over its legitimating, albeit mythical, narratives in ways that threaten its foundation and preservation. Third, I discuss how this crisis in legitimacy has led to the rise of two divergent trends conceived as alternative modes of political organization: transnationalism and devolution. I conclude that neither of these trends pose an ideal alternative to the state but rather reinforce its necessity.

Truth and Fiction: The Making of the Nation-State

The most definitively accepted feature of the modern nation-state is the Weberian notion of a human community that can monopolize the legitimate use of violence within a given territory. This understanding of the state is incomplete, at best. Although state actors may acquire power through violence, violence in and of itself cannot legitimate the state. To maintain violence, notes Vincent Della Sala, the state must also monopolize *"the narratives of what constitutes legitimate political authority, where it comes from and who has the right to enjoy its collective goods."*[10] To create a nation or a group that can contemplate itself as a collective within the borders of state is to instrumentalize the use of fiction, particularly political mythology. Myths are formidable political tools for galvanizing the masses.[11] According to Henry Tudor, a myth is a story told in dramatic prose that is believed to be true regardless of the veracity of its content to help people "come to grips with reality" and make sense of their present conditions.[12] Myths provide individuals with ways to identify politically and generate solidarity among those who share that identity. They develop links between the governing entity and its subjects by telling a story about who has the legitimate right to govern and why obedience is warranted.[13] A collective is forged through both the content of the story and its transmission and reproduction by members of the political community.[14] In this process, truth may be entirely subordinated to political efficacy, even when what is asserted lacks any plausibility.[15]

Perhaps the most salient myth at the heart of every nation-state is what Carl Schmitt identifies as the friend-enemy distinction that marks the legal boundaries of a state and gives birth to a political community within it. Schmitt argues that the "phenomenon of the political can be understood only in the context of the ever present possibility of the friend-and-enemy grouping, regardless of the aspects which this possibility implies for morality, aesthetics, and economics."[16] The nation-state remains the decisive political entity insofar as it possesses the "right to demand from its own members the readiness to die and to unhesitatingly kill enemies."[17] This demand for self-sacrifice distinguishes nation-states, and by extension, national conscript armies, from other historic forms of statehood and defense. Membership within this political community requires an unwavering identification with whatever substantive characteristics mark the identity of a group.[18] What Schmitt fails to cast light on, however, is how this binary is generated and reinforced. Identifying a collective enemy group in need of annihilation is neither intrinsic nor logical, since "there exists no rational purpose, no norm no matter how true, no program no matter how exemplary, no social ideal no matter how beautiful, no legitimacy nor legality which could justify men in killing each other for this reason."[19] The degree of courage, passion, and self-sacrifice required to pursue a cause that individual entities have little or nothing to gain from cannot be explicated through parochial pragmatism. It is not rational analysis that impels violence; it is rather the "*pouvoir moteur* of a great myth."[20]

If the friend-enemy principle is the distinction that solidifies the borders of the state, then the social contract is the myth that governs relations within it. Schmitt's distinction works on the condition of self-sacrifice; members of a political group commit themselves to the greater sociopolitical good by pledging to oppose a common enemy. To do so, they must first identify as a collective and acknowledge the state's ultimate authority in governing relations of life and death on behalf of this collective. This agreement derives from the social contract, or the negotiated settlement between the rulers and the ruled. However, to speak of a nation-state in terms of a social contract is contingent on the a priori existence of a "social," an order of social being they commit to uphold. In reality, the social contract is neither negotiated nor consensual. It is, rather, the product of force, historical circumstance, and unequal power relations, a convenient fiction passed down from one generation to another, to lend credence to state power, to justify the state's monopoly on power. In his account of social contract theory, David Hume argues that the concept of a social contract is a convenient form of fiction:

> As no party, in the present age can well support itself without a philosophical or speculative system of principles annexed to its political or practical one; we accordingly find that each of the factions into which this nation is divided has reared up a fabric of the former kind, in order to protect and cover that scheme of actions which it pursues.[21]

Few if any nations were not consolidated through state-sanctioned violence ranging from slavery to genocide and the illegitimate seizure of indigenous lands. Such historical realities, however, tend to be overlooked in the origin of the social contract, all in the cause of preserving the foundational good that is the myth of origins. For this reason, Fredric Jameson opposes political theory. According to Jameson, political theory is nothing without the nation-state, and so the discipline inevitably fails to constitute the object of its study—which is the collective.[22] "Owing to our individualization as biological entities," Jameson reminds us, "the collective is, as such, impossible to conceptualize."[23] The "social contract" as a reflection of the "general will" is the "singling out" of "the moment when a collectivity comes to 'maturity'" by appropriating the new sociopolitical formation for its own end through a "deliberate and collective act."[24] The collective is thus transient, incapable of being represented in the moments following this act—a constituting fiction. It is born in resistance to temporal conditions of oppression but is unlikely to endure in their aftermath once liberation from those commonly identified circumstances has been achieved. Any attempt to manufacture a lasting collective must thus appeal to the affective power of fiction to sustain itself.

Fiction articulates a nation, but too much fiction without immanence is a difficult sell. What prevents a population from collectively rising against the state's coercive penetration of social life is its ability to be of use to its constituents. The success story of the state can be recast as one of centralization, concentration, and absorption. Its survival stems from its unprecedented—but not unchallenged—ability to organize into singularity the social, military, and economic functions once distributed across multiple and possibly disparate institutions.[25] In other words, the state's power and influence is, in part, derived from these institutions but in the process acquires a degree of autonomy that enhances its utility.[26]

The provision of public goods lends truth to the fictional construct of a nation and compels its citizens to act as a collective to defend its—and their—existence. Access to education, security, and health care, among other collective goods, is how members of a political entity are led into thinking of themselves as a collective, with the requisite avenues of communal expression. In other words, adopting William James's invocation of pragmatism, truth is "*happens* to an idea."[27] In this sense, the state and society, much like nation-building and state-building, are inextricably intertwined and mutually reinforcing. As Michael Mann concludes, "Where states are strong, societies are relatively territorialized and centralized. That is the most general statement we can make about the autonomous power of the state."[28]

The Crisis of the State

In much of the twentieth century—a *longue durée* that marked the pinnacle of state power and autonomy—the state was based on a Keynesian-style state capitalism, or social democracy, aimed at balancing the tripartite forces of state, capital, and labor.[29] This post–World War II agreement was made possible by a decisive shift in the balance of class power that integrated workers into political processes, ameliorating the labor conflicts that marked much of the world after the Industrial Revolution.[30] The Keynesian state, later designated as the welfare state in some contexts, created a collective out of the ruins of empire and the persistent class conflicts that were a feature of economic life from the second half of the nineteenth to the postwar era.

In addition, it made possible the ideal of liberal democracy. For democracy to flourish, insists Rousseau, the power differential within a people must "not be so great that they can be wielded as violence." This entails that none may "be so rich that he can buy another and none so poor that he is compelled to sell himself."[31] An orientation toward democracy in the context of capitalism required state support for the redistribution of wealth and strong prophylaxes against corruption by wealth. The state thus assumed a more active role by intervening in the domains where deeply entrenched inequalities (often the result of monopolies and crude market outcomes) threatened the quasi-egalitarian social prerequisites necessary for democratic life. The amelioration of class, racial, and gendered inequalities gradually became the rhetorical promise of the state.[32] For the state to survive and thrive, Adam Smith's "invisible hand" of the market was to be mediated so that neither markets themselves nor winners within them could monopolize power. The triumph of the welfare state was the realization that the pursuit of social justice, a prerequisite for political equality, nurtures the facade of a loyal collective.

The welfare state compromise had the effect of solidifying national identity, reducing class confrontations, and suppressing the rise of the international proletariat. The more the promise of political equality and social justice in capitalist economies was promoted, the easier it became for citizens to support the discourse of national identity and its accompanying allegory, the shared social contract. Toward the end of the twentieth century, however, the welfare state model increasingly came under threat by the advance of the neoliberal paradigms.

For Michel Foucault, neoliberalism is the art of "governmentality" whereby "political economy reflects on governmental practices themselves." It does not question market principles to "determine whether or not they are legitimate in terms of right. It considers them in terms of their effects rather than their origins."[33] Governance was adapted to serve markets; markets were to be constructed, propped up, and occasionally even rescued by political institutions. Keynesian policies "formed the adversary and target of neoliberal thought, that which it was constructed against or which it opposed in order to form itself and develop."[34] The premise of neoliberalism according to its intellectual vanguard, the likes of Friedrich Hayek, Milton Friedman, and other thinkers in the Chicago School, was an outright attack on the social or any attempt to create one and by extension, the welfare state that nurtured it. Whether by privatizing public goods (as in the Ronald

Reagan–Margaret Thatcher revolution), devolving its scope of intervention (though the United Kingdom's Big Society and George H. W. Bush's thousand points of light), or dissolving the administrative state (the underlying logic behind Donald Trump's presidency), the ideal of the social was rendered an unintelligible fallacy, to be replaced by traditional morals that organically arise from market relations and family structures.[35] Practically and conceptually, the existence of society—or the very foundation of a nation as an appropriate site of group solidarity, social justice, and commonwealth—was abhorred.[36]

Friedman and Hayek were determined, and perhaps sincere, in their attempts to debunk the myth of a social. It remains, nonetheless, a myth that is essential to the endurance of the nation-state. Dismantling "society" affected statehood in different ways. In more developed nation-states, it threatened the already fragile notions of political equality by undermining democracies, leaving in their stead oligarchies. It gave rise to xenophobic and exclusionary right-wing parties intent on preserving those vestiges of the social advantageous to their agenda. As antidemocratic and populist political figures arose, they generated a grotesque political landscape, plagued by powerful economic interests and populist zeal. The battle cry to "get government off our backs" transformed into a sweeping antagonism toward the political; it animated a movement of authoritarian liberalism in some domains and reactionary authoritarian moralism in others.[37] As Wendy Brown notes in describing the unintended effects of neoliberalism's attack on the social:

> Instead of being insulated from and thus capable of steering the economy, the state is increasingly instrumentalized by big capital— all the big industries, from agriculture and oil to pharmaceuticals and finance, have their hands on the legislative wheels. Instead of being politically pacified, citizenries have become vulnerable to demagogic nationalistic mobilization decrying limited state sovereignty and supranational facilitation of global competition and capital accumulation. And instead of spontaneously ordering and disciplining populations, traditional morality has become a battle screech, often emptied of substance as it is instrumentalized for other ends.[38]

For newer postcolonial states, the results have been even more detrimental. Structural adjustment programs put an end to government spending in all the domains through which a collective can be realized. The production of a nation was severed before its consolidation.[39] The expected benefits of statehood were especially questionable in postcolonial states where the Weberian state has yet to exercise the full force of its authority and establish legitimate control over the means of violence. Estimates show that as much as 80 percent of the world's population lives in areas of limited or failed statehood where the state's most basic function—the monopoly over the means of violence—simply does not exist or is significantly undermined by nonstate actors.[40] States are therefore left with the unachievable goal of pursuing the common good without a state, a reality that Colin Ward characterizes as "anarchy in action."[41] Universalizing the neoliberal paradigm through extractive neocolonial processes impeded the government's ability to procure any tangible gains for its population. Instead, it increasingly rendered the very notion of the state inept and exclusively violent in nature—in short, ruling through sticks without the incentive of carrots. In such contexts, the state itself becomes the biggest source of insecurity for its inhabitants, waging war against dissidents through legitimate or illegitimate use of violence to preserve the neocolonial pact between local elites and their Western counterparts.[42]

Apart from the domestic turbulence caused by neoliberalism, another critical implication arises from its global saturation. It has fundamentally reconfigured what is deemed political by altering the nature of relations among states. Under neoliberalism, states do not relate to each other as enemies or imperial rivals but as "competitors in the marketplace."[43] In seeking to eliminate the possibility of war between states, neoliberalism eschewed and obscured the friend-enemy distinction that grants the state its political value. Despite its attempt to dispose of the political by denouncing the mechanisms through which it is articulated and performed, it has failed to dispose of the conditions that generate political grievances. "Economic antagonisms can become political," Schmitt warns us, because "when the exploited and the repressed attempt to defend themselves in such a situation, they cannot do so by economic means."[44] In unleashing a plethora of economic grievances, a historically unparalleled level of inequality, and a range of social injustices, it has made the political inevitable.

Through the dual forces of globalization and technology, the friend-enemy distinction is being reconfigured by actors who do not adhere to the conventional rules of warfare. Increasingly democratized access to communication technology, coupled with migration and diasporic ties, frays social bonds and disperses relations through material and immaterial transborder links.[45] As noted by Philip Cerny and Alex Prichard, "Awareness of what is happening across the world is, thus, leading to an uneven mixture of convergence and diversity, the breakdown (and reinvention) of old and the formation of new bonds and identities."[46] The political—that is, making the sacrifice of death to defend a political community—is therefore reconfiguring itself through transnational alliances, the rise of terrorism and nonstate militias, and reactionary claims to theocracies that challenge the very notion of territorial sovereignty (such as ISIS). As technology exposes citizens to information that threatens the myth of a nationally defined collective by breaking down our perception of the Other, the state's ultimate authority of defining and declaring whom its enemy ought to be increasingly diminishes. The more its influence wanes, the less the state will control its own destiny, and the more the state will cease to be the main object of the political.

Notwithstanding these challenges however, the state is far from obsolescence. Like capitalism, it has proved capable of reinventing itself in times of crisis, often through the very apparatuses and mechanisms that generate them. To understand the state's enduring salience, irrespective of the challenges to which is has subjected itself, I turn to a Foucauldian approach of decentering the state as a departure point for the study of political power. This does not entail reducing the state's importance as a site of political action but rather recognizing that the state acquires its power only in relation to other existing modes of power and social relations that are both supported by and lend support to it.[47]

For Foucault, the state's concrete reality is incarnated through the work of its agents and inscribed in the central issues and discourses of its time.[48] The technologies of power, which grant the state its authority, are anchored in relationships that are "invented and organized from the starting points of local conditions and particular needs" and took shape in a piecemeal fashion.[49] The state "has no . . . inherent propensities; more generally, the state has no essence."[50] Rather, it is engaged in an indefinite process of defining and redefining its functions and ethos in relation to other forms of power. According to Stephen Sawyer's interpretation of Foucault, the state's history,

> is the result then not of accumulating a monopoly on legitimate means of violence, but is instead part of a *necessarily more incomplete process in which the construction of hierarchies and legitimacy takes place through the process of invoking the state itself.* As a result, state processes cannot take place without constant interactions with other sources and practices of power.[51]

Instead, then, of positing the state's incommensurability in relation to its constitutive elements, it may be more constructive to embark on an investigation of where the state has surfaced as a problem, by whom it is invoked, and in what ways it appears to be a solution. A deeper understanding of temporal threats facing the state allows us to probe the dispute mechanisms available to it and shed light on the possibilities of its trajectory, considering the realities of our day.

Globalization and Fragmentation

I have established that the state was once able to deliver on whatever achievements it made—and one cannot deny that in some contexts the achievements were remarkable—because for most of the twentieth century there was a workable fit among politics, economy, and control over information, which were all managed at a national level.[52] Centralized national authorities possessed the power to reinforce the myth of a collective while channeling economic and ideological synergies toward real human ends. Yet such possibilities have now become relics of a bygone era. The threats facing our world today—climate change, pandemics, migration crisis, terrorism, internet governance, and global market shocks—have produced, somewhat contradictorily, a liberal dream: state interdependency and global governance. Simultaneously, the loss of state legitimacy, the breakdown of national identities, and the destabilizing effects of modernization among communities have released a reactionary strand of reinvented tribalization. To resuscitate itself, the nation-state has had to relinquish some of its authority by moving toward decentralization and devolving some its power back to local communities. With pressure from the Bretton Woods Agreement institutions, the International Monetary Fund, the World Bank, and other international development organizations, decentralization was prescribed as a mechanism for implementing structural adjustments; strengthening democracy and good governance; and accommodating and appeasing ethnic, religious, and cultural minorities demanding greater autonomy over their decision-making processes. By the end of the 1990s most governments across Latin America, Africa, East Asia, and Central Europe oversaw some transition from centralized to decentralized modes of governance.[53]

The state thus finds itself ensnared between two divergent trends; transnationalism, or the attempt to amalgamate individual nation-states in a broader political community, and devolution, or the transfer of authority, responsibility, and accountability from central governments to local authorities. These trends diametrically oppose each other—one espousing greater representation, the other espousing direct participation; one favoring transnational cooperation and solidarity, the other favoring local solutions to local problems; one creating more bureaucracy, the other resisting bureaucracy; one seeking to *supersede* state power, the other seeking to dilute its influence—but both ultimately aim to undermine the state's hegemony and control. James N. Rosenau casts these tensions between "globalization and localization, centralization and decentralization, and integration and fragmentation" as the ongoing interactions constitutive of our epoch.[54] Sometimes they are cooperative but, more than not, they are conflictual.

Neither of these trends, however, is inherently novel; both have been operative since the inception of the nation-state and have maintained a tenacious hold on discussions about state power. The unsustainability of the state in its modern form was particularly palpable to those leading the decolonization movement in the mid-twentieth century. Postcolonial leaders perceived a twofold challenge in the Westphalian states they inherited: states too large to allow for meaningful democratic participation yet too small to address centralized global power.[55] Consequently, they channeled their efforts into experimental forms of direct democracy while also embarking on regional and transnational economic blocs and alliances to enhance their global leverage in the face of neocolonial capitalist exploitation.

Anticolonial leaders were forced to think beyond the nation-state and become *internationalists* to secure independence.[56] They understood the state as an instrument for upholding international racial hierarchies but used it as a medium for instituting a "radical rupture" in pursuit of a "reconstitution of the international order" to address deep-seated global inequalities.[57] To bypass legal, political, and economic hierarchies and assert a claim to self-determination, former colonies constituted regional federations such as the Organization of African Unity, the United Arab Republic, and the Caribbean Economic Community. These federations would lay the foundation for a more integrated and egalitarian international order that challenged the Westphalian state model, liberal democracy, and Eurocentric notions of absolute state sovereignty.[58] Kwame Nkrumah secured independence for Ghana in 1957 only to later propose that Ghanaians relinquish some of their sovereignty to the short-lived Union of African States. Eric Williams founded the West Indies Federation in 1958 in tandem with the British colonial office. Léopold Senghor in French West Africa made a similar move with the establishment of the Mali Federation in 1959. All these projects, albeit transient, outlined the need for transnational alliances and solidarity to avoid the predatory exploitation these nation-states were susceptible to under capitalism.

Reconstruction of an egalitarian international world order was doomed to fail, however, if it was not people centered or if the state became more powerful than the sum of its citizens. For postcolonial elites, the challenge of the state was how to reconcile meaningful democratic participation, which commences at the local level, with the centralization of state power. What is now termed devolution or decentralization manifested itself in rural-centered initiatives that sought agency-centered development and grassroots control. Notable examples include Gamal Abdel Nasser's agrarian land reforms, Muammar Gaddafi's establishment of popular commit-tees and people's congresses, and Julius Nyerere's *villagization* of the forces of production.[59] All these policies aimed to devolve state power and wealth by enhancing the capacity for direct participation in decision-making pro-cesses. Retrospectively, they were based on the faulty premise that the inter-ests of the state and its large peasant populations are aligned; a premise that was incessantly undermined by the state's distrust of the masses and a fail-ure to reconcile the shortsighted goals of the rural masses with the long-term developmental agenda of the state. Even the most ambitious and com-prehensive of these attempts failed to yield their intended developmental and political outcomes. Take, for instance, Nyerere's *Ujamma* policies, which at first espoused grassroots control as the foundation for state policy but quickly transformed into a forceful assertion of state authority in the name of development.[60] This was necessary, it was argued, because large parts of the peasantry showed little inclination to collectively organize themselves in pursuit of the state's long-term interests, a reality that Marx had warned of almost a century earlier.[61]

Yet postcolonial elites soon discovered that the barriers hindering direct participation were not only upheld by tensions between the central and the local or between the base and the superstructure; they were also embedded *within* local structures. In particular, the predatory influence of local chiefs who became the enforcers of a "peculiarly authoritarian version of tradi-tion" deprived the peasantry of meaningful participation in state-centered decision-making processes affecting their lives.[62] The centralization of state power in postcolonial Africa became a necessary means of liberating the rural peasantry from the regressive and authoritative influence of local chiefs and traditional authorities whose positions were strategically institu-tionalized through indirect colonial rule and later through the introduction of multiparty democracy.[63] Mahmood Mamdani argues:

> Even if the central state was reorganized as a representative parlia-mentary democracy, the local state continued to function as a de-centralized despotism. The same peasants who could elect their representative in parliament had little choice about who would be their chief wielding despotic power on the ground.[64]

Resolving the perennial dilemma posed by the dichotomous relation-ship between representation and participation entailed abolishing the influ-ence of intermediary traditional authorities who regulated the relationship between the state and its rural subjects. Attempts to draw the peas-antry directly into the domain of state power were rooted in a "militant anti-colonialism" that "linked militant urban-based nationalists to varied peasant struggles against chiefship and its corruption of 'tradition.'"[65] Paradoxically, devolving state power became directly tied to the state's ability to exercise its power directly over local populations and transform them into political subjects through a mixture of persuasion (often disguised in nation-building rhetoric and activities), coercion, and elimination of competitors. The promise of participation was an exercise in centralization. Across the board it became increasingly clear that the local must first be subsumed into the orbit of the national before the ideal of local empowerment could be realized. Needless to say, the aftermath of centralization rarely succeeded in fostering a revolution from below and was often accompanied by the imposition of a one-party system that was far from democratic.[66] Reforming localized despotism turned into centralized despotism.[67]

Such lessons demonstrate the complexities embedded in striking a balance between participation and representation that devolution seeks to reconcile. More importantly, they affirm Foucault's understanding of political hierarchies and legitimacy as being derived through complex processes that *invoke the state itself.* Another crucial flaw, however, remains in the paradigm of decentralization as a charted path to development in contexts where the state has yet to exercise the full force of its authority: how can one effectively *de*centralize what was never effectively centralized? In other words, how can decentralization manifest itself as anything other than a self-defeating exercise in the acquisition of state power and its subsequent negotiated concession to those made violently its subjects? Where statehood is limited or incomplete, the source of marginalization and disenfranchisement cannot be attributed to centralized state power. Rather, the source of the problem is citizen remoteness or exclusion from the center where the decision-making process and the redistribution of wealth is negotiated. If there is a need to decentralize power, it is preceded by the need to centralize it.

The alternative promise of transnationalism, in contrast, is currently rooted in the Kantian belief that the conditions for securing a "perpetual peace" could be constructed if all states embrace the tripartite forces of liberal democracies, liberal economies, and liberal international institutions of governance as the foundation for an international world order. Its rationale is bolstered by the democratic peace theory, which posits that liberal states tend to be prone to peace in their relations with each other yet prone to war in their relations with nonliberal states (and nonliberal states are prone to war with each other).[68] The democratic peace theory is arguably the most debated thesis in international relations, but there is ample evidence, albeit contested, affirming the proposition that the spread of democracy increases the likelihood of peace between states.[69] What the theory fails to account for, however, is the highly anti-liberal process through which this complex order was derived and institutionalized in the first place. Who is included in the making and representation of the discourses deemed international? What notions of democracy are accepted under this world order and what criterion qualifies states to fall into the reprimanded antithetical category of rogue states? How exactly are we to distinguish between peace derived through economic integration and peace derived through economic dependency and the exploitative flow of raw materials from the periphery to the core?

Such questions only reinforce the importance of the state. The power of individual states determines their leveraging position in the international landscape, enabling them to weigh in on the terms of peace and reap its benefits. At the very least, this is because concepts such as the universal, the international, and humanity that liberalism claims to be acting in the name of presuppose a state of peace but cannot in and of themselves become instruments of peace. As Schmitt reminds us, the concept of humanity—as it manifests itself politically—will always be politicized and instrumentalized to serve power struggles. "Humanity as such cannot wage war because it has no enemies. The concept of humanity excludes the concept of the enemy, because the enemy does not cease to be a human being."[70] In liberal rhetoric, the propensity for war is disguised as the need for military confrontations with rogue states and actors, a responsibility to protect from crimes against humanity and military invasions authorized under the pretext of spreading democracy, a notable example being the internationally sanctioned invasion of Iraq in 2003. So long as the prospect of war is eminent, then, the concept of humanity is politicized and stripped of its metaphysical essence. Schmitt exposes these contradictions in liberal theory, writing:

> When a state fights its political enemy in the name of humanity, it is not a war for the sake of humanity, but a war wherein a particular state seeks to usurp a universal concept against its military opponent. At the expense of its opponent, it tries to identify itself with humanity in the same way as one can misuse peace, justice, progress, and civilization in order to claim these as one's own and to deny the same to the enemy. The concept of humanity is an especially useful ideological instrument of imperialist expansion, and in its ethical-humanitarian form it is a specific vehicle of economic imperialism.[71]

A liberal transnationalism may prove capable of achieving a tenuous peace, enshrined through liberal imperialism and political pacification, but it cannot claim a set of universal values as reflective of humanity insofar as these values are deployed in contexts of governance and war. Liberal international organizations can raise the stakes of war, introduce new possibilities for warfare, and sanction wars under specific contexts, but they cannot eliminate the possibility of war and hence the political.

As far back as 1995, the French diplomat Jean-Marie Guéhenno and the Japanese organizational theorist Kenichi Ohmae separately published books titled *The End of the Nation-State*. Power, they predicted, would be ceded to supranational bodies such as the EU or dwindle down to regions and cities.[72] In the decades since these arguments were made, some of their predictions have been incrementally crystallizing, but the state's salience and resilience have demonstrated that these trends need not undermine its relevance. If anything, it has shown that *the only way out is through*. The nation-state, like capitalism, has yet to establish the full scope of its potential for the question of its demise to be a tangible reality in the near future. The fruits of neither transnationalism nor decentralization can be sowed in the absence of a strong state—one capable of exerting authority over its population through some sort of constructive hegemony or "predominance by consent."[73] Transnational organizations such as the United Nations and EU are only as strong as the sum of their states. If the power differences between states are too great, small states risk being exploited by their counterparts, a reality that postcolonial elites were highly cognizant of in their quest for self-determination. For decentralization to deliver on its promise of restoring a grassroots approach to state power, the state must first be able to exercise the full force of its authority and draw more people into its orbit. In other words, states remain the main actors on the global and local stages, even if they are no longer the *only* main actors.

The Way Forward

While some states are more functional than others, it is a reality that the state has become a site of insurmountable discontent globally. In every corner of the world, it is in crisis and governments are struggling to meet their challenges. Yet in nearly all the forms of resistance against the state (uprising, protests, revolutions, armed rebellions, political apathy), few, if any, are explicitly calling for an alternative to the it. Resistance remains, largely targeted toward the state: its capture, its reform, and its expansion but hardly ever its dissolution. Even those who live in the margins of the state, those to whom the state remains an elusive abstract entity with little bearing on their everyday lives, are being increasingly lured into its domain by struggling to assert a claim to its privileges, adopting its language of representation, and demanding recognition by those hoarding power.

It is an enigma that even in the most radical forms of resistance against the state, it nonetheless remains the object of dissent and desire; it is identified as both the problem and the solution. This predicament was elucidated by Hugo Albuquerque's description of how Luiz Inácio Lula da Silva's attempts to empower excluded minorities in Brazil eventually backfired by strengthening acts of resistance against state power. Despite observing an increase in their quality of life, it was as if this very improvement had become the catalyst for resistance:

> The central issue is less that people objectively "improved their lives" . . . but rather that they feel authorized to desire and therefore, desire without authorization. . . . No repressive formula is capable of containing the intense investment of desire—at least not for long.[74]

There are of course some exceptions to this. For instance, James Scott's prominent study *The Art of Not Being Governed* reveals how the disparate groups residing in the Zomia highlands of Southeast Asia have structured their social organization, agricultural practices, and cultural norms in ways that allow them to evade state power.[75] If these populations are "stateless" and "barbaric" as some would have us think, argues Scott, it is by intentional design.[76] Yet Scott nonetheless acknowledges that the intensification of state enclosure after World War II now makes such cultures of resistance a rare, if not extinct, phenomenon.

At least in the realm of desire, the state has perhaps managed to capture the imaginary of its constituents and its personae non gratae. If we adopt Hegel's proposition that all desire is ultimately a desire for recognition of a self that is always constructed through and within networks and discourses of power, then the state becomes an indispensable domain for the production and recognition of our desires. Once people are drawn into the domain of the state, whether violently or constructively, directly or indirectly, what emerges is a desire to be recognized by it. The state increases the scope of desire and empowers people to act on them; it destabilizes and uproots but also allows its constituents to identify with causes and clusters beyond their limited surroundings; it operates through power but inevitably provides opportunity for people to assert a claim to this power. As Slavoj Žižek notes, "Desire is always a desire for its own nonsatisfaction: its ultimate aim is always to reproduce itself as desire."[77] Perhaps, then, the question is not how to dismantle state power but how to broaden its scope to accommodate the vicissitudes deriving from this process.

If the virtues of statehood have been questionable, then current events—the COVID-19 pandemic and the international uprising against police brutality sparked by the Black Lives Matter movement—have added another level of complexity to the debate. In the midst of this global pandemic, it is difficult to perceive how the virus could have been contained without the state's ability to exercise control over movement and borders, enforce rigorous lockdowns, halt all economic activity (in an unprecedented milestone that granted primacy to human lives over capital), or offer testing, relief, vaccinations and shelter to those affected by the pandemic. If the legitimacy of state power was once in question, one would have to address the question of how the state was bestowed with the legitimacy to accrue unprecedented mandates that ranged from increased monitoring and surveillance, imposing mandatory testing and isolation, and the authorization of force to impose rigorous lockdowns. Such measures are an expansion of the biopolitics and disciplinary power at the heart of Foucault's modern state which are likely to have a lasting impact on individual freedoms, even in the aftermath of the pandemic. Where protests have erupted in relation to these drastic measures taken by the state to combat the virus, their genesis is not a question of the government intervening too much but of the government intervening *too little*. The pandemic not only demonstrated the indispensable nature of the state and its bureaucracy, particularly the medical component, but the need for its expansion. Medical workers are being hailed as the new soldiers, and their role in delivering on the state's promise of public safety and order has been avowed.

COVID-19 has managed to elucidate the state's indispensability in the realm of *human* security, but its role in arbitrating traditional mechanisms of security is becoming increasingly contested. The ongoing murder of African Americans, Latinos, and other minorities at the hands of police has incited global debates about police brutality and systemic racism, both of which are an indistinguishable feature of the modern state and international world order. These protests pose a critical juncture in state discourse as people target the very apparatuses, the policy and the military, that until recently have been the foundations of the modern Weberian state. The longstanding and futile paradigm of police reform has now shifted toward police abolition: a complete defunding of the police and security institutions to enable the rise of a new model for public safety that challenges the state's role as the sole arbitrator of institutionalized violence. What will be the role of the state in a post-Weberian order where the state's monopoly over the means of violence has lost it discursive appeal and legitimacy? The answer is yet to be determined. However, the demands of protesters worldwide offer some insight into the tangible alternative to coercive state power. By diverting police funding into impoverished communities, health care systems, education, and job creation, the state's basic function ought to be transformed from being the arbitrator of violence to being the arbitrator of social justice. In other words, to survive, it will become necessary for the state to restore funding to all avenues through which a *collective is created and rectify the sins of its past by incorporating those who were excluded in its making.* It is a question of redefining the terms of our collective existence *within* the state and *among* states, of rethinking the relationship between the nation and the Other outside it and the exclusionary friend-enemy distinction that has for too long served as the basis for collective action. The new collective may not buy into the fallacy of a life or death binary distinction between those inside and outside its borders, but if the material benefits of their subscription to a nation are materialized, this may be enough to render its existence one worth preserving by its imagined collective.

NOTES

1. Haskell Fain, "The Idea of the State," *Noûs* 6, no. 1 (1972): 15.

2. G.W.F. Hegel, *The Philosophy of History* (New York: Dover, 1956), 39.

3. Michael Bakunin, "Social and Economic Bases of Anarchism," in *The Anarchists,* ed. Irving L. Horowitz (New York: Bell, 1964), 143.

4. David S. D'Amato, "Understanding the Modern State," Libertarianism.org, August 10, 2018, https://www.libertarianism.org/columns/understanding-modern-state.

5. Meyer Fortes and E. E. Evans-Pritchard, introduction to *African Political Systems,* ed. M. Fortes and E. E. Evans-Pritchard (London: Oxford University Press, 1961).

6. Michael Mann, "The Autonomous Power of the State: Its Origins, Mechanisms and Results," *European Journal of Sociology* 25, no. 2 (1984): 185–213.

7. Benedict Anderson, *Imagined Communities: Reflections on the Origins and Spread of Nationalism* (London: Verso, 1983), 5.

8. Anderson, 5.

9. Depending on the content of its imagining, the nation can take the shape of a political community (French nationalism), a cultural entity (German nationalism), a linguistic affiliation (Arab nationalism), a racial group (black nationalism), or an ethnic affiliation (Kurdish nationalism).

10. Vincent Della Sala, "Political Myth, Mythology and the European Union," *Journal of Common Market Studies* 48, no. 1 (2010): 9; emphasis added.

11. Henry Tudor, *Political Myth* (London: Macmillan, 1972).

12. Tudor, 17.

13. Geoffrey Hosking and George Schöpflin, eds., *The Myths of Nationhood* (London: Hurst, 1997), 22–23.

14. Della Sala, "Political Myth, Mythology and the European Union."

15. Jeffrey Andrew Barash. 2000. "Political Mythologies of the Twentieth Century in the Perspective of Hermann Heller, Ernst Cassirer, and Karl Löwith," *Bulletin du CRFJ,* no. 6 (Spring 2000): 121–133.

16. Carl Schmitt, *The Concept of the Political,* trans. George Schwab, expanded ed. (London: University of Chicago Press, 2007), 35.

17. Schmitt, 46.

18. Schmitt, 43.

19. Schmitt, 49.

20. Tudor, *Political Myth,* 14. *Pouvoir moteur*: driving force; to empower through motivation. Tudor borrows from Georges Sorel's understanding of myths as "expres-

sions of the will to act" and the driving force of political violence. Georges Sorel, *Reflections on Violence* (Cambridge: Cambridge University Press, 1908), 19.

21. David Hume, *Essays, Moral, Political, and Literary*, part 2, essay 12, *Of the Original Contract* (1777).

22. Fredric Jameson, *An American Utopia: Dual Power and the Universal Army* (London: Verso, 2016), 23.

23. Jameson, 23.

24. Jameson, 23.

25. D'Amato, "Understanding the Modern State."

26. Mann, "The Autonomous Power of the State."

27. William James, *Pragmatism: A New Name for Some Old Ways of Thinking* (New York: Longman, Green, 1907), 201.

28. Mann, "The Autonomous Power of the State," 212.

29. Sandra Halperin, *War and Social Change in Modern Europe: The Great Transformation Revisited* (Cambridge: Cambridge University Press, 2003).

30. Halperin, 283.

31. Jean-Jacques Rousseau, *The Social Contract*, trans. Maurice Cranston (London: Penguin, 1968), book 2, p. 96.

32. Wendy Brown, *In the Ruins of Neoliberalism: The Rise of Antidemocratic Politics in the West* (New York: Columbia University Press, 2019), 28.

33. Michel Foucault, *The Birth of Biopolitics: Lectures at the Collège de France, 1978–1979*, ed. Michel Senellart, trans. Graham Burchell (New York: Palgrave Macmillan, 2008), 15.

34. Foucault, 217.

35. Brown, *In the Ruins of Neoliberalism*, 28.

36. Brown, *In the Ruins of Neoliberalism*.

37. Brown, 59.

38. Brown, 84.

39. See Adebayo O. Olukoshi and Liisa Laakso, eds., *Challenges to the Nation-State in Africa* (Uppsala, Sweden: Nordiska Afrikainstitutet, 1996).

40. See Thomas Risse, ed., *Governance Without a State? Policies and Politics in Areas of Limited Statehood* (New York: Columbia University Press, 2011); and Marianne Beisheim and Andrea Liese, *Transnational Partnerships: Effectively Providing for Sustainable Development?* (London: Palgrave Macmillan, 2014).

41. See Colin Ward, *Anarchy in Action* (Oakland, CA: PM Press, 2018).

42. 'Funmi Olonisakin, "A Human Security Approach to Peacemaking in Africa," *Strategic Review for Southern Africa* 37, no. 1 (2014): 3–8.

43. Foucault, *Birth of Biopolitics*, 7.

44. Schmitt, *Concept of the Political*, 77–78.

45. Few counties, including China, foresaw the threat from communication technologies that spurred new forms of collective action. Some have opted to circumvent these technologies' destabilizing effects by banning foreign-owned social media platforms and urging citizens to instead rely on government-monitored communication technologies, which are also sometimes government funded. This, however, requires coordinated, centralized effort and a highly authoritative mode of governance to implement. See Gary King, Jennifer Pan, and Margaret E. Roberts, "How Censorship in China Allows Government Criticism but Silences Collective Expression," *American Political Science Review* 107, no. 2 (May 2013): 326–343.

46. Philip G. Cerny and Alex Prichard, "The New Anarchy: Globalisation and Fragmentation in World Politics," *Journal of International Political Theory* 13, no. 3 (2017), https://journals.sagepub.com/doi/full/10.1177/1755088217713765.

47. David Macy and Michel Foucault, *Society Must Be Defended* (London: Picador, 2003), 28.

48. See Didier Fassin, *Juger Réprimer Accompagner: Essai sur la morale de l'Etat* (Paris: Seuil Back Matter, 2013).

49. Michel Foucault, *Power/Knowledge: Selected Interviews and Other Writings, 1972–1977*, ed. C. Gordon (New York: Pantheon Books, 1980), 158–159.

50. Colin Gordon, "Government Rationality: An Introduction," in *The Foucault Effect: Studies in Governmentality*, ed. Graham Burchell, Colin Gordon, and Peter Miller (Chicago: University of Chicago Press, 1991), 4.

51. Stephen W. Sawyer, "Foucault and the State," *Tocqueville Review* 36, no. 1 (2015): 147; emphasis added.

52. Rana Dasgupta, "The Demise of the Nation State," *The Guardian*, April 5, 2018, https://www.theguardian.com/news/2018/apr/05/demise-of-the-nation-state-rana-dasgupta.

53. G. Shabbir Cheema and Dennis Rondinelli, eds., *Decentralizing Governance: Emerging Concepts and Practices* (Washington, DC: Brookings Institution Press, 2007).

54. James N. Rosenau, "The Governance of Fragmegration: Neither a World Republic Nor a Global Interstate System," *Studia Diplomatica* 53, no. 5 (2000): 16.

55. See, for example, Muammar Qaddafi's remarks on the restoration of direct democracy in his political manifesto the "Green Book" (http://openanthropology.org/libya/gaddafi-green-book.pdf), in which he promoted the establishment of people committees and popular congresses as the path to "direct democracy . . . the ideal method of government" (23).

56. Adom Getachew, *Worldmaking after Empire: The Rise and Fall of Self-Determination* (Princeton, NJ: Princeton University Press, 2019).

57. Getachew, 17.

58. Getachew, *Worldmaking after Empire*.

59. See, for example, Gamal Abdel Nasser, "The Charter," in *Nasser Speaks, Basic Documents*, trans. E. S. Farag (London: Morssett Press, 1972), 90–151; and Julius Nyerere, *Freedom and Development* (Oxford: Oxford University Press, 1973).

60. Leander Schneider, "Freedom and Unfreedom in Rural Development: Julius Nyerere, Ujamaa Vijijini, and Villagization," *Canadian Journal of African Studies Revue Canadienne Des Études Africaines* 38, no. 2 (2004): 344–392.

61. See Marx's remarks on peasantry's inability to represent itself and establish a class consciousness in *The Eighteenth Brumaire of Louis Bonaparte* (1852).

62. Mahmood Mamdani, "Historicizing Power and Responses to Power: Indirect Rule and Its Reform," *Social Research* 66, no. 3 (1999): 877.

63. Mamdani, "Historicizing Power and Responses to Power."

64. Mamdani, 877.

65. Mamdani, 878.

66. Mamdani, 880–882.

67. Mamdani, 882.

68. See Immanuel Kant, *Perpetual Peace: A Philosophical Sketch* (1795).

69. See Zeev Maoz and Bruce Russett, "Normative and Structural Causes of the Democratic Peace, 1946–1986," *American Political Science Review* 87, no. 3 (September 1993): 624–638.

70. Schmitt, *Concept of the Political*, 54.

71. Schmitt, 54.

72. Kenichi Ohmae, *The End of the Nation-State: The Rise of Regional Economies* (New York: Simon and Schuster, 1995); Jean-Marie Guéhenno, *The End of the Nation-State*, trans. Victoria Elliott (Minneapolis: University of Minnesota Press, 1995).

73. See Valeriano Ramos Jr., "The Concepts of Ideology, Hegemony, and Organic Intellectuals in Gramsci's Marxism," *Theoretical Review*, no. 27 (March–April 1982), https://www.marxists.org/history/erol/periodicals/theoretical-review/1982301.htm.

74. Hugo Albuquerque, "Becoming-Brazil: The Savage Rise of the Class Without Name," *South Atlantic Quarterly* 113, no. 4 (2014): 856–857.

75. James C. Scott, *The Art of Not Being Governed: An Anarchist History of Upland Southeast Asia* (New Haven, CT: Yale University Press, 2009).

76. Scott, 8.

77. Slavoj Žižek, "The Seeds of Imagination," in *An American Utopia*, ed. F. Jameson (Verso: London, 2016), 283.

4

Insurgent Practices in Contemporary Francophone Africa

Emerging Critical Challenges

Kasereka Kavwahirehi

This chapter reflects on citizen movements that have emerged within the public and social sphere in sub-Saharan Africa since the early 2010s, more specifically in francophone countries such as Burkina Faso, Senegal, the Democratic Republic of the Congo, Gabon, the Republic of the Congo, and Chad. While it seeks to highlight their political meaning as well as their singularity by examining their context of emergence and demands, the ultimate aim is to shed light on the challenges these movements present for African political thinkers regarding the postcolonial state. In-depth analysis of this shifting political landscape remains limited. Scholarship has yet to fully examine these movements in terms of their methods of protest and resistance or their social and political grievances and therefore has not fully considered the new theoretical issues being imposed on African critical and social thought. Given the objectives of this chapter and the nature of these movements—which are particularly evocative of what Félix Guattari calls "micropolitics"[1]—my approach resembles what Fabien Eboussi Boulaga calls "thinking spatially," which consists of discovering that what is to be thought and done is out there every day, before our very eyes.[2] In other words, thinking spatially involves renouncing the countless theoretical fictions associated with diversion and alienation and turns instead toward "the surface (the visible), the near, the ordinary: these are the centers of interest, the theoretical and practical places that our situation fixes for us."[3]

This approach prevents us not only from colonizing events or phenomena by reducing them to the conventional or the already established but also from inadvertently neutralizing the possibilities they may contain. It is the same pitfall that Geoffroy de Lagasnerie faces in the introduction of *The Art of Revolt: Snowden, Assange, Manning*.[4] Lagasnerie suggests that the difficulty of making space for new concepts in the political sphere can be explained "by the fact that, when a singular movement emerges, the odds are that it will not be recognized for what it is. Its specificity and unprecedented character derail categories of perception and therefore escape notice. Movements of this kind often wind up being explained, even by those actively pursuing them, by way of preexisting terminologies rather than being grasped as original."[5] To overcome this tendency toward totalization, which consists of colonizing struggles, relying on outdated frameworks, and forcing events to be interpreted through globalizing and all-encompassing theories, it is crucial to undertake critical analyses that emphasize the importance of thinking in terms of singularity, specificity, and therefore, rupture.

Context of Emergence

In the 2010s, several youth-led movements came to the forefront of the political and social scene in francophone Africa. Although these young people are typically from civil society, they consider themselves autonomous and assert their independence from the latter because they deem it complicit with the very powers from which they seek liberation. These grassroots movements include Burkina Faso's Balai citoyen (Citizen's Broom), Senegal's Y'en a marre (We're Fed Up), the Democratic Republic of the Congo's Filimbi collective and Lucha (Lutte pour le Changement; Struggle for Change), Chad's Ça doit changer (Things Must Change), Gabon's Ça suffit comme ça (That's Enough), and Cameroon's Generation Change. In addition to these movements, many politically engaged musical artists have also expressed their quest and support for political and social change, including Tiken Jah Fakoli (Ivory Coast), Lexxus Légal (Congo-Kinshasa), Valsero (Cameroon), Luati Bereirao (Angola), and Keur Gui (Senegal). These artists use rap and reggae to denounce political leaders who not only perpetuate systems of violence and social inequality as a means of maintaining their hold over society as a whole but also condemn young people to social marginalization. To fully grasp the novelty and importance of these movements as they relate to African experiences of democratic invention (as well as intervention) and the quest for social change, we must consider them within a broader African history of social movements. Positioning them within such a history helps refute allegations that these organizations are devoid of historical depth.

The origins of these social movements in francophone Africa date back to the colonial period, with the most well known having been associated with national liberation and decolonization. In general, scholars have tended to concentrate less on the movements themselves and more on anti-colonial nationalisms and their contributions to nation building.[6] Furthermore, they have focused their attention on the political elites, to the detriment of the lower classes, who were relegated to the sidelines once independence was achieved.

In *The Black Man's Burden: Africa and the Curse of the Nation-State*, the British historian Basil Davidson provides a thorough analysis of this process. He shows how, after having won the national struggle with the support and sacrifice of the popular masses, nationalist elites stopped thinking about social struggles and ultimately cast peasants aside. These elites were quickly transformed into the national bourgeoisie and began to deploy forces of law and order against the masses when they demanded fundamental social transformation. The national bourgeoisie presented these grievances as threats to national unity and state stability.[7] Frantz Fanon correctly states that the new national bourgeoisie fed only nationalism to the masses, but what the masses actually sought was freedom and social justice. It would appear that nationalist leaders forgot that, while nationalism provided the impetus needed and was a major catalyst for the revolt against the colonizer, national consciousness needed to be transformed into social consciousness once independence was achieved.[8]

Thus, those very same Fathers of Independence were quick to downgrade and even silence social movements under the guise of nation building and the establishment of state institutions. From the mid-1980s, financial donors began to view civil society as the panacea for African democratization. However, civil society is not beyond reproach, since it might be partially responsible for some of those failed democratic transitions. As Francis Akindès and Ousmane Zina explain, "Dominated by international and local nongovernmental organizations, [civil society] represents a space for negotiating aid, a market, distanced from the popular masses who are supposed to lead the fight for democratization through sacrifice. Less dissenting, this 'civil society' supports the State rendered minimalistic by structural adjustment programs, in its logic of capturing international aid."[9] When issues with the existing system are raised, these criticisms often lapse into what Lagasnerie calls "systemic critique, that is to say, assertions that, despite the appearances and intentions of their proponents, are actually in line with the very systems they think they denounce, and thus, they reinforce them." This means that "there are discourses that, while being critical and true, constitute tricks of conservative reason."[10]

The mass protests of the Arab Spring that led to the collapse of the authoritarian regimes of Tunisia and Egypt in 2011 and of Burkina Faso in 2014 and the mobilization led by the citizens' movements Y'en a marre in

Senegal and Lucha and Filimbi in Congo against a third term of President Abdoulaye Wade and President Joseph Kabila, respectively, signaled the failure of political elites and the rise of new kinds of social movements on the continent. Indeed, while nationalist mobilizations and civil society in the past were led by nationalist leaders and intellectual elites, the movements begun in the 2010s are spearheaded by students, artists, and recent graduates who are often unemployed and, for the most part, lack social ties. These youth seek not to take power but rather to form an opposing force, acting as whistleblowers who occupy streets, virtual spaces, and social networks and whose rallying power remains epitomized by the Arab Spring.[11]

The movements' founders are cognizant of their historical roots. According to Alioune Sane, cofounder of Y'en a marre, this movement is the outgrowth of lengthy trade union struggles and long-standing Senegalese opposition to the single-party system that brought Léopold Sédar Senghor and Abdou Diouf to power. Balai citoyen, for its part, claims the legacy of the Sankarian revolution and the uprising of January 3, 1966, which overthrew the corrupt regime of Maurice Yameogo, the first president of Burkina Faso, then known as Upper Volta. Finally, Filimbi and Lucha are both steeped in a tradition of protest and a drive for social change, influenced by the March of Hope held in Kinshasa, Democratic Republic of the Congo (DRC), on February 16, 1992. Those peaceful protestors sought the reopening of the National Conference, which had crystallized popular hope for a new social and political order. The National Conference, whose mission was to reestablish a democratic state, had been unilaterally suspended by Mobutu Sese Seko, who saw himself stripped of what he considered to be his rightful power.

But there is more worth noting. While the young Burkinabe members of Balai citoyen take inspiration from Captain Thomas Sankara's revolution, and members of Y'en a marre relate to the Senegalese trade union struggles, Filimbi and Lucha members often refer to Patrice Lumumba, Simon Kimbangu, and Kimpa Vita, three historical figures who symbolize the fight for liberation and dignity of Black people. These allusions to historical figures—who at critical moments epitomized the importance of rebelling against the intolerable and who perished before seeing the outcomes of their respective projects—are of the utmost importance from the perspective of a philosophy of history and a memory of the future. They represent the will and desire of young people to bring forth a future dedicated to their fallen colleagues. By reappropriating the struggles of their predecessors, these youth seek to bring their stalled projects to fruition. Thus, to invoke Walter Benjamin, with the enemy vanquished, the dead will be protected and be at peace.[12]

As Ernst Bloch would suggest, for young people who are aware that they are part of a history of struggle and that they must move forward, it becomes a matter of blending "with the past in a living way," so that "others also come back to life, metamorphosed; the dead are resurrected."[13] In other words, one must find the traces of those past dreams of a better world and transform them into potentialities. At stake here is what Jean Ladrière refers to as "the call of history," which arises from the unrealized that is contained in the present world as a possibility waiting to be actualized:

> It is because we are able to bring a certain historical past to life within ourselves—made manifest by words, institutions, works, events, feelings, and collective presentiments—that we enable ourselves to carry the future of a time that is not strictly our own within our own anticipations. By taking the historical past into our own hands, which is also first and foremost that of others, we open ourselves in our own future to the future of history, which will become by virtue of our actions, that of others.[14]

Bloch, in "Notice to the Reader" that opens *Thomas Münzer, théologien de la révolution*, further explains that "all the past that deserves to be recounted exists to assign us a task, to inspire us, to support our ongoing project ever more broadly." To which, he adds:

> We never want to be anywhere but where we belong. Even then, our gaze is not retrospective. We mix with the past in a living way. And in this way, the others also come back to life, metamorphosed; the dead are resurrected; with us, their deeds will once again be carried out. Münzer saw his work brutally shattered, but his will opened up to far-reaching perspectives. . . . Above all, Münzer represents history in the most fertile sense of the word: he and his work, and all the past that deserves to be recounted, exist to assign us a task, to inspire us, to support our ongoing project ever more broadly.[15]

The Blochian conception of history as a repository of possibilities representing living options for future action—more specifically, that the unrealized potentialities of the past can direct present subjects toward a better and more desirable future—sheds light on the relationship that African youth have with certain figures from the colonial and postcolonial past.

This feature, common to popular citizen movements, can also be found in the novels of young African novelists, such as In Koli Jean Bofane's *Congo Inc.: Le Testament de Bismarck* (*Congo Inc.: Bismarck's Testament*, 2014), Sinzo Aanza's *Généalogie d'une banalité* (Genealogy of the mundane, 2015), and Fiston Mwanza Mujila's *Trame 83* (*Tram 83*, 2014). In a kind of insurrectionist style, these authors—confronted by endemic social crisis coupled with the deadly violence that pitilessly ravages the DRC—reexamine Congolese modern history through literature, using the Berlin Conference (also known as the Congo Conference, held 1884–1885) as the departure point. As they move through the past, they seem to look for the springboard that will launch them toward the Congo of their dreams. By narrating their country's history, they hope to uncover a vision for the future to invent. One might even say that these novels are, in one way or another, supported by what Walter Benjamin asserts, in his essay "Critique of Violence," "The critique of violence is the philosophy of its history—the 'philosophy' of this history, because only the idea of its development makes possible a critical, discriminating, and decisive approach to its temporal data."[16]

These young activists and novelists remind us that concealing the past, or more precisely obscuring the historical experience of a people, is a way of distancing them from themselves, of depriving them of all lucidity about themselves, as well as about their present, future, and their roots. This ultimately leads them to suppress themselves as spontaneity itself, as subjects endowed with power, or as potential subjects of revolt. Unsurprisingly, this tactic was used by the founding fathers and dictators, who acted as though they were the alpha and the omega and who even went so far as to banish the memory of those who had truly fought colonialism and were the actual progenitors of independence.

By widening the scope of our analysis, it becomes clear that the insurgent practices emerging during the 2010s had already manifested themselves, albeit more symbolically, in literary production from the end of the 1970s onward. Novelists such as Sony Labou Tansi (*La vie et demie* [*Life and a Half*], 1979; *Les yeux du volcan* [The volcano's eyes], 1988), Boubacar Boris Diop (*Les Tambours de la mémoire* [The drums of memory], 1987), and Pius Ngandu Nkashama (*Le pacte de sang* [The blood pact], 1984; *La mort faite homme* [Death made into man], 1986; and *L'empire des ombres vivantes* [The empire of living shadows], 1991) developed a disconcerting aesthetic, one of discomfort, inversion, and transgression of things once considered taboo. These authors also cultivated a new relationship with language, one that breaks with convention to produce new forms of meaning. Their narratives are rife with strange beings, madmen, victims of sinister powers, and characters haunted by nightmares. Yet a fervor for the future remains. Sony Labou Tansi's opening to *The Shameful State* reveals the passion that dwells within, making these authors representatives of what Herbert Marcuse calls "radical subjectivity" or precursors of "new sensibility":[17] "I've heard it said that the novel is a work of the imagination. Even if that is true, this imagination must still have a place somewhere in reality. One could say that I write, or rather that I cry out, as a way of forcing the world into the world."[18]

To cry out or to write in order to force a better world to come into being! Sony Labou Tansi's words were open to adoption by francophone rappers, Rastafarians, and youth participating in the citizen movements. In his warning to the reader, Labou Tansi reaffirms the need for radical change or at least a new beginning ("forcing the world into the world"), one that must be rooted in the subjectivity, intelligence, passion, and emotion of individuals themselves. Declaring that one writes "as a way of forcing the world into the world" suggests that the present world is merely a shameful caricature—a kind of prehistory, from which true history and the real world is yet to come. A similar sentiment can be found in the works of artists like Bodys Isek Kingelez, who in the mid-1980s began sculpting *City of the Future*, which had neither police nor cemeteries. The Congolese artist was undoubtedly outraged and appalled at seeing *Kin-la-belle* (Kinshasa the beautiful) becoming more and more akin to *Kin-la-poubelle* (Kinshasa the rubbish bin).

Toward a New Consciousness

The youth-led citizen movements, driven by a common desire for social and political change, increasingly showed signs of new awareness or, more accurately, a new political consciousness. This awareness comes from the hardships and injustices the people have endured and the inner wounds stemming from the possibility that their dreams of recognition could be dashed at any moment. But this new consciousness is also the consequence of a radical breakdown of trust in traditional political and social actors and, more particularly, the consequence of their betrayal by greedy and hedonistic elites, whose sense of the common good is negated by the desire to accumulate unlimited wealth, culminating in the privatization of hope. Hence, the leitmotif that guides the Filimbi movement: "The Congo belongs to us all!" Their motto can be connected to "We're fed up!" from Dakar's young people, who refuse to accept the utter arrogance of governmental power, which starkly contrasts with the social inequalities and plight facing the broader population.

By occupying the streets, by challenging legislation proposed by ruling powers intended to further consolidate their hold on the state and its wealth (what is now known as state capture), by going from house to house to raise awareness and inviting citizens to join the resistance, these movements herald a new era of activism on the continent, a new era of politics: the politics of the street. This new political consciousness is also the natural outgrowth of the postcolonial African state that features the hypertheatricalization of state representatives alongside the erasure of the people to such an extent that the Latin *potentia* (the power of the people) is supplanted by the *potes-*

tas (the power that must be exercised by delegation). Thus, what should logically and chronologically come first (the people) ends up coming last (second) and what should be the end ultimately becomes the means. This also explains the fetishism that characterizes political power supposedly derived from the ballot box. Fetishism, in this sense, refers to "the absolutization of the 'will' of the representative, which ceases to respond, ceases to base itself on and link itself to the 'general will' of the political community it represents: 'Thus I wish it, thus I order it; the will (of the governor) takes the place of *reason* (as foundational).'"[19]

In such a political context, African youth movements represent what one could call insurgent or oppositional subjectivities. They do not want the future of the city or the debate on collective issues to be the prerogative of a corrupt elite. Their aim is to reappropriate the rights that have been denied for a long time to ordinary citizens. That is the meaning of Filimbi and Lucha's cry, which contests the way the DRC has been governed by Presidents Mobutu and Kabila as private property: "This country belongs to all of us. The land of our ancestors is not to sell." This cry is the expression of a new feeling, one that bypasses those very political elites whose debauchery has overwhelmed their senses to the point that they live shuttered in gated mansions, completely disconnected from reality. This new feeling is made clear by these young citizens not being afraid of jail when arrested by agents of the status quo. As Eboussi Boulaga would put it, the new feeling announces a new era to come:

> It is indeed, thanks to feeling that the dawn of a new era is announced in the decline of the preceding one. It is in the sentiment of revolt that great revolutions are initiated and plotted. Even when sentiment stutters and shows in the trappings of the bygone period, its message about the future may still be deciphered. It looks weak in the face of established reason, rational equipment and arrangements; it eventually gets the better of them, because of its correspondence to the actuality of being.[20]

The Cameroonian philosopher goes on to add:

> The tardiness gap of things on signs and symbols that feeling instantly captures creates an aspiration to being, a program defining what ought to be and is to be done. Dream and utopia, expressive of feeling, are transformative forces mightier than rationality insensitive to itself and its limitations, nurturing the illusion of being eternal on account of its abstraction and timeless, more than that rationality, fettered and blocked.[21]

One could connect this with Marcuse's reflections on liberation: "We rid society of its systems of domination by ridding it of the forms of subjectivity formed by those systems and replacing them with new forms of subjectivity. . . . The new sensibility is the medium of social change that mediates between the political practice of changing the world and one's own drive for personal liberation."[22] The young people's refusal to remain subservient to a corrupt political system is a potent symbol of this new sensibility. This explains why members of these movements were systematically hunted down by agents of the established power. Their sometimes inopportune but forceful initiatives, which have been instrumental in ousting tyrants and second-rate leaders from power in Burkina Faso, Congo, and more recently, Mali, remind us that democracy is not just about putting a piece of paper in a ballot box; it is above all "this singular reversal of the order of things, according to which those who are not destined to take care of common things start to take care of them"[23] in order to block the duplicity of an elite devoid of honor, dignity, and a sense of the common good.

The Insurrection of Vulnerable Bodies

Other manifestations of this new sensibility cannot be ignored. In the DRC, the spouses of soldiers, to claim the unpaid salaries of their husbands at the front, demonstrated nude or almost so on the public highway in Beni (North Kivu) May 9, 2014. The protest was deemed scandalous, indecent, and even lewd. This reaction can be better understood within the context of African cities and towns, where everyday life has a tendency to be aestheticized. The physical body is ever more adorned, sometimes at such cost that one wonders whether it is not a way for self-assertion. By transforming a precarious body into an idealized one, these individuals are perhaps challenging the very institutions producing precariousness.

There is, however, another political interpretation of the event. It is generally understood that the body is not only shaped by the social but also fashions the social in its own right. The body is akin to a text or code, which can be subverted, thereby revealing its inherent performativity. Thus, the public display of a naked body in a place where social norms of decency require females to be covered can be viewed as a gesture of insurrection and resistance to sociopolitical structures and norms, thereby also being an act likely to foster and support social change. Why not interpret this gesture more as a demonstration of the power of women to act, using their vulnerability (and that of the social body itself) as a tool for social and political protest? These women are calling for an end to their social precariousness by exposing their physical vulnerability. The exposure of their vulnerable bodies condemns the indecency of corrupt political elites in power. As Richard Shusterman suggests, in certain contexts, the body speaks and can even endanger social or official discourse by its very presence:

> Like the language of the strong poet, the body is not a wholly private affair. It has been significantly shaped and repressively scarred by history's dominant social practices and ideologies, which also means that it is not free from linguistic markings. But the fact that the somatic has been structured by body-punishing ideologies and discourse does not mean that it cannot serve as a source to challenge them through the use of alternative body practices and greater somatic awareness.[24]

To those who find obscenity in the gesture of mothers exposing their naked, vulnerable bodies on the public highway, one must respond that they remain prisoners of the system of domination or repression that these women denounce. In fact, as Marcuse puts it, "Obscenity is a moral concept in the verbal arsenal of the Establishment, which abuses the term by applying it, not to expressions of its own morality but to those of another. Obscene is not the picture of a naked woman who exposes her pubic hair but that of a fully clad general who exposes his medals rewarded in a war of aggression."[25] Obscenity, in the situation that concerns us, is rather, for the political elites to show brazenly the outward signs of a shameful success, when the ordinary citizens, the children, and the young people are deprived of the bare minimum to survive.

As Marcuse notes, in the context of revolt, "linguistic therapy—that is, the effort to free words (and thereby concepts) from the all but total distortion of their meanings by the Establishment"—is necessary. It "demands the transfer of moral standards (and of their validation) from the Establishment to the revolt against it. Similarly, the sociological and political vocabulary must be . . . methodologically and provocatively 'moralized' in terms of the Refusal."[26] Indeed, revolt, refusal—which is the expression of a radical rejection of the world in its current form—is always carried out on behalf of other values or systems of norms. As Albert Camus aptly remarks, "Not every value entails rebellion, but every act of rebellion tacitly invokes a value."[27]

The Apathy and Arrogance of the Leviathan

As I have already suggested, despite the democratic pretensions of postcolonial African states, citizens' movements are at best tolerated and at worst represented by officials as terrorist groups whose project is to destabilize the state. This increasingly problematic relationship between African states and social movements is highlighted through the outcomes reserved for citizen movements and their requests, in countries like Chad, the DRC, and so on. The state holds a regressive—and repressive—view of the social and political demands represented by ordinary people. According to Eboussi Boulaga, the reason is that the

> African nation-state is constituted by the discordance between the reality experienced by individuals and society and that which is defined and perceived by the State. Contact with the social is lost through the schemas we project onto it. Attempts to act on it operate only in a destructive way, since it is the reality that must be destroyed ... so that the mission and the legitimacy of which the holders of power are the depositaries and which justify their privileges can become evident.[28]

The postcolonial African state seems to suffer from a kind of pathological apathy. Not only do state representatives ignore what their populations endure but they feel no need to listen to their demands. As Partha Chatterjee points out, the overwhelming majority of citizens are, first and foremost, a population for the state to administer and manage, even when they have the right to vote.[29] The state disregards that populations, in reaction to government management, "are constantly inventing new ways of choosing how [they] want to be governed" and developing new political forms that defy the established categories associated with modern politics. "Political struggles that develop, often on the boundary of legality, regarding the recognition of the rights of the governed to redefine policies that affect them,"[30] are treated as nonevents by the state or simply as breaches of public order. This results in "a waste of the collective energies that could be a valuable source of great innovations"[31] in political, social, and philosophical realms.

A keen observer might note that the African state is plagued by three major oversights that ultimately produce a disconnect regarding the aspirations of ordinary people and a resistance to potential sources of transformation. The first issue involves the refusal to recognize that ordinary citizens are endowed with reason and must be regarded as autonomous subjects who are not only objects but also active subjects of justification. In this respect, institutional politics simply cannot ignore their aspirations and moral experience[32] without succumbing to the absurdity of authoritarian social policy that does not account for "desirability" or "viability," to borrow Erik Olin Wright's terminology.[33] The second issue is related to how the state promises change while repressing all social movements. Representatives of the state are not ready to acknowledge that "social action is a vector for change, capable even of removing the obstacles erected by institutions, like rigid forms of organization, meant to impede the transformations and liberties that are sought."[34]

The third major issue consists of attaching almost absolute importance "to politics in the most institutional sense of the term, to the detriment of politics as it could be embodied through social struggle." This tendency is exacerbated when the perspectives of those who govern dominate those of the governed.[35] Ultimately, the governed are reduced to mere effects of the decisions taken from above. Thus, regressive and authoritarian statism severely undermines popular sovereignty, which is most often invoked by those in power only when it operates as an instrument of state sovereignty. While using democratic rhetoric, political rulers act autocratically by controlling and even prohibiting any form of public assembly or protest that might call their policies into question. By drastically limiting gatherings, they also devalue their critical and democratic function.[36] It is as if, by casting a vote, the people completely relinquish their sovereignty, handing it over to elected representatives who govern by sovereign and divine decree.

The Task for Critical Theory

The task of critical theory is twofold: It, first, includes contributing to the strengthening of social movements, the rise of new social struggles, and the development of new strategies of resistance. It, second, aims at a social analysis of institutions as well as of classic categories of politics (legitimacy, popular sovereignty, people, patriotism, democracy, public order, etc.), which are instrumentalized by those in power to conceal domination, transfigure brutality, justify subjugation, and produce obedient and exploitable citizens.[37] The objective of this thinking would be to uncover "non-justifiable social and political relations, hence not only political relations in the narrower institutional sense but also economic or cultural relations. By this is meant all those more or less institutionalized social relations and structures which do not measure up to the standard of reciprocal and general justification and are marked by forms of exclusion, by privileges and domination."[38] The culmination of this critical undertaking would be the exposure of the very political philosophy that produces these categories and leaves little space for social movements and protests.

Indeed, the political philosophy that continues to resonate with African political thinkers remains one that is heavily informed by the state and the maintenance of law and order. It is not a discourse of freedom, independence, or the individual but rather one of obedience, based on the legitimization of the sovereign—or of something that represents sovereignty. This political philosophy is not on the side of social struggle and cannot provide tools for resistance. Instead, it provides political leaders with discourse granting them the right to govern[39] and the expectation of obedience from the people. This narrative, centered on the state, its authority, and its inviolable qualities, ultimately undermines the requirement of authentic politics for a constant search for methods and means by which social life can be expanded and intensified.[40]

In other words, it is the task of critical and social thinkers to listen to the dominated, provide them with the means through which they can seek emancipation, and establish "a theoretical practice of resistance, struggle, and insubordination."[41] This requires two major conditions. First, critical and social thinkers should not act like "political philosophers, on the side of the state and its rulers, but instead [position themselves] on the side of the governed, alongside their struggles and aspirations."[42] Second, they must put structure of subjugation at the center of their analyses in order to understand how it produces subjectivities. This requirement is crucial because it is only when the deconstruction of subjugation and the extent of the mechanisms producing such structures is uncovered that "it will be possible to provide the governed with the tools needed for emancipation."[43] Finally, criticism must challenge all autonomous political action by reintegrating it into the social, because the social sphere provides the terrain where political representations confront one another.[44]

Clearly, what is at stake here is an analysis of the very type of rationality that underpins the postcolonial African state and politics as a whole. Broadly speaking, the guiding philosophy providing the foundations and justifications for francophone African states seems to be one that covers the state with a mantle of transcendence, that puts it beyond the reach of individuals (and especially of their social struggles). Thereby, decisions about what society can and should be—or cannot be and should not be—are reserved for the few, who, by virtue of their "knowledge" and "expertise," remain the authorized makers and interpreters of the necessary rules and laws to which everyone should submit.[45]

Within this framework, social movements are unimaginable. They are reprehensible in all respects as long as they exist despite the ban. This is precisely what happened in Congo, where members of citizen movements have been hunted down like criminals. This type of political rationale bears an intrinsic resemblance to how colonial institutions claimed to save native inhabitants from the darkness of sin and ignorance without ever actually listening to, or hearing, them. Eboussi Boulaga confirms this viewpoint by suggesting that the postcolonial African state is a product of a kind of technological engineering. It is split "from the historical community of which it is the organization, the constitution of the operation, or the collective action that produces it as a result."[46] This situation comes from the fact that the postcolonial state reproduces colonial and slavery order under the guise of a new order to be established by sublimating it, under the species of a possible necessary, to an a priori regulator, in transcendental condition of any "social object", whatever it may be. An ill-conceived doctrine provides it with a set of principles, norms that enter into the formation of definite types of enunciations, which forbid others, just as they authorize certain perceptions, even prescribe them, and make them blind or insensitive to others. What does not fit into this guidance matrix is deemed nonexistent or turned into waste. A correlation to this theory is a discipline that orders rule following, submission to constraints and to techniques with controlled appellations, to accomplish what is necessary in the right way.[47]

To oppose this type of thought that, in its very principle, prohibits individuals from believing themselves free and from imagining it possible for them to claim their desire, that opposes the claims of individuals to laws of "necessity," critical theory must develop a "thought of immanence (and therefore of the invention of the social—and therefore of the law—by individuals and above all by their collective struggles)."[48] This is possible only if it is able to listen to the social movements and struggles that emerge, to take into account the issues they raise, in order to radicalize them by proposing new ways of acting so as to dismantle mechanisms that support the transcendentality of the state. The task of critical thinkers is to accompany this movement to increase their effectiveness.

To be clear, I am not recommending the fusion of the critical philosopher with social movements or activist groups. Instead, I am advocating for what Max Horkheimer calls the "dynamic unity of theory"[49] and social movements. This means that, as an "element of praxis aiming to establish new forms of social organization,"[50] critical thought must develop within or from a historical context to which it is destined to return as a driving factor of the struggle taking place. Didier Eribon follows a similar line of thought when writing about Michel Foucault: "Not only is theoretical work inseparable from political efforts; it is provoked by them (new political mobilizations raise new theoretical questions), and its function is to support and serve them: according to Foucault, theoretical work is born of conflict and must return to conflict."[51] He adds, "Philosophical work is embedded in the movements taking place in society, as well as in the critical questions and mobilizations that appear and develop there. The critical philosopher does not occupy a lofty position. He does not regulate the practices or knowledge of others. He transforms himself through contact with these practices and this knowledge."[52] The tension between critique and social actors represents "a process of reciprocal influence."[53]

It seems to me that this is the posture that must be adopted by the African thinker concerned with taking part in and supporting the movements that fight for emancipation and social justice. The challenge is to break with the dominating gaze that reifies social actors. An observer can note that, just as the state and its representatives believe that the demands of individuals and what they endure in society do not deserve to be taken seriously, francophone African thinkers do much the same. Generally, they avoid taking the insurrectionary practices and languages of ordinary people as objects of analysis and, by so doing, contribute to the loss of their critical and emancipatory potential. This is probably why it remains difficult to find in-depth and substantive philosophical or critical analysis on popular movements and other insurgent practices that have become widespread in francophone Africa in this century. Favoring normative theories and questions on the ideal principles of a just exercise of political power, African philosophers leave aside the analysis of society as it is with its pathologies and daily struggles for a better life. By proceeding in this way, they not only reproduce in their discourse the silence of institutional politics on the moral experiences of the dominated and their aspirations but support, inadvertently or not, the status quo.

An analysis of everyday life, which aims to develop an understanding of the codes that govern the lives of ordinary people may be a very important philosophical task today. In states that are ruled by authoritarian political figures, as is still the case in francophone Africa, struggles for survival take place in the sphere of daily life. Ordinary individuals, who foresee the possibility of another world, subtly transgress the established order. Social groups tend to challenge established forms of domination as well. But one cannot forget that also in everyday life the state ceaselessly tells us what must be done and how it ought to be done. And as Didier Eribon explains, "We allow the social order to function through each of our responses to the official, unofficial, or tacit questionnaires that we receive in daily life; through each of our spontaneous reactions, each of our judgments of value and taste, and so on." The social order is us, because it shapes what we are and how we are in the world.[54] This means that the critical analysis of everyday life remains crucial in bringing to light the insidious apparatuses that reproduce the established order, which are sometimes present in us even when we think we are fighting against it. If there is indeed some hope of social change, it probably resides in the "ever-renewed theoretical analysis of the mechanisms of domination, in their innumerable cogs, registers and dimensions, allied to an ineradicable desire to transform the world in the direction of greater social justice." This ever-renewing theoretical analysis "will allow us to resist the various forms of oppressive violence as much as possible and to implement a system that can finally legitimately be called democratic."[55] The challenge facing African thinkers concerned with social change is to develop a theoretical critique of African societies and imagine a new type of social intelligence that serves the continued struggles for emancipation on the continent.

NOTES

1. Félix Guattari and Suely Rolnik, *Micropolitiques* (Paris: Les Empêcheurs de penser en rond/Seuil, 2007). Unless otherwise noted, all translations are mine.

2. Fabien Eboussi Boulaga, "Éditorial," *Terroirs: Revue africaine de sciences sociales et d'études culturelles* 4 (2004): 5.

3. Eboussi Boulaga, "Éditorial," 4.

4. Geoffroy de Lagasnerie, *The Art of Revolt: Snowden, Assange, Manning* (Stanford, CA: Stanford University Press, 2016), 10.

5. Lagasnerie, *The Art of Revolt*, 11.

6. Nathalie McSween, "Repenser l'analyse des mouvements sociaux africains," March 2010 (Québec: L'Alliance de recherche université-communauté/Innovation sociale et développement des communautés), http://w3.uqo.ca/crdc/00_fichiers/publications/cahiers/ARUC/ARUC_R32.pdf.

7. Basil Davidson, *The Black Man's Burden: Africa and the Curse of the Nation-State* (London: James Currey, 1992).

8. Frantz Fanon, *Les damnés de la terre* (Paris: Seuil, 1962), 193.

9. Francis Akindès and Ousmane Zina, "L'État face au mouvement social en Afrique," *Revue projet* 6, no. 355 (2016): 86.

10. Geoffroy de Lagasnerie, *Penser dans un monde mauvais* (Paris: Presses Universitaires de France, 2017), 72.

11. Akindès and Zina, "L'État face au mouvement social en Afrique," 85. For more information about citizen movements like Y'en a marre, Balai citoyen, Filimbi, and Lucha, see Kasereka Kavwahirehi, "Y'en a marre! Philosophie et espoir social en Afrique" (Paris: Karthala, 2018), 173–179.

12. Walter Benjamin, *Sur le concept d'histoire*, suivi de *Eduard Fuchs, le collectionneur et l'historien et de Paris, Capitale du XIXe siècle*, trans. Olivier Mannoni (Paris: Payot, 2013), 60.

13. Ernst Bloch, *Thomas Münzer, théologien de la libération* (Paris: Prairies ordinaires, 2012), 25.

14. Jean Ladrière, *Vie sociale et destinée* (Gembloux, Belgium: J. Duculot, 1973), 73.

15. Ernst Bloch, *Thomas Münzer, théologien de la libération* (Paris: Prairies ordinaires, 2012), 25.

16. Walter Benjamin, "Critique de la violence," in *Œuvres, I*, trans. Maurice Gandillac, Rainer Rochlitz, and Pierre Rusch (Paris: Gallimard, 2000), 241–242.

17. Herbert Marcuse, *An Essay on Liberation* (Boston: Beacon Press, 1969), 23.

18. Sony Labou Tansi, *The Shameful State*, trans. Dominic Thomas (Bloomington: Indiana University Press, 2016), frontmatter.

19. Enrique Dussel, *Twenty Theses on Politics*, trans. George Ciccariello-Maher (Durham, NC: Duke University Press, 2008), 30–31.

20. Fabien Eboussi Boulaga, *Muntu in Crisis: African Authenticity and Philosophy* (Trenton, NJ: Africa World Press, 2014), 215.

21. Eboussi Boulaga, *Muntu in Crisis*, 215.

22. Herbert Marcuse, *Arts and Liberation, Collected Papers of Herbert Marcuse*, vol. 4, ed. Douglas Kellner (London: Routledge, 2007), 234.

23. Jacques Rancière, "Les hommes comme animaux littéraires," in *Pensées critiques: Dix itinéraires de la revue Mouvements 1998–2008*, ed. Étienne Balibar et al. (Paris: La Découverte, 2009), 51.

24. Richard Shusterman, *Pragmatic Aesthetics: Living Beauty, Rethinking Art* (Lanham, MD: Rowman and Littlefield, 2000), 200.

25. Marcuse, *An Essay on Liberation*, 8.

26. Marcuse, *An Essay on Liberation*, 8.

27. Albert Camus, *The Rebel*, trans. Anthony Bower (New York: Vintage Books, 1956), 26.

28. Fabien Eboussi Boulaga, "Introduction Générale," in *Le génocide rwandais: Les interrogations des intellectuels africains*, ed. F. Eboussi Boulaga (Yaoundé, Cameroon: Clé, 2006), 15.

29. Partha Chatterjee, *The Politics of the Governed: Reflections on Popular Politics in Most of the World* (New York: Columbia University Press, 2006), 27–52.

30. Christophe Jacquet quoted on the back cover of the French translation of Chatterjee, *The Politics of the Governed*.

31. Theodor Adorno, quoted in Didier Eribon, *D'une révolution conservatrice et de ses effets sur la gauche française* (Paris: Éditions Léo Scheer, 2007), 82.

32. See Rainer Forst, *Justification and Critique: Towards a Critical Theory of Politics*, trans. Ciaran Cronin (Cambridge: Polity Press, 2014), 7–8.

33. See Erik Olin Wright, *Envisioning Real Utopias* (London: Verso, 2010).

34. J.-P. Cometti, *La démocratie radicale: Lire John Dewey* (Paris: Gallimard, 2016), 117–118.

35. Eribon, *D'une révolution conservatrice*, 68.

36. Judith Butler, *Rassemblement: Pluralité, performativité et politique*, trans. Christophe Jacquet (Paris: Fayard, 2016), 203–204.

37. See Geoffroy de Lagasnerie, *La conscience politique* (Paris: Fayard, 2019).

38. Forst, *Justification and Critique*, 7–8.

39. Geoffroy de Lagasnerie, *La dernière leçon de Michel Foucault: Sur le néolibéralisme, la théorie et la politique* (Paris: Fayard, 2012), 134.

40. See Kasereka Kavwahirehi, "La philosophie sociale ou le chapitre manquant de la philosophie africaine," *Philosophiques* 46 no. 2 (Fall 2019): 339–357.

41. Lagasnerie, *La dernière leçon de Michel Foucault*, 139.

42. Lagasnerie, *La dernière leçon de Michel Foucault*, 148.

43. Lagasnerie, *La dernière leçon de Michel Foucault*, 138.

44. Franck Fischbach, *Manifeste pour une philosophie sociale* (Paris: La Découverte, 2009), 132.

45. Eribon, *D'une révolution conservatrice*, 128.

46. Fabien Eboussi Boulaga, *Les conférences nationales en Afrique noire* (Paris: Karthala, 1993), 102.

47. Eboussi Boulaga, *Les conférences nationales en Afrique noire*, 103.

48. Eribon, *D'une révolution conservatrice*, 128.

49. Max Horkheimer, *Théorie traditionnelle et théorie critique*, trans. Claude Maillard and Sibylle Muller (Paris: Gallimard, 1974), 48.

50. Eribon, *D'une révolution conservatrice*, 49.

51. Didier Eribon, *Hérésies: Essais sur la théorie de la sexualité* (Paris: Fayard, 2003), 46.

52. Eribon, *Hérésies*, 46.

53. Horkheimer, *Théorie traditionnelle et théorie critique*, 48.

54. Didier Eribon, *Principes d'une pensée critique* (Paris: Fayard, 2016), 96–97.

55. Didier Eribon, *La société de verdict* (Paris: Flammarion, 2014), 254.

5

Tampered Witnessing

Visual Agency and the African American Poet

Gregory Pardlo

Countee Cullen's first poetry collection, *Color* (1925), has been out of print and rare for decades.[1] Princeton University owns one of the few library copies available in the northeastern United States. It arrived, at my request, in a cellophane wrapper secured by a stubborn strip of glue. This level of care only heightened my reverence for the object, the contents of which I knew well in advance, half hoping to find Cullen's spectral thumbprint somewhere among the pages. An inscription identified the book as having belonged to Dr. Hamilton Cottier, a professor of English at Princeton University from 1925 to 1962. On the flyleaf, Cottier quoted a passage from a review he considered relevant enough to memorialize but not important enough to provide attribution. "Interestingly reviewed," Cottier prefaces, and quotes, "Good, but quite unremarkable poetry—were it not by a negro [*sic*] and chiefly about the Negro, it would not be worth printing.—6/27/26."

I find the quoted review interesting for the pretense of analysis that cannot veil its condescension. "Good, but . . . unremarkable" creates a polite clearing in which the entire collection may be dismissed as having, not literary, but sociological value. This is not to suggest, necessarily, that Cottier himself held a condescending view of Cullen's work but that, in quoting that passage, he conjured a particular animus that is very much at home in the criticism of African American poetry.

Cottier's note, an attempt to muffle Cullen's voice or possibly silence it altogether, makes Cullen's prefatory poem all the more poignant. "To You

Who Read My Book" assumes this out-of-print collection will continue to reach readers long after the poet has passed. Here, Cullen appeals to the reader, book in hand, to remember the poet fondly and reflect, "Though his throat is bare, / by death defiled, / song labored there / and bore a child" (Cullen 1925, xvi). While there is no question whose profile in American literature prevailed, it is difficult not to see Cullen's and Cottier's as competing voices from beyond the grave.

Perhaps fittingly, *Color* also contains one of Cullen's most canonical poems, "Yet Do I Marvel," which laments the disproportionate cost of that competition. The poem wonders why God would "make a poet black, and bid him sing" (3). The terms, the poem suggests, are at cross-purposes and thus punitive. Cottier's animus, a hostile genie, takes up residence between "poet" and "black" to ensure that they remain antithetical. The poem acknowledges an alien presence in the poetic imagination that seeks to regulate the exercise of that imagination. "Yet Do I Marvel" extends a trope in African American poetry by which we take for granted this hostile genie inhabiting the imagination and well-nigh naturalize its presence. While there were indeed hostile economic and cultural forces restricting his access to publication, and as Cottier proves, critical forces poised to stymie the work's reception and interpretation, why should we presume either force (or some combination of the two) could reach into the poet's psyche and work its toxic spell on the very site where the literary imagination emerges?

I am reminded of Phillis Wheatley's (1793, 65) poem "On Imagination," which refers to an oppositional force allegorized as "Winter" that "forbids me to aspire." The poem's last line, "Cease then, my song, cease the unequal lay," surrenders the imagination to this oppositional force, which reads as Wheatley's conceptualization of Cottier's genie. The penultimate stanza of George Moses Horton's 1865 poem "George Moses Horton, Myself" reads "My genius from a boy, / Has fluttered like a bird within my heart; / But could not thus confined her powers employ, / Impatient to depart" (1982, 10). Paul Laurence Dunbar's (1895, 21) "We Wear the Mask" famously laments "We sing, but oh the clay is vile / Beneath our feet, and long the mile." Indeed, one could play this game at length, hopscotching through the canon of black poetry, cataloging poets' various confrontations with the virulent genie.

In a 1975 lecture at Portland State University, Toni Morrison metaphorized racism as "the red flag that the toreador dances before the head of a bull. Its purpose," Morrison elaborates, "is only to distract, to keep the bull's mind away from his power and his energy, to keep his mind focused on anything but his own business. Its hoped-for consequence was to define black people as reactions to White presence." We might read this "White presence" as a counterpart to the "Africanist presence" Morrison finds haunting white writers (*Playing in the Dark*, 1992). The Africanist presence in turn reprises the "brown specter" Zora Neal Hurston perceives haunting her white friends.[2]

Although Hurston differs from others in her appraisal of the costs the racial imaginary exacts on the American writer, that the argument needs to be made at all is tacit acknowledgment of the dominant perception that the greater adversity rests with the African American writer. Perhaps it is self-evident that the African American poet would experience the imaginary "White presence" as hostile because the ongoing social violence it represents is deeply imprinted on the black imagination while the Africanist presence represents more of a fetishistic preoccupation for white writers like the magical powers white planters ascribed to communities of escaped blacks in the mountains of Jamaica who wreaked havoc and vengeance on those planters' persons and property. Considering what was (and in many ways, continues to be) at stake, is it any wonder that those in the cultural and intellectual vanguard would seek to introduce this malware, to use an anachronistic concept, into the black poetic imagination that would reproduce itself in plain sight as self-evident fact?

Might we make possible a more dynamic black imagination, and thus more robust black futures, if we were to demystify the motives and operation of this Althusserian genie that seems to increase its obstructionist power as it decreases its legibility in the poet's text? Is there a paracritical practice that we might adopt to disarticulate the genie from the text and, reflexively, from literary production itself?

> Misery is often the parent of the most affecting touches in poetry. —Among the blacks is misery enough, God knows, but no poetry. Love is the peculiar oestrum of the poet. Their love is ardent, but it kindles the senses only, not the imagination. Religion indeed has produced a Phyllis [sic] Wheatley; but it could not produce a poet. The compositions published under her name are below the dignity of criticism. (Jefferson 2018)

In his 1785 *Notes on the State of Virginia*, Thomas Jefferson (2018) disparaged Phillis Wheatley's poetry as being "below the dignity of criticism." In so doing, he established the rubric against which black poetry would be evaluated, as we have seen, well into the twentieth century and arguably beyond. The dignity of criticism Jefferson withheld was tantamount to human dignity. Poets and critics of African American poetry following Jefferson have built a tradition on the tacit acceptance of the premise that one of the functions of black poetry was to prove the humanity of black people and earn the "dignity of criticism" while being denied access to the very disciplinary paradigm in which it could be authorized.

Why should it be that black musical forms, from spirituals to R&B and hip-hop, have made relatively easy strides toward earning the dignity of criticism while black poetry continues to press its case? The critical analysis black music demands does not privilege it within the ocularcentric European paradigm. According to this paradigm, black music, primal and instinctual, confirms black stereotypes. Thus, black excellence in music could be acknowledged and even celebrated because it does not directly challenge what Nicholas Mirzoeff (2012, 2) calls "visuality." For Mirzoeff, "visuality" is the conceptualization and policing of the imaginative field of history, essentially the conceptual archive of the cultural imaginary, which I read here as the shared imaginative field on which the humanity of the black subject is dialectically contested and normalized. "This practice," Mirzoeff writes, "must be imaginary, rather than perceptual, because what is being visualized is too substantial for any one person to see and is created from information, images, and ideas" (2). It seems appropriate, then, that for Mirzoeff visuality originates on the slave plantation, where he claims that the slave master as sovereign employed a surveillance network to restrict slave movement physically and imaginatively and to maintain a living tableau of domination and abasement that would in turn produce a modern division of labor. Enslaved laborers, British planters in Jamaica went so far as to decree, were prohibited from "imagin[ing] the death of any white person" (8).

Quoting Jacques Derrida, Mirzoeff (2012, 1) suggests that visuality opposes "the right to look. The invention of the other." As the right to look represents the autonomous exercise of the imagination that is anathema to visuality, we can expand the concept of visuality to encompass the figurative realm of literary production so that we might analyze the effects of the contested "right to look" on poetry and the poetics of race in America.

Whiteness, as a hegemonic force, proliferates by establishing an ocular regime in which black subjects are enjoined to perform a lack of visual agency and self-awareness compulsorily rendered as ignorance and naivete. We can reason that white poets and critics, consciously or not, are invested in the production of blackness because one of the affirmative functions of whiteness is to promulgate a vision of blackness that authorizes the status quo. Conversely, as subjects actively engaged in autonomous exercises of the imagination, black poets and critics necessarily claim the right to look that opposes the dominant visuality of blackness. Out of this confrontation emerges our popular and normalized, however stereotypical, conception of black subjectivity. To claim that popular images of what it means to be black are incorrect or flawed misses the point, because those depictions are constructed a priori. To evaluate poetry in terms of who has the authority or right to inscribe those depictions is to engage in the very dialectic that maintains the status quo. What impact do these negotiations have on the black poet who, to access the material resources of a white supremacist regime, must first recognize some of its most toxic images, then reflect for that regime a visuality of blackness that sufficiently concedes to the status quo, then further, visualize the self not as Other, but as an assimilable and sanctionable cultural novelty?[3] At what point does such a performance become authenticated?

The reassuring (to whites) performance of an inhibited or chastened right to look is what W.E.B. Du Bois (1903) metaphorizes as the veil. Paul Laurence Dunbar (1969) offers us the image of the mask. While these and other metaphors concretize an abstract perceptual hindrance, they largely invest the black subject with that hindrance exclusively, thus reaffirming the white positionality that the Negro problem resides with the Negro him- or herself. The always contested formal conventions of rendering black subjectivity—whether as docile and happy-go-lucky or as aggrieved and hostile; with ironic, performative distance or with confessional sincerity—present a significant field of study, the topography of which, even when theorized by black critics and poets, is nonetheless shaped by the material and transhistorical imperatives of whiteness.

The music historian Ronald Radano, in his 2003 study *Lying Up a Nation: Race and Black Music*, reveals the way essentialist critiques of black music place the genre beyond the scope of conventional criticism and thus outside history. Rather than point to some indefinable quality like soul, Radano suggests black music is a product of "racio-social discourse" (11). This argument constitutes a prolonged critical negotiation that allows the delineation of a discursive space in which a thing such as black genius or black excellence may be articulable. While Radano applies this analysis to music, I suggest we might devise a similar lens for reading African American literature, poetry in particular.

By establishing some discursive parameters for analyzing and evaluating the visual practices of poets and writers concerned with race in America,[4] I hope to also offer an alternative to the dangerously essentialist tradition of evaluating black literature in terms of its lyricism and orality. The much-celebrated combination of orality and lyricism of black poets is both a cultural inheritance and evidence of black poets' confrontation with social proscriptions placed on their vision/ary power and a restriction on what the black subject is permitted to observe. Put simply, orality is both ceded to and claimed by black writers *in lieu of* full access to the enlightened and illuminating right to look. By often coding it in essentialist terms, the privileging of orality in black literature is also complicit in critical practices that, while they uncover many aesthetic choices of black writers, obscure the role those choices play in producing racial identity.

Out of necessity, black poetry lays claim to the intellectual field on and within which blackness is produced. Jefferson recognized the importance of fending off incursions not simply in the isolated case of Phillis Wheatley but for all such pretenders to come. Jefferson viewed Wheatley as a standard-bearer for the autonomous black imagination attempting to establish itself within Enlightenment's ocularcentric paradigm. Jefferson's defense, which Cottier's mystery critic invoked, was elegant, hinging, not on poetry, but on the determination of who gets to write it. As I have suggested, it is a two-part defense. First, Jefferson claimed that "among the blacks" there was "no poetry." Next, it was important for Jefferson to eliminate love and religion as ground that might theoretically give rise to a black poet because, in love and religion, we find logic for the abolitionists' prevailing arguments against slavery.

Colonial-era abolitionists argued that blacks were equal to whites in every way and that they would contribute meaningfully to civilization if they were granted the love of human kindness that slavery denied them. Adding greater authority to their case, abolitionists argued that Christianity could civilize the savage who was already held, in God's estimation, in equal esteem as whites. Wheatley (1793, 18) herself employed this argument. "Remember *Christians*, *Negros* black as *Cain*," she writes in "On Being Brought from Africa to America," "May be refin'd, and join th' angelic train." Ever the legal mind, Jefferson refused to, in his words, grant Wheatley, and thus her race, the "dignity of criticism" because to do so would open the door to reasoning that would imperil the entire complex of plantation thought and principles, a complex that is coextensive with the visuality of blackness. Jefferson's interest in Wheatley was not axiological. It was ontological.

I propose that we think of the production of blackness in America as a shared, and perhaps even democratic, effort. Blackness, like gender, is not fixed. It is only locatable in the deictic sense and is therefore largely theoretical. It comprises a field that is unimaginable by any single subject. Its production is far more collaborative than we commonly admit. Blackness is always being rewritten and overwritten. The production of blackness is an adversarial process, to be sure, undertaken by parties with competing claims and interests in the ways that blackness, an essential commodity in racial capitalism, should figure in our civic, social, and cultural lives. If the United States can be said to have a collective cultural disposition, that disposition is characterized by the ongoing struggle over blackness.

20 And Noah began to be an husbandman, and he planted a vine-
  yard:

21 And he drank of the wine, and was drunken; and he was uncovered within his tent.

22 And Ham, the father of Canaan, saw the nakedness of his father, and told his two brethren without.

23 And Shem and Japheth took a garment, and it laid upon both their shoulders, and went backward, and covered the nakedness of their father; and their faces were backward, and they saw not their father's nakedness.

24 And Noah awoke from his wine, and knew what his younger son had done unto him.

25 And he said, Cursed be Canaan; a servant of servants shall he be unto his brethren.

26 And he said, Blessed be the Lord God of Shem, and Canaan shall be his servant.

27 God shall enlarge Japheth, and he shall dwell in the tents of Shem; and Canaan shall be his servant. (Genesis 9:20–27, King James Version 1900)

The story of Noah cursing Ham is a core element in the visuality of blackness. The story has been used in various ways by apologists for slavery. I am repurposing it here as a hermeneutic of racism's prescriptive force and the legacy of trauma it imprints on the black imagination.[5] The story of Noah cursing Ham, on its own, presents several interpretive challenges, one of which is pertinent to this chapter: How do we make sense of Noah's sudden rage toward Ham for, apparently, having seen Noah compromised by drink? It would seem that Noah projected his shame onto Ham to avoid taking responsibility for his shameful intemperance. Perhaps it is because of such aporia that, before the advent of scientific racism—that is, before the Enlightenment wrested visuality from the church and assigned it to a secular and political whiteness—apologists for slavery looked to the Bible as an authority, and to Genesis 9:20–27 in particular, for moral justification for the violence needed to maintain slavery. In tandem, racism and the Bible mutually reinforce each other. For what else but American racism could make sense of Noah's behavior? What, other than a mystifying and gratuitous biblical curse, could justify American slavery?

According to the exegesis endorsed and promulgated by Southern slaveowners, in Genesis 9:20–27, Noah's wife was "black," however retrospectively. Among her three sons, Ham (a name in Hebrew that some interpret to mean "dark," "burnt," or "hot") alone inherited her racial condition to become the progenitor of all black Africans. Ham's unique blackness justified Noah's anger at having been seen naked by Ham. Noah's curse—not on Ham, but on Ham's son Canaan—was then used to justify the determination that all descendants of Ham, black Africans, were divinely tasked, according of the terms of the curse, to be the servants of Shem's and Japheth's (white) descendants. This rendering of Genesis 9:20–27 also figures blackness as a genetic defect indicative of spiritual failing that condemns its bearer to a subordinate and servile status indefinitely, the very recipe necessary for lifetime enslavement. Although nothing in the Bible extends Noah's curse to Canaan's descendants in perpetuity, and there is not an explicit connection between Ham and black Africans, the curse of Ham would remain the most enduring evidence for the divine ordination of black subjection in the West.

Presented in this way, Noah is not simply condemning them to a life of servitude by turning Ham's descendants into slaves. The symbolic nature of the punishment renders Ham's descendants incapable of exercising visual agency. For it is important to note that Ham was punished for allegedly claiming the right to look. Just as Ham's gaze is semantically figured as illicit, and its indiscriminate expression is subject to punishment, the black gaze enjoys a narrow range of sanctionable applications. Ham's curse allegorizes the very real subjection that conditions black visual agency. We must now consider how this moral encumbrance of the black gaze is performed, contested, recorded, and archived for enduring effect by poets who choose to step into that accursed worldview.

Through patterns of inversion and projection, what stereotypes of blackness connote—namely, emotional and intellectual opacity and all manner of figurative blindness—become the inward experience of black subjectivity *as imagined by* Americans of all races. For some poets, mostly black, these are stereotypes to be resisted and demystified. For other poets, mostly white, they serve as guideposts that inform and affirm the metaphysics of race. What role does this metaphysics play in the creative process? How do we do more than marvel at its complexities? Although responded to in vastly different ways, this metaphysics is not the province of any particular identity group. We will not be able to chart a new poetics until we can fully assess the adaptable, but transhistorical yoke of what I am calling Ham's curse on the creative imagination. I do not suggest that black poets today continue to struggle under this metaphorical curse or that the curse may be lifted through further metaphors. The emergent concept of unapologetic blackness, however, in its logical formation, admits to the lingering consciousness that there might at some point have been a reason to apologize.

"Slavery," as Mirzoeff (2012, 7) concludes, "is the removal of the right to look." Social and legal injunctions prohibited free blacks from serving on juries or giving testimony except against other black people and black women from naming (and thus witnessing) the white men who fathered their children. In those places where it was not illegal for a black person to meet a white person's eye in the antebellum American South, it was still a punishable affront. The potentially mortal repercussions of exercising the black gaze, in addition to impediments to its interpretive faculties, induce a preoccupation, an awareness at the very least, in the black poet that is distinct from double consciousness and that delineates for each black poet the realm of the seeable. Such boundaries may be transcended but not without risk.

Setting aside the story of Ham's curse, and the metaphors of the veil and the mask, we can turn to the obscurantist orthographic conventions of Negro dialect poetry, which offer yet another figuration, a formal trope to visualize racism's postdiluvian curse—namely, the authority whiteness claims over the visuality of blackness. Attempts to invest the golem of black subjectivity with living breath produce a legible topography, a phrenological surface on which we may begin our interpretive process. Dialect poetry is an ideal context within which to study the mechanics of visuality.

Dialect, like the Creole that concerns Martinican critic Édouard Glissant, "bears the stamp of coercion" (1976, 95).[6] In other words, Negro dialect poetry employs a form of discourse that evolved out of the unchecked expressive needs of white subjectivity. As Glissant explains, because Creole is the result of oppositional forces, "it is not a language of Being, but a language of Relatedness" (1976, 98). Creole exhibits what Glissant calls "forced poetics" (1976, 95). Glissant juxtaposes forced poetics with *free*, or "Natural," poetics, which he defines as "any collective drive toward expression when it is unthwarted either in what it wants to express or in the language it is using" (1976, 95). Free poetics is a state of equilibrium in which the need to express something the language does not already contain is met with a corresponding invention, intelligible to all and disseminated as expeditiously as a viral video or tweet. "In any traditional culture the idiom (or means of expression) and the language (or attitude of the community toward its idiom) coincide," Glissant (1976, 98) writes.

Conversely, forced poetics "is practiced by a community which cannot express itself directly through an autonomous activity of its members. In order to pinpoint this lack of autonomy, the speaker condemns himself to a kind of non-power and to the impossibility of expression" (1976, 96). A forced poetics emphasizes image over idea, lyric over concept, impulse over reason. A forced poetics struggles with the field of visuality and finds its least resistance in acquiescing to stereotypes. Resisting the coercive power of forced poetics, and thereby claiming the right to look, a speaker risks slipping into the realm of the nonsayable or even nonsense. What happens when a subject whose language is conditioned by the practice of free poetics attempts to enter or reproduce the effects of a forced poetics as would be the case with, for example, a white poet writing in black dialect?

Operative behind the fixed mask of dialect's orthographic novelty is the poet's socially conditioned subjectivity. Subjects formed within a community whose poetics are "free," in Glissant's term, will necessarily visualize the world differently from subjects formed within a community whose poetics are "forced." The poet who identifies with the majority culture will indulge freely and without irony in the dominant view of, in the example of the white poet writing black dialect, black subjectivity. The poet who condemns him- or herself "to the impossibility of expression," as Glissant puts it, the poet who finds with James Weldon Johnson (1931) that Negro dialect poetry is indeed incapable of rendering nuanced emotions beyond humor and pathos, will find that form restrictive and self-erasing. These subjects will visualize differently given their differing relationships to language. Is it possible for a black poet to produce work that meets the white supremacist threshold of sayability—the articulable—while resisting its dominant, coercive, and limiting conception of the imagined field of figurative possibilities? Or as Mirzoeff (2012, 2) phrases the question, "How can we think with and against visuality?" How can we make a poet black and bid her or him sing, and in Negro dialect, no less?

Negro dialect poetry is an invention of the white imagination. Nineteenth-century abolitionist poets and Southern writers of the Plantation tradition whose agenda was to redeem a disgraced way of life both strove to make their representations of blackness an authenticating subject position. In other words, dramatic irony was rare in the hands of the white poet of Negro dialect. These portrayals were intended to be as realistic as a daguerreotype.

The first to be celebrated for his "accuracy," the Southern white poet Irwin Russell was a pioneer of Negro dialect poetry. Born in 1853, in Port Gibson, Mississippi, Irwin Russell was a short-lived but influential poet. His Negro dialect poems were preceded in print by the work of the abolitionist poet John Greenleaf Whittier and the light verse of the Southern poets Thomas Dunn English and brothers Sidney and Clifford Lanier,[7] but their dialect work is widely considered, ironically enough, below the dignity of criticism. As Jean Wagner writes approvingly, "Russell's importance lay not merely in his having been the first writer to discover a rich vein of inspiration in the Negro and in his dialect, but also in having built an enduring foundation for the stereotypes of the black in the American literary tradition." As was common among dialect poets of this time, Russell was deeply influenced by his "idol" Robert Burns. Like Burns, Russell experimented with Scottish and Irish literary dialects. And like Burns, Russell was drawn most to the dialect that he found representative of the peasant class among his people—in Russell's case, this class was best represented by Negro dialect. Russell differed from Burns in that, while Burns wanted to elevate the peasant dialect he most favored, Russell was bound by racist customs and habits of mind—the mandates of prevailing visuality—to travesty his imagined black subjects. Far from producing uniquely nuanced and idiosyncratic speakers, Russell creates simulacra, copies of one black subject barely distinguishable from the next in tone or temperament. Russell's subjects are projections masked with inventive orthography.

Russell is most famous for his long poem "Christmas-Night in the Quarters" (1956). In this poem, Russell's omniscient narrator describes, in standard English, a Christmas party among slaves in the idealized terms of pastoral poetry. More than simple narrative, the poem examines the festivities with anthropological fascination and alternates between dialect and standard English. Those characters speaking in dialect are subordinated to the omniscient narrator who serves to oversee—that is, a figure who is authorized to order and visualize the inner lives of the black characters.

One such subordinate character, Booker, the banjo player, plays the evening's final tune and, "in melody and rime," tells the story of how the banjo was invented. The story satirizes the story of Ham, "de only n—— whut wuz runnin'" on Noah's "packet," which, in this embedded narrative, Russell imagines as a Mississippi steamboat.[8] Russell's Ham was employed as a barber on the steamship, a job traditionally held by black men. According to the story, one lonely day, Ham decided to fabricate a musical instrument, the yet-to-be banjo. It is an origin story, after all, meant to celebrate black ingenuity and creativity within the strictures of the prevailing visuality of blackness and all that that entails: the biblically ordained and juvenile servility, the pseudoscientifically established inferiority, the scope of vision and imagination that is limited to what is materially at hand and subject to improvisation, and so on. This popular section of the poem is often excerpted bearing the title "De Fust Banjo."

Booker, a character given permission to speak by the standard-English-speaking omniscient narrator of the framing poem, adopts the mask of yet another, derivative omniscient narrator. Booker's narrator speaks in dialect and on behalf of the banjo, not Ham, whose music conveys that instrument's fictive origin story. Booker's narrator imitates or translates into Negro dialect the banjo's narration. We see, even in this embedded story, it is necessary to withhold the power of narrativity from either Booker or Ham, the two most obvious candidates to tell the story, which would confer the power to visualize a history. Lest anyone quibble that, logically, Russell has indeed made Booker the narrator, Russell locates the source of that voice in the sanctionable realm of music. One wonders if it could be heard otherwise. The spectral narrator whimsically addresses an audience made up of animate and inanimate, but nonetheless sentient, objects:

Go 'way fiddle! folks is tired o' hearin' you a-squakin'.
Keep silence fur yo' betters!—don't you heah de banjo talkin'?
About de 'possum's tail she's gwine to lecter—ladies, listen!—
About de ha'r whut is n't da, an' why de ha'r is missin'. (1956)

In the banjo's multiply mediated story, Noah reads the local newspaper to discover the river is forecast to overflow from an incoming storm. Noah builds the steamboat and gathers a great store of livestock and forest creatures. Once the steamboat is underway and they are caught in the storm, lonely Ham invents the banjo to amuse himself and others. He uses the hair from an opossum's tail to string the improvised instrument, which explains why the animal's tail is hairless today. The narrative assigns agency to the instrument, almost divine in its inexplicability, which wills itself, and as a consequence Ham's art, into being by using Ham as a bored and thoughtless vessel. Instrument and creator are reversed.

Russell's work is successful in this regard not only because Russell is himself white. Much of "Christmas-Night in the Quarters" consists of stock themes supplied by the Plantation School, but Russell's lyric facility is the thing on display. Ultimately, our attention is on Russell rather than his evocations of the black subjects' purportedly lived experiences. The nesting and imbricated masks of speakers further prove the artifice while contributing to the illusion that we have penetrated the otherwise opaque (because it is wholly imagined and imaginary) subjectivity of blackness. Russell's speakers are indistinguishable because he wants to claim for himself the authority to inscribe blackness. And in the echo chamber of race, the blackness Russell means to inscribe is his own.

Many conventions of dialect poetry are designed to alienate black subjectivity from the privileged norms and standards of literary production that would otherwise reveal an interiority recognizable enough to warrant empathy. No dialect is accurate in poetry,[9] certainly not in poetry that is rhymed and metered. Yet by employing the discourse of accuracy and authority, critics shunt Negro dialect poetry off to the realm of ethnology and dodge the actual work of close reading and analysis, thereby upholding Jefferson's prime directive. The graphic, which is not to say phonetic, agenda of dialect poetry resists transparency and reminds the reader of the material nature of the text. To invoke Rodolphe Gasché's (1997) formulation, when the silver backing becomes visible, the mirror loses its ability to reflect. Dialect poetry endeavors to make the silver backing visible, so to speak, so the reader cannot see him- or herself in the work.

Reading Dunbar's 1969 "When Malindy Sings," the novelist Gayl Jones (1991) notes Malindy's physical absence as evidence of a defect in dialect as a form. The form resists the revelation of interiority, Jones claims, and "therefore share[s] the *consequences* if not the *intentions* of the Plantation Tradition" (18). Jones is correct in her critique; however, she makes a fundamental category mistake when she observes that "Dunbar's lack of plasticity carries beyond the impulses of the language itself to the potential of character revelation; the interior landscape of character is not yet visible" (18). What Glissant calls "free poetics," Jones, borrowing the term from James Weldon Johnson, calls "plasticity." Although she does not define plasticity, we might take her to mean this as a kind of mobility of perspective that we associate with the novelistic free indirect discourse generously employed by Irwin Russell. By ignoring Dunbar's historical moment and positionality, Jones employs a New Critical reading that alienates the work from relational concerns of audience and authorial intention.

Whether Dunbar is writing in dialect or not, we understand he is writing within a white visuality of blackness that was indeed monolithic in its expectations regarding the performance of race. Dunbar had to write within and against the dominant feature in the visuality archive, the linguistic tropes of minstrelsy. Dunbar's contemporary audience was largely incapable or unwilling (or both) to suspend disbelief in relation to the artifice of the presentation when the depiction of black characters strayed too far beyond minstrel conventions. Dunbar's work suffers critical inattention today, despite his being regarded as an important literary figure, because it traffics in the tropes of minstrelsy, appearing to capitulate to this dominant force. Few readers today have the patience to suspend disbelief long enough to interpret and contextualize the various ways Dunbar works within the form. Had he chosen to write outside minstrel conventions (as he did on occasion and was reproached for having done so by black and white critics alike), Dunbar's work would have been dismissed as irrelevant or even suppressed as antagonistic to the dominant sensibilities of the day. Because he cared to be popular or even relevant, he had to negotiate with the rigid expectations of his audience. By reading Dunbar against literary conventions he was not allowed to access, Jones reaffirms Jefferson's categorical exclusion. It is further unfair, then, for Jones to expect Dunbar to transcend the literary fashions of his day given how disempowered he was in relation to the kinds of work his reader would accept and given that, by all accounts, when Dunbar wrote in dialect he did so under duress.

J. Saunders Redding, in his 1939 *To Make a Poet Black*, gives us a sense of the time and adumbrates the intermingling issues of essence and audience:

By a sort of natural development the "d——y" sketches [on the stage], now [late nineteenth century] so intimately a part of American minstrelsy, hardened into the recognized speech of the Negro, into glee and jamboree songs that were immediately characterized as "c——n" songs, into sentimental ballads which were considered especially representative of the colored people, and finally into a pathetic kind of "d——y" poetry. Thus were set up the limits to the Negro's media of expression. Thus was focused the picture of the Negro as a slapstick and a pathetic buffoon. . . . It was not long before [the Negro] discovered that in order to be heard at all he must speak in the voice and accents that his hearers recognized. The picture of Paul Laurence Dunbar as a thwarted poet . . . is fairly composite.[10] (1988, 51)

Redding notes not only the artificiality of dialect but that it was a coauthored form.

Gayl Jones's first mistake in her reading of "When Malindy Sings" is that she assumes Malindy is the exclusive subject of the poem. The very fact that the poem is written in dialect qualifies it as a persona poem or dramatic monologue. From the standpoint of the crafting poet, the foremost subject of every persona poem is the character of the speaker. The weight of Dunbar's creative intelligence is brought to bear on his crafting of the mask— that is, his crafting of the visuality of blackness evoked by the rhetorical and epistemological features assigned to the speaker. The interior character we are meant to engage in a persona poem typically belongs to the speaker. When the speaker is black, however, the representation of that interior must be negotiated. These were the terms on which Dunbar challenged the dominant visuality of blackness. While Russell insisted on obscuring the interiority of his black speakers, Dunbar invested his speaker with a powerful balance of intellect and affect without overly offending white readers' sensibilities.

We can be fairly confident that Dunbar was reading Russell. Russell's poems appeared widely in major magazines and enjoyed great popularity in their time. Perhaps more telling, however, is the structural similarity of the openings of each poet's most popular poem. Russell's "De Fust Banjo" begins, as we recall, "Go 'way fiddle! folks is tired o' hearin' you a-squakin'." The first line of "When Malindy Sings" reads, almost in response to Russell, "G'way an' quit dat noise, Miss Lucy—." This is not dispositive of a salute to Russell, but it contributes to my confidence that Dunbar looked to Russell, just as Russell had looked to Burns, for various forms of scaffolding.

As Dunbar's objective in the poem is to trouble the notion of white superiority, he employs rhetorical argumentation as well. Dunbar's speaker tells his auditor, "Miss Lucy," that she can practice until she's old and gray, but she will never be able to sing like Malindy. Miss Lucy simply does not have the natural faculties—the gifts—that a black woman has for song. By extension, we understand that Miss Lucy is representative of Dunbar's white audience and that Malindy is representative of Dunbar's visuality of blackness. In matters of culture, then, according to Dunbar's logic, blacks are superior to whites. That Dunbar camouflages this sentiment by misdirecting the reader's attention toward Malindy (this is what Glissant calls "detour") and her necessarily vaguely drawn character is evidence of the coercive counterforce with which Dunbar was in contention inside his literary practice.

We can examine a poem such as "Accountability" with similar results. The misdirection, the detour, in this poem of Dunbar's is the humorous rationalization of the stage Negro's propensity for stealing chickens. The counterpoetic disruption Dunbar employs is that Dunbar's speaker espouses a philosophy that is fundamentally at odds with the very logic of stereotypes behind this, one of the most entrenched and stereotypical masks projected onto the black subject, the chicken thief. As a result, we can read the poem as radically subversive. Although the speaker announces, in the last line, that he has stolen "one o' mastah's chickens," he rationalizes this act as a consequence of his God-given station in life. "We all fits into places dat no othah ones could fill, / An' we does the things we has to, big er little, good er ill." So weighted with intellection, the dialect in these two lines threatens to collapse under the weight of Dunbar's argument against the collectivizing opacity of black subjectivity. Almost too wise, the jester nearly breaks character.

Returning to "Malindy," Jones mistakes the persona for the poet when she refers to "*Dunbar's* lack of plasticity." This fundamental misstep prevents us from reading dialect poetry with the requisite skepticism. Jones's rhetorical slippage occurs in part because dialect poetry is a textual representation of a nonstandardized idiom. Dialect poetry exists in the border territory between orality and written expression and lacks a predictable system of ciphering. Without codification there can be no confident distinction between surface meaning and subtext, sincerity and irony. As a result, dialect poetry is always subject to overvaluation on one hand and to derision on the other. Dialect poetry is the prototypical briar patch, which is to say, it is, in a manner, *all* subtext; it is replete with counterintentional sentiment. The only thing we can be certain of with dialect poetry is its artifice. For Jones to suggest, on the basis of the evidence of his poems, that Dunbar himself lacks some quality or characteristic is misguided because it is a personal rather than a literary critique.

Dialect poetry does make for slippery analysis, however, when used in service of racial uplift, the conventional mission of African American literature. Without sincerity it is difficult for the reader to infer conviction from the poetic speaker. Indeed, it is difficult for the reader to take the speaker of a dialect poem seriously at all. This is how we arrive at the famous "two stops" notion proffered by James Weldon Johnson (1931), who contends that dialect poetry is capable of conveying only comedy or pathos. It is no wonder, then, that dialect poetry has been written off as ineffectual if not irrelevant in service of the big mission, as I call it, to counter Jefferson's prime directive. The dialect poems of Paul Laurence Dunbar suffer a lack of critical attention accordingly.

Many commentators claim folk traditions for the root of African American poetry. Any black poet writing after World War II who aspires to canonicity feels a pressure that is "well-nigh irresistible," to use Johnson's words. This pressure to align her work with folk expression, no matter how foreign such expressions may be to her idiomatic inclinations, results from the system of patronage, which seeks to maintain the dominant visuality of blackness.

The definition of blackness has always been contested. The contest is now visible because black people are on the offense, targeting white statuary, symbology, historical narratives, and the composition of public space (Black Lives Matter plazas, for example). Black poets have begun to shift their strategies in this contest from proving black parity to limiting and policing white access to the visualization of blackness. White interests resist such strategies by deriding them as the fruits of an oppressive and draconian cancel culture.

Technology, however, is an increasingly powerful tool in black poets' struggle to inscribe the visuality of blackness. Technology amplifies and allows black subjects to exercise an outsize influence over the visuality of blackness, one that exceeds what might be possible in real life. In *Distributed Blackness* (2020), André Brock Jr. suggests that in the twenty-first century the visuality of blackness is mediated through technology. Blackness is visualized, in theory and in practice,[11] via social networking platforms like Twitter, where one can refer to "Black Twitter" as an arbiter of online cultural norms. "Black online culture and sociality," Brock writes, "are more easily visualized today thanks not only to the hashtag and other algorithmic means but also to the near infrastructural use of social networking services as well as older online artifacts, such as messaging services, blogs, and bulletin boards, where one could see articulations of the Black identity across digital networks" (2). The technological field has come to replace the metaphor of visuality with an inscribable surface on which revision and erasure are exponentially more difficult to enforce.

NOTES

1. In 2021 it was republished by Mint Editions of Berkeley, California.

2. "The position of my white neighbor," Hurston writes in her 1928 essay "How It Feels to Be Colored Me" (2015), "is much more difficult [than mine]. No brown specter

pulls up a chair beside me when I sit down to eat. No dark ghost thrusts its leg against mine in bed. The game of keeping what one has is never so exciting as the game of getting."

3. I argue that, because the white-produced black subject is characteristically unacceptable to black subjects themselves, every expression of that subject produces a new Negro, so to speak.

4. Arguably, not writing about race in America is simply one more strategy for contesting the prevailing visuality of blackness.

5. I regret the rhetorical slippage suggested in essentializing terms like "the black imagination." I employ these terms so as not to distract from the larger argument.

6. Glissant, Edouard. "Free and Forced Poetics." *Ethnopoetics*. Eds. Michel Benamou and Jerome Rothenberg. Boston: Alcheringa, 1976. 95–101.

7. Sidney Lanier is known for a poem titled "The Power of Prayer; or, The First Steamboat Up the Alabama" spoken in the voice of a blind black man who mistakes the sound of a steamboat for the devil.

8. I have obscured slurs.

9. To evaluate the historical accuracy of a literary dialect is to make a category mistake. One cannot evaluate the historical accuracy of a fictional event.

10. I have obscured slurs.

11. I'm thinking here of the Althusserian notion of ideology as praxis.

WORKS CITED

Brock, André, Jr. 2020. *Distributed Blackness: African American Cybercultures*. New York: New York University Press.

Cullen, Countee. 1925. *Color*. London: Harper.

Du Bois, W.E.B. 1903. *The Souls of Black Folk*. New York: Penguin.

Dunbar, Paul Laurence. 1895. *Majors and Minors*. Toledo, OH: Hadley and Hadley.

Gasché, Rodolphe. 1997. *The Tain of the Mirror: Derrida and the Philosophy of Reflection*. Cambridge, MA: Harvard University Press.

Glissant, Edouard. 1976. "Free and Forced Poetics." *Ethnopoetics*. Eds. Michel Benamou and Jerome Rothenberg. Boston: Alcheringa.

Horton, George Moses. 1982. *Naked Genius*. Greensboro, NC: Chapel Hill Historical Society.

Hurston, Zora Neale. 2015. *How It Feels to Be Colored Me*. Carlisle, MA: Applewood Books.

Jefferson, Thomas. 2018. *Notes on the State of Virginia*. N.p.: Franklin Classics.

Johnson, James Weldon. 1931. *The Book of American Negro Poetry, Chosen and Edited, with an Essay on the NEGRO'S Creative Genius*. New York: Harcourt, Brace.

Jones, Gayl. 1991. *Liberating Voices: Oral Tradition in African American Literature*. Cambridge, MA: Harvard University Press.

Lanier, Sidney. 1999. *Poems of Sidney Lanier*. Athens: University of Georgia Press.

Mirzoeff, Nicholas. 2012. *The Right to Look: A Counterhistory of Visuality*. Durham, NC: Duke University Press.

Morrison, Toni. 1992. *Playing in the Dark*. Cambridge, MA: Harvard University Press.

———. 2014. "Portland State, 'BLACK Studies Center Public DIALOGUE. Pt. 2' May 30, 1975." *SoundCloud*, January 24, 2014. soundcloud.com/portland-state-library/port land-state-black-studies-1.

Radano, Ronald M. 2003. *Lying Up a Nation: Race and Black Music*. Chicago: University of Chicago Press.

Redding, J. Saunders. 1988. *To Make a Poet Black*. Ithaca, NY: Cornell University Press.

Russell, Irwin. 1956. *Irwin Russell's Christmas Night in the Quarters: And Other Poems*. Arranged by Lillie Varetta Barton. Dallas, TX: American Guild Press.

Van Evrie, John H.. *Negroes and Negro "slavery:": The First an Inferior Race; the Latter Its Normal Condition*. United States, Van Evrie, Horton & Company, 1861.

Wagner, Jean. 1973. *Black Poets of the United States: From Paul Laurence Dunbar to Langston Hughes*. Translated by Kenneth Douglas. Champaign: University of Illinois Press, 1973.

Wheatley, Phillis. 1793. *Poems on Various Subjects, Religious and Moral*. London.

Subverting Colonial Aesthetics

Frantz Fanon, W.E.B. Du Bois, and Janelle Monáe

SARAH THEN BERGH

To theorize the historical conditions that lead us to think Africana studies is first and foremost to engage questions of the human—to ask who is accounted for as (being) human. Such questions have and continue to lie at the very heart of the intellectual project that is Africana studies. Its long-standing history in examining racializing processes alongside the psychosocial effects of slavery and colonialism are steeped as much in an exploration of different dehumanizing representations of bodies, spaces, and cultures and their ties to particular narrations of blackness, as they are in commitments to a disruption of such practices of policing through the creation of a "new language and a new humanity."[1] Inherently entangled, the stakes of this twofold project that is Africana studies are high. On the one hand, it rests on a probing of various, often overlapping, political and social fabrics in view of the distribution of their members and the parts they play that either allow or deny them the ability to be recognized as human—that is, the ability to assert themselves and the ability to be heard. On the other hand, this project rests on continuous efforts to disrupt existing distributions both ontologically and epistemologically. In doing so, Africana studies does not merely seek to alter which members hold the ability to assert themselves and be heard but it also fundamentally alters the relationship among said members.

Reflections on such practices of distribution take on a particular aura in a political moment that is engaged in a renewed public discourse over who cannot breathe in our contemporary sociopolitical fabric and whose assertion of this experience is left unheard in the most urgent moment. This is a disquieting question in relation to the murder of George Floyd in 2020 or that of Eric Garner in 2014. It is also a disquieting question in relation to a global pandemic resulting from the spread of a coronavirus whose infection leaves those it entraps unable to breathe and whose measurable impact has been contingent on a disproportionate distribution of access to medical equipment both within and across states. We are left, then, with a political moment that highlights anew the importance of considering the different modes that structure our sociopolitical fabrics and the means through which those distributed within them seek to make themselves heard such that they are accounted for as human.

This chapter takes up these questions of the human as questions of distribution at the heart of Africana studies and examines them through the lens of audiovisual aesthetics. To this end, I engage the theoretical and artistic contributions of Frantz Fanon, Aimé Césaire, William Edward Burghardt Du Bois, and Janelle Monáe to explore how these thinkers' conceptual reflections are shaped by an interplay between two complementary analytic approaches: first, by an analysis of the colonial aesthetic of a spatial and temporal stasis[2] that marks racialized lines of division among the enslaved and slaveholder much as the colonized and colonizer in the past and, second, by their formulation of a decolonizing aesthetic[3] that functions to disrupt such delimitations in the(ir) present and for the future. To trace these two elements in the scholars' and artists' respective works, the chapter is divided into three main parts.

The first draws on the writings of Frantz Fanon and Aimé Césaire to conceptualize both the aesthetic underpinnings for their analyses of a colonial and racialized order, and their propositions for a decolonizing cultural production. These are respectively marked by an aesthetic of spatial and temporal stasis, and an aesthetic of motion. I move to extrapolate the two core transformational elements that highlight a decolonizing cultural production within Fanon's and Césaire's frameworks. The first is defined by a shift in addressee such that the colonized peoples, rather than the colonial system, become the core audience for the colonized artists' work. Beyond an essentialized argument of authenticity along racial lines, however, this shift in addressee emerges as the final—and indeed only—possible structuring of a cultural production that succeeds in redefining and initiating relationships that disrupt the colonial aesthetic of stasis. It does so by rendering the colonized people as the subjects, rather than the objects, of an artistic production under the confines of a totalizing colonial system. Contingent on the artwork's ability to embody the contemporary lived experiences of the colonized peoples during the liberation struggle of the twentieth century, the second central transformational element of a decolonial aesthetic emerges in its ability to give shape to a trajectory of existence. Emblematic of both an ethical commitment to remembrance and an aesthetic commitment to cultural production as a heterogeneous and fluctuating artistic process, both elements of a decolonizing cultural production disrupt the static aesthetic at play in the colonial order to which a decolonial aesthetic responds.

The following two parts of the chapter extrapolate from and probe the conceptual framework offered by Frantz Fanon and Aimé Césaire through the lens of two musical forms from the African diaspora in the United States: W.E.B. Du Bois's analysis of the "Sorrow Songs" in his *The Souls of Black Folk* and Janelle Monáe's 2013 music video for "Q.U.E.E.N." Both are centrally concerned with a musical and audiovisual shift in addressee as their conceptualizations and performances proceed. And both are fundamentally committed to presenting their audiences with a historical and musical trajectory of existence that underpins their writing, performance, and thought. In reading Du Bois's reflections and Monáe's performance alongside Fanon's and Césaire's theoretical framework of a decolonizing aesthetic, the intention is not to assimilate the histories and experiences of slavery and colonialism that centrally inform the work of these respective thinkers. Nor is it to suggest that these experiences, as well as the spatial and temporal contexts within which they emerge and continue to emerge can necessarily be mapped onto a single conceptual plane. It is, rather, to engage and honor the multidirectional and multisited commitment to "critical and theoretical dialogues" that have marked the historical condition that is Africana philosophy.[4] It is from this web of exchanges that I hope to let this chapter speak.

Colonial Aesthetics and Decolonial Subversions in Frantz Fanon and Aimé Césaire

Colonial Stasis

To enter the world of the colony through the lens of the aesthetic is to embark on a guided visual tour that finds one of its most meticulous and articulate considerations in the writings of Frantz Fanon. His 1961 work, *The Wretched of the Earth*, opens by setting as its scene the motionless and static world of the colony with its corresponding figures, "the native" and "the settler."[5] Through the use of this blanket terminology we find the first indication of the colony as a delineated and confined division of its members and their functions. What emerges is the colony as an aesthetic installation that is marked by spatial and temporal stasis, seeking to eliminate any supplementary part and function beyond those classified as the native and the settler.

In this sense, Fanon's spatial outline of the colony emerges as the first marker of its corresponding aesthetic of stasis. Captured in the "motionless . . . world," that marks the colonial context from which Fanon speaks, he welcomes his readers by introducing the colony as a "Manichean world,"[6] separated into "two zones [that] are opposed, but not in the service of higher unity."[7] More than the colonizer's denial of a Hegelian dialectic in his or her encounter with the colonized, however, the two zones that Fanon outlines mark the spatial, which is to say cartographic and physically divided organization of the colony. Following his writing, we are guided along the "dividing line" that separates the colony into the "settler's town" on the one side and the "native town" on the other.[8] The latter in particular is characterized as "a world without spaciousness [such that] men live there on top of each other, and their huts are built on top of the other."[9] In other words, the native town is marked by the compression of all those who inhabit it and the physical space between them. Read as an indication of the incapacity of motion that concomitantly arises as an indicator of subjugation for colonized subjects within that space that Fanon terms the native town, this serves as the first marker of an aesthetic of stasis in his spatial depiction of the colony as installation.[10]

The consequent "immobility to which the native is condemned"[11] is not, however, of a purely spatial and cartographic nature. Instead, what emerges is a complementary representation of stasis in a temporal sense. This is apparent when we return to Fanon's analogical understanding of the colonial encounter as confrontation. Within Fanon's paradigm, Hegel's conception of sublation (*Aufhebung*) qua (mutual) recognition is stifled in the colonial context because the settler seeks to establish her or himself as the sole meaning-giving entity. Colonial rule, as a quasi-totalizing system, thus reveals the settler's violent attempt to impose on the natives a caricatured representation of themselves. Within the colonial confrontation this manifests as a twofold process.

The first is marked by the colonizer's efforts to hollow out the heterogeneous identificatory processes of the native through a systematic elimination of the natives' national culture. In an attempt to render these practices nonexistent, the settler is not satisfied with a mere denial and the systematic devaluation of the natives' national culture. Perversely, the colonizer demands that the natives themselves acknowledge the supposed "inferiority" of their national culture.[12] In this way, the colonizer's project is to ensure that the colonized recognize the "unreality" of their culture and begin to devalorize, "in the last extreme, the confused and imperfect character of his [or her] own biological structure."[13] Not unlike the process of natal alienation that Orlando Patterson lays bare in *Slavery and Social Death*,[14] this systematic eradication of cultural ties among the natives marks the precondition for the second step in the settler's attempt to impose on the natives a caricatured representation of themselves: the emergence of the settler as the sole source of meaning making such that the colonizer becomes the sole actor on the colonial stage. "In fact," writes Fanon, "the settler is right when he speaks of knowing 'them' [the natives] well. For it is the settler who has brought the native into existence and who perpetuates his existence."[15]

The twofold dynamic of this violent imposition of an identity on the colonized by those colonizing finds further articulation in the work of Aimé Césaire. Césaire argues that the colonial world is not merely marked by a division that delineates the distinct functions of the master ("maître") and slave ("serviteur") in the colony. Rather, the very historical composition of the colony is at stake. In Césaire's scenario, the colonizer takes on a distinct role within the Manichean world that marks the colony. As the creator of cultural values ("le créateur des valeurs culturelles") the colonizer's function is set against that of the colonized by relegating the latter to the status of mere consumer ("consommateur") of the colonizer's values.[16]

However, more than the settler's attempt to impose the "supremacy of white values"[17] on the native, Césaire's analysis of the hierarchized distinction between the colonizing creator and colonized consumer reveals the colonial system as an attempt to implement a "metaphysics of difference"[18] in which the settler emerges as the sole (discursive) sculptor of the native. This is reminiscent of Fanon's analysis of the capturing white gaze that brings into being the "BLACK MAN!" as "triple person" in his 1952 *Black Skin, White Masks*.[19] The native so conceived is trapped in her or his presupposed ontological inferiority. In this sense, those subjects encompassed by the sweeping categorization of the native are emptied of specification and denied individualization, while attributed excessive signification. The effect of such caricatured categorization is that the figure of the native can be set in direct opposition to and separated from those subjects designated the settler within the Manichean world of the colony. Fixed in their colonial categorization of being, what emerges, for Fanon, is the world of the colony as a "world of statues."[20]

Read through the lens of stasis as the aesthetic regime of Fanon's colonial installation, the static or immobile emerges here in its temporal sense. The rise of the settler as the sole meaning-making entity in any (or all) colonial confrontation with the native denies the latter an identificatory, and thus temporally unfolding, *process* of becoming, both subjectively and culturally. Relegating the native to a hollowed out and *fixed* "objecthood,"[21] the eradication of the natives' national culture serves to establish a static delineation of the statues on display within the spatial and temporal colonial installation that Fanon presents us with. In this sense, both a spatial and a temporal stasis emerge as a primary "aesthetic expression of respect for the established [colonial] order [that] serve[s] to create around the exploited person an atmosphere of submission and of inhibition which lightens the task of [colonial] policing considerably."[22]

Much like Jacques Rancière's notion of a police force, the static aesthetic we encounter as a marker of Fanon's colonial installation functions to establish and maintain a delineation of the sensible that renders the creating colonizer visible and audible while relegating the consuming colonized to a realm of the invisible and inaudible.[23] At stake, then, in Fanon's colonial aesthetic of spatial and temporal stasis, is the founding and manifestation of social relations that are marked by an essentialized distance between the colonizer (as the sole creator) and the colonized (as mere consumer). In this way we arrive at the question of the human as the question of distribution in an aesthetic sense.

Decolonial Motion

The primacy of an aesthetic of spatial and temporal stasis that sets the scene for the colonial installation of the native and settler statues at the outset of *The Wretched of the Earth* is complemented in the book's second part. Here the aesthetic emerges as a decolonial disruption that seeks to transform the colonial order at play. Located in the realm of culture and, specifically, in the reinvigoration of a national culture, the latter emerges as an integral aspect of the anti-colonial liberation struggles in Fanon's framework. Two strategic attempts to disrupt the colonial aesthetic through the reinvigoration of a national culture are undertaken by colonized artists in moments foreshadowing decolonization. However, as we will see, their respective subsumption under, and reliance on, an aesthetic of stasis impedes the success of these early attempts at disrupting and thus transforming the colonial order to which they seek to respond.

The first strategy posits an attempt by the colonized artist to render him or herself visible and heard under the premise of the colonial order itself. In so doing, this first strategy resembles attempts by colonized subjects to inhabit the denigrated caricature of the "BLACK MAN,"[24] or woman, which the "white man had . . . woven out of a thousand details, anecdotes, stories."[25] For Fanon, this points to the only way in which colonial subjects are able to make themselves known within the sociopolitical fabric of the colonial world. Similarly, the initial response of colonized artists to the colonial system is marked by their attempt to perform the fantastical cultural forms and categories that the colonizer attributes to the colonized peoples. Yet, in this attempt the colonized artist serves only to advance "an artisan style [that] solidifies into a formalism which is more and more stereotyped."[26] Arrested in a cultural essence, the artistic forms that the colonized artist pursues are imposed on him or her by the colonizer and thus "marked off by fences and signposts."[27] Consequently, neither the pursuit of different artistic styles nor the development of existing artistic forms are available to the colonized artist. Instead, the colonized artist is condemned to replicate the very aesthetic of stasis that defines the colonial and racialized installation and pits the colonizer as the creator of cultural values against the colonized as the consumer of said values. Militating against any disturbance in the colonial order, the colonized artist is once more engulfed by the colonial aesthetic regime at play, thus only reinforcing it.

The second strategy to reinvigorate a national culture is pursued through the colonized artist's explicit endeavor to counteract the devalorizing narratives that seek the total elimination of the natives' national culture. To this end, the colonized artist pursues a reinstatement of natal ties through a restoration of prior cultural forms, largely preserved through traditions of dress and other customs. While Fanon acknowledges in this second phase the beginnings of a "demonstration of nationality,"[28] its attempts to reinvigorate a true national consciousness and national culture are nonetheless set to fail. Thus, its reliance on a return to, and preservation of, "abandoned traditions"[29] once more maintains an aesthetic of stasis. Temporally, we encounter this stasis through a stagnation of cultural forms, where the preservationist strategy constitutes a "throw-back to the laws of inertia."[30] Beyond the commensurate immobilization of artistic aesthetics and styles, at stake in this cultural inertia is its inability to transform existing social relations or to initiate new ones. In the attempt "to get back to the people in that past out of which they have already emerged," the preservationist strategy fails to attend to "that *fluctuating movement*" that marks the experiences of the people in the contemporary moment of their liberation struggle.[31] Consequently, "there is no taking of the offensive and no redefining of relationships. There is simply a concentration on a hard core of culture which is becoming more and more shrivelled up, inert and empty."[32] As a result, this second strategy to reinvigorate a national culture, too, is condemned to an aesthetic of stasis, similar to that which is reproduced by the colonized artist who attempts to establish him- or herself from within the colonial order itself.

Collectively, the aesthetic of stasis within which these earlier strategies are embedded impedes their success at transforming the colonial order through a redefinition of social relationships. This is largely due to these endeavors remaining premised on an attempt to address the colonial system itself. Whether the colonized artist seeks to establish him- or herself quietly, by imitating the fantastical artistic forms and styles that the colonizer attributes to the cultural realm of the colonized, or whether the colonized artist seeks to counteract the devalorizing narrative that the colonizer attempts to instill in the colonized culture, both strategies are premised on addressing the colonial system itself. Given its sociopolitical organization, both strategies are compelled to address the colonial order's static aesthetic, and in doing so, they reproduce it.

Yet if this illustrates why the two initial attempts by colonized artists to reinvigorate a national culture in moments foreshadowing the liberation struggle fail, it also explains the eventual success of such attempts. For Fanon this triumph lies in an artistic shift of the addressee such that a new focal point of the colonized artist, and her or his work of art, is established. Consequently, the true formation of a national consciousness and reinvigoration of a national culture emerges in the final instance only when the colonized artist seeks to address the lived experiences of the colonized peoples during the liberation struggle. Doing so requires that the colonized artists capture precisely that "fluctuating movement"[33] that a preservationist strategy fails to attend to. The unleashed motion that underlies this movement—a movement that is consequently both formally and aesthetically decolonial—reinvigorates the cultural production among colonized artists and breaks its ties to a colonial aesthetic of stasis. Both a source of legitimacy for the artist and that which gives the artistic work shape, the address of the artist to his or her own people allows a redefinition of existing relationships and an initiation of novel social ties.

Rather than adhere to an essentialized argument of cultural authenticity along racial lines, however,[34] at stake in Fanon's insistence on this shift in artistic addressee is the rendering of the colonized people as the *subjects*, rather than the *objects* of the artistic production under the totalizing colonial system. In its ability to redefine existing relationships and initiate new social ties, a shift of the artistic addressee thus subverts the fixed and delineated classification of the settler and the native, much as their allocated functions. In doing so, a shift of the artistic addressee posits the first central element of a decolonial disruption in the colonial aesthetic of stasis, thus allowing for a reinvigoration of a national culture. The second element grows out of the first and emerges from the ensuing necessity to embody and give shape to the contemporary lived experiences of the colonized peoples during the liberation struggle, within the artwork itself. This requires that the colonized artist break with essentialized and atemporal cultural forms and attributes that stifle the living transformation of cultural production relegating it to the realm of tradition and custom, and return instead to the fluctuating movement that underpins the people's lived experiences.

Fanon's framework of a reinvigorated national culture highlights motion as an imperative condition for its success as a decolonial disruption to the colonial aesthetic of stasis under a totalizing colonial system. Premised on an ethical commitment to contemporary remembrance, and on an aesthetic commitment to cultural production as a heterogeneous and fluctuating artistic process that sediments in the artwork itself,[35] a shift in addressee at the heart of this artistic constellation posits the (lived experiences of the) colonized peoples, much as the artist who gives shape to these experiences, as creator. This subverts the static distribution that pits the statue of the colonizing creator against that of the consuming colonized within the preceding colonial installation. What emerges is an artistic tracing of fluctuating human conditions of existence that moves beyond the confines of simplified and isolated forms of tradition and cultural custom.

The following section focuses on a concrete example of this aesthetic anamorphosis through a consideration of W.E.B. Du Bois's writings on sorrow songs.

W.E.B. Du Bois's Sorrow Songs

Considering the musically decolonizing aesthetics through the writings of W.E.B. Du Bois in *The Souls of Black Folk* is to begin and end in song, more specifically, with the "Sorrow Songs."[36] Placed at the beginning of each chapter, these songs receive their due analytic attention in the book's final chapter. Tracing the structural layout of *Souls*, we find that the sorrow songs function as a means of reframing the scenes and performances of a racialized primary aesthetic that Du Bois simultaneously invokes and transforms through them. This emerges on three main fronts.

The first significance of these songs for a decolonizing aesthetics emerges in their placement as epigraphs to each chapter of *Souls*. Their epigraphic prominence and recurrence identifies this music as conceptually indispensable to Du Bois's sociological and theoretical explorations. In conjunction with epigraphic verses from mostly European and Euro-American writers of the eighteenth and nineteenth centuries, the musical notes from the sorrow songs emerge as a source of thought that attributes them equal standing with European and Euro-American writers.

In this way, we encounter the first marker of disruption in the politics of Du Bois's decolonizing aesthetic regime. Its emergence lies in Du Bois's ability to invoke a "strangeness"[37] through the conjoined placement of *"Negro" music* in relation to *"American" literature* and its European genealogy—his two critical sources of thought.[38] In doing so, Du Bois "breaks with the sensory self-evidence of the 'natural' order"[39] under a racialized regime. The latter places the visual as the mode of rationality and thought, as well as the European and Euro-American as the body/part in its command, against the aural as a mode of the merely sensual (the animalistic), embodied through the category of the Negro. Read as a clash of two sensory orders, this brings into relief "the color-line"[40] as the manifestation of a policing order that seeks to separate these two spheres so as to denote the former as the sole creator of thought. In disrupting this delineation, Du Bois's structuring of *Souls,* much like the sorrow songs that drive his writings therein, "stirs"[41] those who witness and experience this strangeness. Revealing the aesthetic regime of Du Bois's decolonizing politics, these twinned epigraphs, in their dual function as both introduction and inscription, offer a new dramaturgy or topology of the intelligible that reframes the scene of a racialized nineteenth-century United States and its trajectory. Consequently, *The Souls of Black Folk*—in the sense of a lived experience and sensibility—speaks and is heard in new registers.

The second significance of a decolonial disruption in Du Bois's sorrow songs emerges from the first and appears as the interwoven shift in artistic addressee and artistic subject that results from the ability to speak and be heard through song. Du Bois offers this analysis of the sorrow songs in the final chapter of *Souls,* when he asserts that "these songs are *the articulate message of the slave to the world.*"[42] The significance of decolonial subversion arises here through a conception of these songs as a revelatory articulation that inserts the collective we of the "slave"—a signifier that is reappropriated in this very act of musical articulation—into that racialized order in which previously they had had no right of address. In transforming the perceived noise that accompanies the "rhythmic *cry* of the slave"[43] into "the *voice* of exile"[44] that "spoke to *men,*"[45] the sorrow songs appear as a new dramaturgy of the intelligible. This places "the slave" as the heterogeneity of the (articulated) multiple, against the singularity of classified identities and their allocated functions in the racialized police order of chattel slavery and its afterlife. "The slave" (and their lived experiences) thus emerge as the artistic *subjects* of the sorrow songs by inserting them, to borrow from Hannah Arendt's terminology, into that space of appearance that reveals the plurality of human subjectivities, who had previously been unaccounted for as such.[46]

Third, so conceived, we find in Du Bois's conceptualization of the sorrow songs an inauguration of what Paul Kottman has called a politics of the scene. Kottman derives his notion of the scene from Hannah Arendt's analytic framework of speech and action as that which politicizes and thus reveals the subject to the social fabric that preceded its arrival. Similarly, Kottman conceives of the politics of the scene as an initiation of human interaction such that "a singular relationship or web of relationships is brought into being, sustained, or altered among those on the scene."[47] In other words, the defining element of the scene is the address of one of its witnesses to another "in ways that confirm a shared relation—one that has emerged on a prior scene or on prior scenes."[48]

More than a mere insertion through speech,[49] however, this address instills a temporality *l'avenir*, where the speaker exposes him- or herself to the "eventuality of another's response."[50] Much like Rancière's politics of aesthetics, this response is neither deliberately desired nor demanded. Nonetheless, it is in the possibility of a "future testimony *among witnesses from the original scene*"[51] that Kottman locates the political significance of a response. in this way, the political significance of the scene does not lie in its creation of (a historical) testimony for those who were absent. Rather, it requires the address and response of the living witnesses—often, though not exclusively, those of victim and perpetrator. Only in this living form can the scene retain its political sense as the "ongoing condition of possibility"[52] for the inauguration of new and altered scenes and thus as a reframing of the distribution of parts and their allocated functions.

Initially, this insistence on the centrality of an address among *living* witnesses posits the sorrow songs as an unlikely example of Kottman's framework. Indeed, Du Bois's own insistence that they pass from one generation to the next, the meaning of their lyrics mystified by this genealogy of transmission, make these songs more likely instances of Kottman's conception of classical narration. The latter emerges for Kottman in the account of protagonists' life stories who are no longer able to act as living, speaking witnesses and whose audience "is not made up of contemporaries, co-actors, acquaintances, or peers of the hero [protagonist] but rather is composed of future generations."[53] However, the example that Kottman proposes, in distinguishing the speech of a scene from the historical transmission of life stories through classical narration, resituates the sorrow songs as scene. By invoking *Hamlet*, and more specifically, the ghost of Hamlet's father who returns to implore Hamlet to remember him, Kottman insists that the "meaning of speech in Hamlet does not arise . . . from its capacity to transmit the meaning of a dead hero's life to future generations" but rather in "being able to address, here and now, those with whom one shares or has shared the world stage."[54]

Two elements in Du Bois's analysis present the sorrow songs as an instance of this shared world stage and thus as an inauguration of the scene among living witnesses. The first appears when we consider Du Bois's introductory remarks in his final chapter in *Souls*:

> Before each thought that I have written in this book I have set a phrase, a haunting echo of these weird old songs in which the soul of the black slave spoke to men. Ever since I was a child these songs have stirred me strangely. They came out of the South unknown to me, one by one, and yet at once I knew them as of me and of mine.[55]

Much as Hamlet's father acts in Kottman's exemplary reading of the play as an instance of scenes, rather than narration, the sorrow songs appear in Du Bois's conception as a ghostly return, a haunting echo. Understood in their acoustic sense as a returning sound that is reflected, the sorrow songs resonate with Tsitsi Ella Jaji's interpretation of "literature of the slave dungeons [to] actually function[] as echolocation, an acoustic operation where transmitted signals, when reflected back as echoes, give an indication of the transmitter's relationship to his or her surroundings."[56] For Jaji, this captures the mode of pan-African identification that continuously marks the forging of new forms of solidarity.[57] Applied to Du Bois's self-positioning in relation to the sorrow songs, his perception of them as echoes locates Du Bois beyond the confines of an engaged listener in the audience of a classical narration. Rather, Du Bois emerges as the songs' respondent, as one body—among presumably many—from whom these songs reverberate, thereby both maintaining existent relationships with and through them and creating the conditions of possibility for new and altered relationships in the futurity of the emergent scene.

The second way in which the sorrow songs emerge as an inauguration of the scene on a shared world stage in Kottman's sense appears when we return to their use as a structural framing for Du Bois's *Souls*, such that his decolonizing aesthetics begin and end in song. Previously, I noted the songs' significance as epigraphs for each chapter, and as the analytic content of the final chapter of *Souls*. However, their centrality for the framing of Du Bois's writing extends to their explicit and implicit references in the "Forethought" and "After-thought" sections, respectively. Introducing the songs' haunting echo in his "Forethought," we might understand Du Bois's plea to "let the ears of a guilty people tingle with truth"[58] as an implicit reference to this music in his "After-thought." Thus, for Kottman, Primo Levi's writings, specifically his trajectory of publication in Germany, represents an instance of the centrality of the living addressees that posit "*those* Germans" as the politically meaningful witnesses to their and Levi's previously shared scene under a racializing National Socialist regime.[59] We find its counterpart in Du Bois's appeal to the ears of a (European and Euro-American) signified people, which consequently posits them as the second intended addressees of the message of the slave that is articulated through the sorrow songs.

In this way, "the problem of the twentieth century"—and events this century certainly lead us to want to extend this temporal marker further—as "the problem of the color-line" that Du Bois extrapolates and anticipates in *Souls*[60] is set on and emerges from a world stage that encompasses witnesses from both sides of the divide. Addressing them musically, the sorrow songs aim to transfigure this world stage and alter the web of relationships unfolding on it such that "sometime, somewhere, men will judge men by their souls and not by their skins."[61] This, according to Du Bois, constitutes the clear meaning of these songs.[62]

Janelle Monáe's "Q.U.E.E.N."

A consideration of the theoretical framework of Frantz Fanon, Aimé Césaire, and W.E.B. Du Bois provides an analysis of a racialized and colonial aesthetic of stasis. It further provides a framework through which to identify those elements of cultural production that succeed in invoking a decolonial disruption to this colonial and static aesthetic—a disruption that is marked by a simultaneous shift in the artwork's addressee, and an ethics of remembrance that centers the lived experiences of those colonized or enslaved. If in the proceeding analysis both elements of this framework speak from, and to, the historical context of the authors' own times, we find a contemporary reiteration of its tenets in the audiovisual construction of Janelle Monáe's 2013 music video for "Q.U.E.E.N."

We are introduced to the video through the sounds of the first bars of the Adagio in Joseph Haydn's Cello Concerto in C Major. Only a few seconds into the piece, a British-accented female voice begins to speak. She introduces herself as a member of the "time council," which as we are told in her opening lines, "prides" itself in having "stop[ped] rebels that time travel."[63] Her voice trails off for a few seconds and the first visuals of the video appear. We follow two black women who enter the scene, which soon reveals itself as an exhibition hall. The British voice, now visibly belonging to a white woman on a screen located at the front center of the museum hall, begins to speak again. Acting, not unlike Frantz Fanon in the first pages of *The Wretched of the Earth*, as a guide to the exhibit on display, she welcomes us to the "living museum." The theme of its exposition is advertised as "legendary rebels from throughout history [who] have been frozen in suspended animation."[64]

As the first indication of an aesthetic of stasis at play in the opening scene of Monáe's music video, the suspended animation to which the museum guide refers is quickly reinforced through the proceeding visuals. Four close-up frames appear, featuring two pairs of motionless bodies, before zooming in on the equally frozen Janelle Monáe and "her dangerous accomplice, Badoula Oblamgata" (Erykah Badu).[65] The first set of bodies are nude with the exception of a red loincloth draped over their hips and white makeup that covers their bodies entirely. The second set of bodies features two black men on display within a showcase. Their suspended animation freezes these pairs in an expressive and projecting gesture, on the one hand,

and the only apparently mundane gestures of walking and speaking, on the other.

On first view, this scene appears as a musical and visual reference to Madonna's 1990 music video accompanying her single "Vogue." As in Monáe's "Q.U.E.E.N.," the opening scene in "Vogue" depicts a series of bodies in stillness, who "strike a pose" amid paintings and ancient Greek statues. The production popularized voguing, a dance style originating in the Harlem ballroom culture of the 1960s among predominantly black and Latino LGBTQ+ communities. Both Madonna's video and the ballroom culture it depicts are referred to—and in this sense, presumably reclaimed[66]— throughout Monáe's "Q.U.E.E.N." Beyond the opening scene, there are allusions of this kind in Monáe's own dance choreography; her iconic tuxedo outfit;[67] and her opening lyrics, in which "walk in a room they throwing shade left and right"[68] is an explicit reference to the black queer vernacular and ballroom practice of "reading an insult."[69] In this way, we arrive at the title of the song itself. According to Monáe, "Q.U.E.E.N." constitutes an acronym, where the Q stands for the queer community; the U signifies the untouchables; the two Es stand for emigrants and the excommunicated, respectively; and the N for negroids.[70] Read phonologically, rather than as a mere acronym, the song's title may simultaneously refer to performers of drag and highlight the trajectory of (LGBTQ+) pop culture that shapes the performance aesthetics of the song's opening scenes.

Nonetheless, this is not the only historical trajectory on which Monáe draws in the opening scenes of "Q.U.E.E.N." Rather, the stasis that captivates the bodies in suspended animation, on display in the museum hall reiterates a global historical trajectory of colonization not unlike that analyzed in the conceptual framework of Frantz Fanon and Aimé Césaire. This is particularly striking when mapping the visuals of this opening scene against its sonic underpinnings. Accompanied by Haydn's Adagio, the British museum guide remains the only speaking character throughout the video's opening scene. Understanding these two entities as simultaneous representations of Europeanness and whiteness, the guide emerges as the sole narrator (author), which is to say *creator*, of "Q.U.E.E.N."'s visual installation. This includes the two pairs of motionless black bodies on display, who—*consequently*, we might say—find themselves in "suspended animation."

Read in this light, the opening scene of "Q.U.E.E.N." emerges as an audiovisual gesturing toward a historical trajectory that leads from so-called freak shows and ethnological exhibitions touring colonial Europe and the United States at their commercial peak in the nineteenth and twentieth centuries to contemporary natural history museums.[71] All three have served, and continue to serve, to exhibit and racialize indigenous peoples from northern Europe, from European colonies, and members of the African diaspora for both entertainment and pseudoscientific purposes. Relegating members of these communities to the "observed-Other side of the glass,"[72] all three share the intent to present visitors with *carefully constructed reenactments* meant to demonstrate the varied nature of human [existence] and experience in the exhibited region," such that performing "participants were clearly actively *'created'* out of the viewer's own obsessions and fantasies."[73] Understood in terms of Césaire's critique of colonization as an attempt to maintain a distanced and static relationship between the colonizer as sole creator and the colonized as passive consumer, these ethnological exhibitions are signified through the museum guide in her role as the exclusive speaker. In this way, the video's opening scene establishes the colonial and racialized aesthetic of stasis on the basis of the colonial creator-consumer relationship.

This constellation is reinforced visually through the absence of the museum guide in an embodied sense. Her relegation to mere presence on a screen forecloses her proximity to the physical space of the installation, as well as those on display, and removes her from the immediacy of the scene that she nonetheless actively produces as its sole narrating voice. Reinstating a relationship of distance, the temporal arrest of those on display does not simply emerge from the suspended animation of their bodily movements. Rather, their arrest derives further from the defining and essentializing properties that the museum guide attributes them, such that the temporal unfolding inherent to an identificatory process of becoming is foreclosed in their classification as "dangerous" and "notorious" "rebels." Further, the long shots and tableaux vivant that mark the cinematographic gaze in the video's opening scene ensure that it invokes a distanced stillness such that we, as viewers, too, become spectators of the "carefully constructed" audiovisual installation that the museum guide leads us through. Once again, we enter a world of statues governed by a racialized and colonial aesthetic of spatial and temporal stasis.

We would be remiss, however, to overlook the decolonial disruptions that underlie the opening scene's historical link to the era of formal European colonialism, its coincidence with ethnological exhibitions and its corresponding aesthetic of stasis. In this sense, we encounter in the video's opening scene as much a depiction of a racialized and colonial aesthetic of stasis as an ethics of remembrance that constitutes the first component of a decolonial disruption in Monáe's "Q.U.E.E.N." While the video itself is set in our future such that the guide's description of Monáe's "musical weapons program in the 21st century"[74] constitutes the historical object on display, its association with historical ethnological exhibitions draws us back into our own (not so distant) past that marks the era of European (settler) colonialism. Invoking time travel, this points to a core aesthetic element of the Afrofuturist genre, which seeks to disrupt a distanced understanding of history that classifies the past as a static and autonomous spatiotemporal entity distinct from the present and future.[75] Read in this way, reference to the racialized aesthetic of stasis as a marker of unfreedom under a colonial order in the video's opening scene acts as a catalyst for its further unfolding. As we will see, these latter scenes are fundamentally informed by a visual and sonic shift in artistic addressee that introduces the second core component of a decolonial disruption in Monáe's "Q.U.E.E.N."

The most immediate marker of this disruption emerges in the video's musical transition itself. Instigated by the two black women whom we initially follow onto the video's opening scene, their visible frustration with the exposition on display leads them to approach a skull exhibited at the back of the museum hall. Revealed to be a turntable, they place a needle on the vinyl and Monáe's own music begins to play. With no pause between Haydn's Adagio and Monáe's "Q.U.E.E.N.," the first note of the latter replaces the concluding keynote of Haydn's introductory bars. Rather than a seamless musical transition, however, the suspended keynote of Haydn's Adagio disrupts its harmonic line. This denies the listener any possibility for a moment of consonance and leaves the audience with an unsettling sense of dissatisfaction and discomfort.[76] In short, we are forced to reorient ourselves harmonically. Read as a shift in the sonic rather than merely visual focus of the song's opening scenes, this musical transfiguration introduces a new harmonic journey that transforms what the audience listens for in tracing its trajectory.

A similar musical reorientation can be discerned in the rhythmic transition from Haydn to Monáe. The shift from the Adagio to "Q.U.E.E.N." does not initially suggest an abrupt rupture. The trochee meter and pulse remain parallel in the two musical pieces that accompany the video. Nonetheless, "Q.U.E.E.N."'s rhythmic texture serves to disrupt and disturb that of Haydn's preceding Adagio. Along with its introduction of hemiolas, syncopation, and an increased tempo, placing the beginning of "Q.U.E.E.N."'s lyric lines at the end of the bar significantly shifts the rhythmic focus from an emphasis on the first beat in the Adagio to the fourth beat in "Q.U.E.E.N." Contrasting the rhythmic structure of Haydn's piece (customary among the Viennese classic style of composition to which he contributed more largely), Monáe's rhythmic aesthetic comes to disrupt and indeed transform that of Haydn.

The significance of this harmonic and rhythmic reordering for our understanding of a decolonial shift in addressee appears when this sonic transformation is set alongside the video's coinciding visuals. Zooming in on

Monáe as the opening notes of her own song start to play, we are drawn to her eyelashes, which begin to move. Hesitantly and carefully at first, she regains motion in her fingers, and soon her head begins to turn. Next to her, the two bodies covered in white makeup similarly start to unfreeze, and picking up their instruments, they begin to play the accompaniment to Monáe's voice, who now sets out to sing. As the song progresses, all other bodies formerly suspended in their animation regain motion in their limbs. By the time the song reaches its third stanza, the audience is welcomed to a view of the former exhibition hall, now transformed into a dance floor, where both former museum spectators and former "exhibits" are dancing alongside each other, with each other, and thus facing one another.

Two elements in this emergent dance scene are integral to understanding the music video of "Q.U.E.E.N." as decolonial disruption. The most apparent of these resides in the dance movements themselves. A colonial and racialized aesthetic of temporal and spatial stasis formerly trapped the bodies and subjects on display in their suspended animation. This contrasts with the dance that these very bodies and subjects engage in to display a ceremony of freedom as the "capacity of motion."[77] Consequently, the dance breaks both the physical and the identificatory confinement of those on display under the (colonial) order of the visual installation in the video's opening scene. Presenting the viewer instead with an arrangement of dancers that is spontaneous and fluctuating, this later scene is suggestive of a communicative yet self-determined relationality among the dancers. No longer rendered distanced and static by a narrating museum guide or the glass of showcases, the relational expressiveness of the dancers marks a rearrangement of their bodies in ways that engage and face each other through dance. As a redefinition of existing relationships, when contrasted with the video's opening scene, this emerges as the first indication of a shift in addressee and thus as a decolonial disruption in Monáe's music video.

The second reflection of a shift in addressee emerging in this dance scene, appears if we take seriously the notion of an embodied and experiential knowledge that Monáe denotes through her recurrent lyric line, "But you gotta testify / Because the booty don't lie."[78] Viewed through this lens, the rearrangement of dancers' bodies such that they now face each other not only redefines their relation to one another in a spatial sense. The dance itself becomes a mode of exchange that narrates the rhythm, which is to say the lived reality, of those on the scene and consequently posits the dancers as artistic subjects rather than objects on display. Conjointly, the dancers' spatial repositioning for the purpose of experiential exchange positions them, in Kottman's sense, as living witnesses who address one another "in ways that confirm a shared relation—one that has emerged on a prior scene or on prior scenes."[79] Thus, both those who acted as spectators and visitors and those who were put on display in the video's opening scene now address each other on the dance floor, such that the "contact of the people [the dancers] with the[ir] *new movement* gives rise to a *new rhythm of life* and to *forgotten muscular tensions*, and develops the imagination."[80] In doing so, the spatial and communicative rearrangement of the bodies on the dance scene redefines existing relationships, as Fanon's decolonial framework proposes.

This is complemented by the creation of new social ties through the altered cinematographic gaze that accompanies the video's musical transition. Repeatedly breaking the fourth wall throughout the video's proceeding narrative, at stake is the viewer's own implication in the unfolding scenes. Through a close-up of Monáe, whose look into the camera serves to address her viewers directly, we are refused the position of mere spectator. Underlying the question-answer format of her lyric lines, the viewers are drawn into the lyrical and visual narrative of Monáe's song that sometimes suggests, at other times seemingly demands, the "eventuality of another's response."[81] Much as Du Bois sees in the sorrow songs the possibility of an address, such that "the articulate message of the slave to the world" that these songs contain may make the "ears of a guilty people tingle,"[82] the breaking of the fourth wall in Monáe's proceeding music video suggests a sense of "response-ability"[83] and accompanying demand for accountability on the part of her audience. Transformed from being spectators of a colonial ethnological exhibition in the "original scene"[84] of Monáe's video, her direct cinematographic address following the emergence of her own song places viewers on the same scene as Monáe herself, in and all those formerly frozen for the purpose of display. Forging new ties between the performers on the screen and those in front of it in ways that resist the static and distanced binary between viewer and viewed, creator and consumer, Monáe's direct cinematographic address implicates us in a shared (historical) world stage that is the colonial and racialized aesthetic of stasis in the music video's opening scene. In doing so, Monáe's "Q.U.E.E.N." fuses an ethics of remembrance that demands the audience to move beyond the original scene of a colonial exhibition and attendant aesthetic of stasis, with an artistic shift in addressee, to propose a "new language"[85] through the motion of dance. Creating new social ties among those formerly viewing and those formerly viewed, we find in the *Gesamtkunstwerk* of Janelle Monáe's "Q.U.E.E.N." a contemporary rendition of Frantz Fanon's and Aimé Césaire's framework of a decolonizing cultural production.

Collectively, the theoretical and artistic frameworks of Frantz Fanon, Aimé Césaire, W.E.B. Du Bois, and Janelle Monáe posit the aesthetic as a configuration of the sociopolitical fabric along sensory and experiential modes that order perceptions and structure their affective responses. In doing so, the aesthetic appears both epistemologically and ontologically as a defining moral universe that dispositions subjects and bodies such that they are either lent the ability to assert themselves and be heard or denied recognition as humans. Consequently, the aesthetic emerges as a productive site of inquiry to engage questions of the human as questions of re/distribution. Whether it emerges as a guardian for or revolutionary against the policing mechanisms of a colonial and racializing stasis, the aesthetic invariably serves as an integral aspect of political life.

Tracing this interplay of aesthetics and perception in Africana theorizing highlights its cumulation in the contemporary political moment as one continuously structured around the questioned presence within the public sphere, of those subjects and bodies who have been made markers of the afterlives of colonialism and slavery. In turn, the attendant assertion that "Black Lives Matter" emerges as an insistence on the legitimate presence of these bodies within the sensory and experiential modes that dominate contemporary political fabrics. Demanding their transformation, the aesthetic thus reveals itself as an indispensable mode through which to theorize the disquietingly recurrent question of who can and cannot breathe within contemporary sociopolitical fabrics and whose assertion of this experience is or is not heard in its most urgent moment.

NOTES

Acknowledgments: I offer my deepfelt thanks to Grant Farred for his close reading and generous engagement with this chapter throughout its multiple stages of development. My thanks equally go to Siba N'Zatioula Grovogui for his many helpful comments and for his continuous intellectual generosity and support. Finally, I thank Samuel Boyles, Lauren Siegel, and Santiago Mollis for their attentive listening and readings.

1. Frantz Fanon, *The Wretched of the Earth*, trans. Constance Farrington (London: Penguin Books, 2001), 28.

2. I use "stasis" here and throughout to denote a sense of stagnation or standstill. While derived therefore from its ancient Greek etymology, its specificity as an Aristotelian term to conceptualize civil wars among different poleis is not what I am after.

3. My use of "decolonizing," "decolonial," or "decolonization" emerges from Constance Farrington's translation of Frantz Fanon's use of the term in the 1961 edition of *The Wretched of the Earth*. Thus, while a framework of "decolonization" is readily associated with the conceptual framework of such scholars as Aníbal Quijano and Walter Mignolo, I resist their close alignment of geopolitical spaces with presupposed ontologies and epistemologies, even as I am indebted to their careful analyses of the ways in which the rigidity of a colonial difference manifests in various areas of human life both during formal colonial rule and in its aftermath (e.g., Walter Mignolo, *Local Histories/ Global Designs: Coloniality, Subaltern Knowledges, and Border Thinking* [Princeton, NJ: Princeton University Press, 2000]). Against this backdrop, I take Fanon's formulation of

decolonization to be both exceedingly materialist and thus structuralist in its approach. My focus on decolonial aesthetics is thus firmly grounded in an understanding of the latter as a reflection of, and shaping of, modes of perception and experiences. Rather than move in the sphere of the merely discursive, therefore, Fanon's insistence on the material conditions of decolonization—including in its manifestation as newly reinvigorated national cultures—alongside his universal approach to anti-colonial struggles that calls for the holistic reconstitution of a global order, emerges as a fruitful framework to think through and with.

4. "History of Africana Studies at Cornell," Africana Studies and Research Center, Cornell University, accessed October 15, 2021, https://africana.cornell.edu/node/1421.

5. I have intentionally retained Frantz Fanon's terminology of "settler" and "native" throughout the chapter to highlight its use in classifying ontologies for the purpose of their stringent delineation under a colonial regime. As I illustrate throughout the text, this significantly underpins what I call a colonial aesthetic of stasis in both spatial and temporal terms. The first appearance of this terminology can be found in Fanon, *Wretched of the Earth*, 28.

6. Fanon, *Wretched of the Earth*, 31, 40.

7. Fanon, *Wretched of the Earth*, 30.

8. Fanon, *Wretched of the Earth*, 29–30.

9. Fanon, *Wretched of the Earth*, 30.

10. Hannah Arendt, *The Origins of Totalitarianism* (New York: Schocken Books, 2004), 600. Specifically, Arendt's conception of freedom as contingent on the "capacity for motion" highlights the significance of stasis—not merely in its sociopolitical and cultural but also in its physical and spatial form—for the purpose of a subjugating colonial rule.

11. Fanon, *Wretched of the Earth*, 40.

12. Fanon, *Wretched of the Earth*, 190.

13. Fanon, *Wretched of the Earth*, 190.

14. Orlando Patterson, *Slavery and Social Death: A Comparative Study* (Cambridge, MA: Harvard University Press, 1982), 26, 31.

15. Fanon, *Wretched of the Earth*, 28.

16. Aimé Césaire, "L'homme de culture et ses responsabilités," *Présence Africaine* 24, no. 25 (February–May 1959): 118.

17. Fanon, *Wretched of the Earth*, 32.

18. Olúfẹ́mi Táíwò, "Exorcizing Hegel's Ghost," *African Studies Quarterly* 1, no. 4 (1998): 11.

19. Frantz Fanon, *Black Skin, White Masks*, trans. Charles Lam Markmann (New York: Grove Press, 1967), 115, 112.

20. Fanon, *Wretched of the Earth*, 40.

21. Fanon, *Black Skin, White Masks*, 109. The term "hollow" is borrowed from Achille Mbembe, *On the Postcolony* (Berkeley: University of California Press, 2001), 173–211.

22. Fanon, *Wretched of the Earth*, 29.

23. Jacques Rancière, *The Politics of Aesthetics*, trans. Gabriel Rockhill (London: Continuum, 2009), 12–19.

24. Fanon, *Black Skin, White Masks*, 115.

25. Fanon, *Black Skin, White Masks*, 111.

26. Fanon, *Wretched of the Earth*, 190.

27. Fanon, *Wretched of the Earth*, 190.

28. Fanon, *Wretched of the Earth*, 191.

29. Fanon, *Wretched of the Earth*, 180.

30. Fanon, *Wretched of the Earth*, 191.

31. Fanon, *Wretched of the Earth*, 182–183; my emphasis.

32. Fanon, *Wretched of the Earth*, 191.

33. Fanon, *Wretched of the Earth*, 183.

34. While Fanon acknowledges the "historical necessity" that leads to an articulation of culture in terms of racialized notions of authenticity, he maintains that the fixed delineation of who or what is imagined to constitute an authentic practitioner, audience, or form of artistic and cultural production stifles the latter and leads to its inevitable demise (Fanon, *Wretched of the Earth*, 172). A similar analysis is offered in the more contemporary writings of Paul Gilroy. Taking as his central analytic category the emergence of black nationalism as it coincides with the production and circulation of different musics in the black Atlantic, Gilroy too asserts that any analysis of this trajectory must attend to the experienced necessity to articulate a unified black culture against the racist assertions that question both its existence and possibility for its emergence. Nonetheless, Gilroy also warns that the "drama of ethnic identity-construction," which he views to be emerging at the time of his writing as a "defensive reaction to [this] racism," runs the risk of resorting to a narration of sameness and symmetry. In doing so, this trend not only replicates "the discourse of the oppressor." More importantly, Gilroy insists, such narrations are contingent on a stifling approach to cultural production and forms, which consequently fail to attend to the "displacements and transformations" that mark the experiences of those subjects in the black Atlantic it seeks to address. It is at this particular moment that notions of cultural authenticity, articulated along specifically racialized lines, lose their validity for both Fanon and Gilroy. Paul Gilroy, *The Black Atlantic: Modernity and Double Consciousness* (Cambridge, MA: Harvard University Press, 1993), 97.

35. Theodor W. Adorno, *Aesthetic Theory* (London: Bloomsbury, 2019), 11.

36. William E. B. Du Bois, *The Souls of Black Folk*, ed. David W. Blight and Robert Gooding-Williams (Boston: Bedford Books, 1997), 185–194.

37. Jacques Rancière, *Dissensus: On Politics and Aesthetics*, trans. and ed. Steven Corcoran (London: Continuum, 2010), 142.

38. The language of "American" as a marker of white/ness, and "Negro" as a marker of black/ness are borrowed from Du Bois himself, thus capturing the "twoness" that divides them and their worlds, which nonetheless conjoin within the bodily spirit of the black American Du Bois describes. William E. B. Du Bois, "Of Our Spiritual Strivings," in *Souls of Black Folk*, 37–44; my emphasis.

39. Rancière, *Dissensus*, 139.

40. Du Bois, *Souls of Black Folk*, 45.

41. Du Bois, 185.

42. Du Bois, 187; my emphasis.

43. Du Bois, 186; my emphasis. The analytic trajectory of perception and thus reception that Du Bois highlights in relation to the sorrow songs is particularly relevant when read in light of contemporary sound studies, such as the analytic framework by Jennifer Stoever. See Jennifer Stoever, *The Sonic Color Line: Race and the Cultural Politics of Listening* (New York: New York University Press, 2016). Fusing Du Bois's conceptual framework with archival research, Stoever explores orality, aurality, singing, and con-

comitant characteristics such as volume, pitch, and timber to argue that sound (including silence) gains significance for racializing narratives, particularly in the context of the United States, from the mid-nineteenth century onward. This, Stoever argues, ultimately serves to police and maintain a public sphere that adheres to normative notions of sonic whiteness. Premised on her notion of the "racializing ear" (7), Stoever employs notions of a habitus of listening to trace various means through which sound is racialized in historical and contemporary settings. On a habitus of listening, see also David Garcia, *Listening for Africa: Freedom, Modernity, and the Logic of Black Music's African Origins* (Durham, NC: Duke University Press, 2017). In similar vein, Jacques Attali has argued that music is inherently a politicized organization of noise that is concomitantly rendered meaningful and coherent for and by particular communities. While the Marxist underpinnings of Attali's framework differ from those of Stoever, both understand sensory orders, particularly those pertaining to the aural and the ear, as a vital analytic entry point to examine unfolding power relations. Jacques Attali, *Noise: The Political Economy of Music*, trans. Brian Massumi (Minneapolis: University of Minnesota Press, 2017).

44. Du Bois, *Souls of Black Folk*, 188; my emphasis.

45. Du Bois, 185; my emphasis.

46. Hannah Arendt, *The Human Condition* (Chicago: University of Chicago Press, 1998), 184–186, 199–207.

47. Paul A. Kottman, *A Politics of the Scene* (Stanford, CA: Stanford University Press, 2008), 10–11.

48. Kottman, *Politics of the Scene*, 147.

49. Kottman (*Politics of the Scene*, 147) attributes this a rather lenient definition, arguing that expressions of emotions—such as tears—may well constitute speech for the purpose of inaugurating, or "making" as he refers to it, a scene.

50. Kottman, *Politics of the Scene*, 23.

51. Kottman, *Politics of the Scene*, 140; my emphasis.

52. Kottman, *Politics of the Scene*, 140.

53. Kottman, *Politics of the Scene*, 142.

54. Kottman, *Politics of the Scene*, 144.

55. Du Bois, *Souls of Black Folk*, 185.

56. Tsitsi Ella Jaji, *Africa in Stereo: Modernism, Music and Pan-African Solidarity* (New York: Oxford University Press, 2014), 152.

57. George Shepperson, "Pan-Africanism and 'Pan-Africanism': Some Historical Notes," *Phylon* 23:04 (1962): 346-358.

58. Du Bois, *Souls of Black Folk*, 195.

59. Kottman, *Politics of the Scene*, 13–14.

60. Du Bois, *Souls of Black Folk*, 45.

61. Du Bois, *Souls of Black Folk*, 192.

62. Du Bois, *Souls of Black Folk*, 192.

63. "Janelle Monáe: Q.U.E.E.N. feat. Erykah Badu [Official Video]," May 1, 2013, video, 00:00–00:11, https://www.youtube.com/watch?v=tEddixS-UoU.

64. "Janelle Monáe: Q.U.E.E.N.," 00:19–00:23. In its entirety, the speech by the narrating museum guide reads as follows: "It's hard to stop rebels that time travel. But we at the time council pride ourselves on doing just that. Welcome to the living museum, where legendary rebels from throughout history have been frozen in suspended animation. Here, in this particular exhibit, you'll find members of Wondaland and their noto-

rious leader, Janelle Monáe, along with her dangerous accomplice Badoula Oblamgata. Together, they launched project Q.U.E.E.N., a musical weapons program in the 21st century. Researchers are still deciphering the nature of this program and hunting the various freedom movements that Wondaland disguised as songs, emotion pictures and works of art" (my transcription).

65. "Janelle Monáe: Q.U.E.E.N.," 00:33–00:35.

66. While voguing and its attendant ballroom culture entered the cultural mainstream through Madonna's "Vogue," its roots lie in the black and Latino LGBTQ+ communities of 1960s Harlem. It is also widely acknowledged, however, that this origin was until recently insufficiently acknowledged in the cultural mainstream.

67. Monica L. Miller, "All Hail the Q.U.E.E.N: Janelle Monáe and a Tale of the Tux," *NKA: Journal of Contemporary African Art* 37 (November 2015): 62–69.

68. "Janelle Monáe: Q.U.E.E.N.," 01:07–01:11.

69. See, e.g., E. Patrick Johnson, *No Tea No Shade: New Writings in Black Queer Studies* (Durham, NC: Duke University Press, 2016), 2.

70. Jeff Benjamin, "Janelle Monae Says 'Q.U.E.E.N.' Is for the 'Ostracized & Marginalized,'" fuse, September 18, 2013, https://www.fuse.tv/videos/2013/09/janelle-monae -queen-interview.

71. An allusion to "freak shows" can be discerned from Monáe's chorus lines as the video proceeds. Structured around Monáe's rhetorical questions, "Am I a freak for dancing around? / Am I a freak for getting down?" these lyric lines are alternately articulated by Monáe and her android alter ego, Cindi Mayweather, to engage in an inner dialogue that navigates experiences of ostracization on the one hand, and self-assertion and indeed celebration, on the other: "Janelle Monáe: Q.U.E.E.N.," 01:39–01:56, 02:35–02:52, 03:29–03:45.

72. Himadeep Muppidi, *Colonial Signs of International Relations* (London: C. Hurst, 2012), 16.

73. Nigel Rothfels, *Savages and Beasts: The Birth of the Modern Zoo* (Baltimore: Johns Hopkins University Press, 2002), 127, 131; my emphasis.

74. "Janelle Monáe: Q.U.E.E.N.," 00:38–00:41.

75. Constantin Fasolt, *The Limits of History* (Chicago: University of Chicago Press, 2004), 9.

76. The unsettling sense of dissatisfaction and discomfort emerges here because of a replacement of the F-major key in Haydn's Adagio by the B-minor key in Monáe's "Q.U.E.E.N."

77. Arendt, *Origins of Totalitarianism*, 600.

78. Miller, "All Hail the Q.U.E.E.N.," 68.

79. Kottman, *Politics of the Scene*, 147.

80. Fanon, *Wretched of the Earth*, 194; my emphasis.

81. Kottman, *Politics of the Scene*, 23.

82. Du Bois, *Souls of Black Folk*, 187, 195.

83. Milja Kurki, *International Relations in a Relational Universe* (Oxford: Oxford University Press, 2020), 85.

84. Kottman, *Politics of the Scene*, 140.

85. Fanon, *Wretched of the Earth*, 28.

Seductive Solidarity

Comrade Lover and Other Demons

Akin Adeşokan

The stuff of fiction.

What can be more rewarding of curiosity than a love affair that an unknown young woman undertakes with a legally married leader of a revolutionary movement, at a time the man is living underground in a foreign country? The curiosity is heightened, though hardly rewarded, as the plot unfolds. The little that is known of the affair emerges only later, in fragments, and from a witness arriving after the fact but who is also the only indisputable proof of that affair. This witness, the child born of the affair, is not interested in the couple's feelings, whatever those might have been. She is concerned with the part that determines her fate: the faint taint of bastardy, the irreparable trauma of a child abandoned to serial abuse, the silence that has descended like a shroud over the circumstances of the revolutionary's death.

A reflection on romantic love as a way of understanding the challenges of political solidarity is at once seductive because rich in curiosities and brittle because matters of the heart are grounds for unresolved emotions, irrespective of the known or hidden details. When some of the dramatis personae are also historical figures, famous and admired, the investigator confronts challenges of a different, political kind. One such challenge is to present those details in ways that do not confuse voyeurism with creative curiosity but that produce, in the process, insights with theoretical potentials.

This challenge is the one chosen here. In this writing, the primary focus is on three decisive stories in Africana intellectual traditions in which political solidarity and romantic love are entangled. These are the friendships between former Black Panther Party activist Sandra Isadore (née Smith) and Afrobeat musician Fẹlá Anikulapo-Kuti in Los Angeles in the late 1960s, the slightly earlier instance of the activist and writer Carlos Moore being brought into a circle of Black women around Maya Angelou in New York City, and the clandestine affair between Cameroonian revolutionary Ernest Ouandié and a Ghanaian woman between Accra and Lagos in the early 1960s.

Better-known accounts of political solidarity or mentoring in Africana worlds have tended to be those constructed around figures like George Padmore and Kwame Nkrumah or Edward Blyden and Samuel Lewis or C.L.R. James and Eric Williams or Elijah Mohammed and Malcolm X. These collaborations are historic and have come to constitute models of intellectual or organizational work without which a credible history of modern politics can hardly be produced. In fact, only the first pairing has been well documented; little yet is known of the context in which Blyden (1994) wrote his farsighted study *Christianity, Islam and the Negro Race* just as the Scramble for Africa got underway in the 1880s and of the work involved in ensuring that it saw the light of day.

However fragmentary, controversial, or incomplete, these are still presented largely as narratives of men at work. Speaking to Stuart Hall (1996, 26) about the earliest meetings of the International African Service Bureau in London, James unselfconsciously remarks that Dorothy Pizer, Padmore's partner and closest associate, "can cook . . . used to cook," causing a contemporary reader wonder if cooking was all she did. Surely, there are less known productive encounters between men and women, with powerful female figures such as Amy Ashwood Garvey, supporting experienced and young African activists in England in the early 1920s. Furthermore, equally consequential stories can be unearthed in the charged situation of civil rights struggle in the United States, with wider ramifications.

These latter stories, of which three form the primary focus here, revolve around the complex emotions of love and sexual attraction. They are appealing for those sensual reasons and count for more, besides. Such stories are common. The relationship between exiled South African musician Miriam Makeba and Stokely Carmichael (Kwame Ture) constitutes a unique chapter in the history of African revolutionary politics. Beverly Axelrod, a San Francisco lawyer, exchanged letters with Eldridge Cleaver, the imprisoned Black Panther Party leader, in which both passionately committed to an affair beyond the professional duty of legal representation. And the ardent letters of C.L.R. James, specially delivered to Constance Webb, written against the background of the revolutionary fervor of World War II as well as communist stirrings in the United States, also reveal a singular effort at self-understanding by a complex political figure. At the other extreme, political activist Bayard Rustin's queer sexuality was a major factor, if not the sole factor, for his marginalized status in the civil rights movement, and the film *Brother Outsider: The Life of Bayard Rustin* (Kates and Singer 2003) offers a telling testimony to the ill treatment.

Love, then, as a route to, or a manifestation of, desires that human agents try to express as they swim through the stormy waters of political struggle. Starting out in this way might seem to reinforce sexuality as the only legible condition for the solidarity between Black women and men. However, this approach has the potential to offer an accurate interpretation of political commitment as a particular kind of emotional investment in life, beyond the merely rational. Besides, the different accounts examined here have incredible power as *stories*, as occurrences so nearly unbelievable in sheer affective potency that they must be retrieved and passed on. As accounts of personal relations of intimacy, they have been subjected to generalized, anecdotal, and sensational retellings, when not deliberately ignored. In looking further into the details, putting the pieces together, one becomes better informed about some of these accounts. If a consequence of this approach is to draw attention to how such complex stories have come to carry particular slants, then it shall have been a worthy effort.

Beyond the facts, still, the more erotic aspects of solidarity among Black people who encountered one another in the field of struggle call insistently for attention. The radical option is already built into the operations of the political solidarity that these friendships entail, so an idea of equality, comradeship, and envisioned freedom is the truly energizing factor. It is even more politically powerful to put love, platonic and romantic, at the center of these friendships, with personal freedom as the guaranteed, nonnegotiable currency in the transactions. The actors are human beings, creatures of the senses, with fears and vulnerabilities, and they can keep going with the fragile but constant hope of gratification that love offers. Moore's account of his friendship with Angelou and her circle of friends is detailed about both the immediate contacts and what sustained his interest, and Fẹlá is similarly graphic about the place where the decisive conversation with Sandra Smith occurred.

The uncertainties of political involvement are such that, to keep going, those who have made that commitment might better endure the uncertainties if they also have fun while at it. Anything psychically demanding finds a cathartic outlet when it allows the sensorial aspects of life, the gratification that is also the assurance to keep going. Uncertainties in personal relationships are not much different. The place of affect in Africana political life need not be limited to the banal forms in which corruption, violence, and disorder feature as dominant themes. Empathy has its place. Giving pleasure, like giving offense, is a matter of life and death.

Fẹlá's relationship with Sandra was perhaps the most controversial, given the context of their meeting and the impact that the relationship had on the musician's art and personality. In Moore's case, we are confronted with a more complex phenomenon. The lover is not one person but a community of Black women, and the sexual gratification was an undelivered, or unsatisfyingly delivered, reward. The gratification was indirectly sought in a bumbling attempt at racial self-discovery, which was also a confused attempt at doing penance for supposed betrayal of the Black woman as a sexual partner. The affair between Ouandié and his Ghanaian lover, Regina Kwedu, was obscure, taking place when the Cameroonian revolutionary was living underground. The world might not have known of it but for the daughter's heart-wrenching revelations in *Leaf in the Wind*, the documentary from Jean-Marie Teno (2013b).

Stories matter. The aesthetic is a crucial factor in the political possibilities that these accounts offer. But the lack of commensurate relations between an episode in a musical career and the birth of a child with circumscribed existence promises more. It upholds the tensions between beautiful seduction and brittle solidarity. In teenager Moore's groping toward self-understanding, the substitution of sex for communal mentoring by strong Black women becomes a form of education, incompletely satisfying as the hunt for gratification sometimes tend to be. Chances are that Moore's experience plays a role in the way he frames the Sandra-Fẹlá entanglement.

"My Lady's Frustration"

Carlos Moore proposed a loaded notion to Sandra Smith. While interviewing her as one of the personalities through whom to construct a rounded portrait of Fẹlá, he said:

> When you met Fela you were therefore very, very aware of your Blackness, of Africa, and looking very intensely for your historical and cultural roots. But when Fela met you he wasn't someone who was that aware of his own Africanness. Fela told me it was you who "Africanized" him. How did you do that? (Moore 2009, 95)

Sandra's answer was less clarifying; at least, she did not say what Moore wanted to hear. "By me being so Black at the time," she replied. "I was so rebellious, then, willing to fight, willing to die. . . . I thought if we Blacks in America had to die for what we believed in, even if it meant your mother and father had to go, then let them go" (Moore 2009, 95). Moore kept up this line of questioning for a while, but Sandra's answers pointed in other directions. They expanded the conversation into a more complex account of that historic encounter between two willful and visionary artists than scholars have embraced.

An intriguing idea lurks between the lines of that conversation, an honest dialogue, on the face of it, between two diasporic Black figures about an individual that they both knew well. It is a commonplace fact that the occasion of a U.S. tour for Fẹlá's Koola Lobitos Band in the final quarter of 1969 presented the musician with the opportunity of meeting Sandra, a former member of the Black militant and self-defense organization, the Black Panther Party. In those closing months of a highly politically charged decade in the experience of African Americans, a largely bourgeois musician from Nigeria found himself a recipient of precious ideological education, courtesy of a woman he had viewed as just another sexual conquest. This was the point of departure for Moore's interview with Sandra. In none of the remaining exchanges with other of Fẹlá's women in *Fela: This Bitch of a Life* did the issue of influence on the musician's life receive the same kind of priority.

Probably following Moore's lead, scholars of Fẹlá's music have framed a clear and accessibly paradoxical picture of the affair as a factor in his ideological education, in political and artistic terms. Michael Veal (2000, 71), in his biography of the musician, writes that the "influence of new ideas from Fela's intense discussions with Sandra—combined with his continued desire for success—forced him to reexamine a number of his own fundamental ideas and ultimately to formulate a new conceptual framework encompassing music, culture, and ideology." Tẹjúmọ́lá Ọláníyan (2004, 29) gives a more critical assessment, emphasizing the irony of "Fẹlá's imperviousness to political influence until now, in spite of his impressionability in other matters [including] that Fẹlá's mother had for decades been an exemplary mode of such commitment." These assessments are not necessarily mistaken. The musician has framed matters in the same way, too, and Moore is correct in his attribution of the claim of the origin of influence. Fẹlá said:

> Sandra gave me the education I wanted to know. She was the one who opened my eyes. I swear, man! She's the one who spoke to me about . . . Africa! For the first time I heard things I'd never heard before about . . . politics, history. (Moore 2009, 85)

Much later, in a famous interview with journalists while he was in detention on murder charges in Nigeria in 1993, Fẹlá repeated this story, with respect to the change in his music from highlife jazz to Afrobeat.

It was my friend Sandra who caused it in 1969. I was lying in bed
with her one day when I made a statement that afterall [*sic*], na white
man teach us everything. She was furious. It was as if I take hammer
knack her head. Didn't you learn anything in school? She said. I tell
am say that was what I was thought [*sic*] in school. Na him she stand
up go inside drawer carry one book give me. It was the *Autobiogra-
phy of Malcolm X* by Alex Haley. . . . Na Sandra show me road. When
I read that book I was sparkling. I said what? Yeah! Malcom [*sic*] X
talk. I speak men. That was in 1969. I come become stupid straight.
I said so I dey take white man sense think all this while. After this
book I come Lagos and bought more books. (*TheNews* 2020)

Sandra's account, in turn, reveals an exchange, a give-and-take. In the
same interview with Moore referred to earlier, she disclosed:

There were so many things I shared with Fela: novels, poetry, politics, history, music. Poems by Nikki Giovanni, The Last Poets . . . ,
Angela Davis, Martin Luther King, Stokely Carmichael, Jesse Jack-
son, Nina Simone's "Four Women," Miles Davis. . . . It was something that happened over a period of time. It was constant talking
every night, every day, over a period of six months. Politics. Love.
Love and politics. Just the two of us. (Moore 2009, 95–96)

The influence was a complex process. It seemed as if Sandra was finding
a way for herself as much as showing it to Fẹlá. When asked how she found
out that she was "Africanizing" him, Sandra replied, "I didn't know at that
time. I found out in 1976 when I returned to Africa to do the 'Upside Down'
album. I realized then that everything in 1970 was upside down. But on my
first trip to Africa [in 1970] I went on with my rhetoric 'cause I was so into
what I was talking about and so happy to be on the continent that I was
like a sponge" (Moore 2009, 96). She said, "We went through a growing
period. He showed me something and, I guess, in turn I showed him something" (102).

She clearly had her own growing up to do. When in Nigeria, being spir-
ited around to escape from the immigration enforcement people (because
she had arrived in the country without a visa, after having cursed out
the Nigerian ambassador in Washington, D.C.), she spent a few days in
Abẹ́òkúta. There, she said, "Fela's mother . . . started me on this religious
thing . . . [and] gave me this communist book to read" (Moore 2009, 104).
She received other gifts as well. In Fẹlá's circles she is still famously known
as Àkànkẹ́ Sandra, the Yoruba personal oríkì meaning "Sandra the Specially Treasured One."

Upon his return to Nigeria, Fẹlá steadily reinvented his sound, infusing it with a complex blend of jazz and other uniquely Africanized forms, facing the decade with what would become an irrevocably political art. The song that came out of that troubled but exciting episode is titled "My Lady's Frustration," and Fẹlá first tried it out during his session at the Citadel d'Haiti, the venue of his performance in Los Angeles. In the assessment of Veal, that song was "the first true afrobeat song." Neither similar to the musician's accustomed highlife-jazz "nor pure rhythm-and-blues," the song was built on a mid-tempo highlife groove with prominent soul-styled guitar rhythms (Veal 2000, 72). Veal calls this new sound a hybrid form, drawing elements from what he was hitherto playing and with ideas of what, in his intense relationship with Sandra, he judged to be his "first African tune" (72).

There is more to the song. Sonically, it is compact, intense, and coherent, longer at seven minutes than the industrial format of radio music that was rarely in excess of five minutes but a lot shorter than the fifteen-minute-long song format that would later become Fẹlá's signature length. The song opens with a guitar-and-drum intro that lasts about ten seconds. A tentative but steadily aggressive horn session follows, accompanying the vocalist's own short, guttural calls (Oh-ho! Eih! Hah!), each monosyllabic exclamation expanding into the boisterous progression of the ensemble. Beyond those huffing-like interjections that would be called scatting if they were not so dominant, Fẹlá does not quite sing, throughout. There is an occasional call of "One more time" when he wants an encore from the saxophone or "Give it to me now" addressed to the drummer. Instrumentals dominate. Between the 2:15 and 5:01 marks, the alto sax has the free range to solo, with the soul-style guitar flowing along as a controlled undercurrent. Commanding over two-thirds of the song's running time, the solo session receives two short boosts from the larger horn ensemble.

There may not have been much singing in the manner that would distinguish him in the years to come, but the albums that followed in the wake of his return testified to Fẹlá's discovery of a style all his own. With the renaming of his band as Afrika '70 came such Afrobeat classics as "Jẹun Koóku," "Yẹyẹ Dey Smell," and "Black Man's Cry." Each of these songs displays with extravagance Fẹlá's hollering style, the throaty spurts of huffing articulations that fit so well with the soul-style fast-tempo guitar and for which 1976's "Zombie" stands as the culmination.

Sandra is also a gifted vocalist, although her actual *musical* contribution to that song is hard to ascertain. The intensity of the relationship tells a story that can be heard on a lower frequency. And she, too, adds something of a subtext, telling Moore about her fights with Fẹlá during this time and of tensions with her devoted parents. Sandra's take on her own attitude was unflattering ("I, too, was so aggressive then. I was a fighter. . . . If you didn't want to hear it my way, I was ready to fight. Physically. Whatever" [Moore 2009, 98]). It might have been all an outlet for her rage against everything she felt was wrong with American society, and the inspiration was clearly paradoxical. It is in the collaboration resulting in the 1976 "Upside Down" that her gifts as a musician are in full display. In thematic terms, the song shares much with "Perambulator," "Shuffering and Shmiling," "Colomentality," and "Original Sufferhead," all critiques of the alienated consciousness of contemporary Black people, especially Africans. This is what Sandra tries to capture and articulate in her statement, "In 1976 . . . I returned to Africa to do the 'Upside Down' album. I realized then that everything was upside down." The song is thus the projection of an outlook for which neither cultural nationalism nor political radicalism is sufficient:

> For oversea
> Where I see
> Communication organized,
> [Pátápátá]
> Electric organized (Kuti 1976)

The poetry ("oversea / where I see"), the rhetorical contrasting of Euro-American efficiency to African or Nigerian social dysfunction are all staple of Afrika '70's output. Sandra's accented pidgin—a case of double defamiliarization—introduces a unique style into Afrobeat. A similar effort with capturing Fẹlá's unique style reappears in Hugh Masekela's remix of "Lady" and eventually points the way to new experimental bands like Antibalas and the Chicago Afrobeat Project.

What is striking about the relationship between Sandra and Fẹlá is less the sexual encounter, gratifying as that might have been for creatures of the senses. Still less decisive is the uplifting narrative of the musical genius having his masculine ego deflated by tutoring from a strong-willed woman. Cultural critics eager to embrace the politically convenient argument about gender sensitivity are fond of this perspective because, as Ọláníyan (2004) points out, it is rich in irony, given the musician's famous self-presentation. The significance of the affair is best sought, I think, in a view of it as a providential meeting of two willful and visionary personalities. Neither Sandra nor Fẹlá was fully aware of what laid within the self or what laid ahead. But the potential of that historic meeting of minds could not have been imagined if, to begin with, the grounds of the encounter were not equal.

That the affair never developed into a full-blown case of routinized matrimony might have been due to a number of factors, including the exigencies of time and location. Perhaps it was a good thing that it did not. They remained friends, nonetheless, and love was never found wanting. At the end of the interview, Moore asked Sandra to describe her love for Fẹlá. She said, "I consider there are two main men in my life: my parental father and Fela. I've been spiritually informed that Fela is my brother. I don't think there's anything Fela could ask me to do that I would refuse him. It's that kind of love" (Moore 2009, 107).

"Little Brother, Don't You Like Black Women?"

The outlook projected in the 1976 musical collaboration between Fẹlá and Sandra brought something equally momentous into focus. Moore, the chronicler of that affair, arrived in Nigeria two years before the album's release, but he had gone through an ideological reconditioning similar to the couple's, only on the other coast of the United States. Born in Central Lugareño, Cuba, in 1942, Moore emigrated to the United States with his family in May 1958, several months before the Cuban revolution. As he saw things, a civil war raged on the island between Fulgencio Batista and Fidel Castro, and moving to New York was a lucky escape for the family. He would return to Havana in June 1961 out of an ardent desire to work for the revolution, and he nearly got eaten by it. Those thirty-seven months in the United States were to prove indispensable to his political and intellectual development. There is ample evidence in *Pichón*, Moore's memoir from 2008, that his relations with women, especially Black women, in those years played a role in the way he narrated the affair between Sandra and Fẹlá.

The years in New York City were Moore's teenage years. Preparing to enter high school, he attended Black teenagers' parties and worked as a dishwasher at a delicatessen (and got fired for demanding a raise). He fell in, then out, with a gang called the Buccaneers, mostly Black teenagers who did not fancy school, and had his first experience of romantic love with Georgia Jeffries, a Black girl who introduced him to African American music. Moore experienced the affair as one of real bliss; it ended in tragic frustration when Georgia, hooked on cocaine and with a helpless mother, disappeared forever. These were also his bohemian years. Out of a desire to appear cool in Greenwich Village, he tried many experiments. He "used skin bleach and hair straighteners," faddishly trying out political rebellion in the dying years of McCarthyism (Moore 2008, 96). Although registered as a high schooler in Brooklyn, Moore did not pay much attention to his studies, preferring to get another kind of education by visiting Lewis Michaux's iconic National Memorial African Bookstore in Harlem and attending meetings with communists and Trotskyites. In 1960, he "entered the world of Communist politics and Revolution" (101) and ended up as a partisan of the revolution in Cuba through his contacts with the Fair Play for Cuba Committee (FPCC).

The political involvements were to lead to involvements of an amorous kind. Here is Moore, accounting for his activities in this regard:

I had developed the habit of dating several women simultaneously, in case one dumped me. Among them was a dark-haired Jewish woman, Lorna, an SWP [Socialist Workers' Party] stalwart I had met at an FPCC rally. . . . Immediately attracted to one another, we began sleeping at once. That was the great thing about those leftist white women: it was hello, a suggestive smile, then bed. (2008, 103)

Thrown in the midst of Trotskyites dedicated to a revolution famous for its nonracial outlook, Moore was a free-floating radical activist, and his incipient outlook was anti-imperial in a general, unanchored way. He was leading a double life. At home he appeared to be fulfilling his parents' expectations, but once out in the streets he turned all his attention to a host of political and sexual escapades. He also religiously visited the National Memorial African bookshop at the corner of 125th Street and Lennox Avenue in Harlem. This was the setting for his meeting with Maya Angelou, "the woman who would send my life into a spin" (Moore 2008, 107).

Moore reports that the first encounter was disorienting for him. Angelou expressed visible excitement when she heard that the young man in front of her was from Cuba. An invitation to a jazz club frequented by Angelou and her friends followed. The performers were none other than Abbey Lincoln and her partner, the drummer Max Roach, but none of this registered much with the teenager. This was odd because Moore had grown to know and like Black music through his short-lived affair with Georgia. In the jazz club, with his white girlfriend in tow, he offended his hosts— Angelou, Lincoln, and Roach—with his behavior. Until this time, Moore and Angelou had met only outside her home, often at the bookstore in Harlem. After the disastrous outing where he displayed his white girlfriend as if a trophy to his African American hosts, he got a second chance with an invitation to Angelou's house at Central Park West.

What he saw and heard during that visit went a long way in nudging him to an awareness of the paradox of freedom and exclusion for Black people in the United States. Full confrontation with that paradox still lay ahead, but at least he knew now that his generous and generalized political identification had limited purchase for him without a grounding in specific experiences of Blackness. He did entertain the fleeting idea that the invitation might be for sex; such was his mindset at the time. The notion disappeared as soon as he settled into the apartment. He found out, for instance, that Angelou was familiar with a host of Black female musicians, including Nina Simone, Odetta, and Miriam Makeba, to whom she made him listen.

The revelations to which this led are worthy of a lengthy quotation from *Pichón* because they were decisive for Moore's journey of self-discovery:

> Maya had left aside one of the LPs, which she now autographed and handed to me, anticipating my surprise. It was her own album, Miss Calypso, recorded four years earlier in 1956, when I was still thirteen. I knew she was a dancer and an actress—she was currently rehearsing for a play called The Blacks—but I had not known that she was a famous singer as well. I was in for a greater surprise when I read the biographical notes on the album's sleeve. "Was born in Cuba twenty-seven years ago. . . . Her father is a full-blooded Watusi, tallest native tribe in the world." Born of a Watusi father? Maya's sonorous laughter inundated the living room as she looked at my astonished face. I too began to laugh: the marketing gimmick on her album sleeve brought us closer together. "I am from the United States," she confirmed. "I was born and bred here." (Moore 2008, 111)

The revelations in this passage are significant for a number of reasons. They may not say much about Angelou's previous career choices, which were more colorful and complex than a suggestion from a pragmatic marketing decision could illuminate. Besides, they say nothing about her growing involvement in pro-Castro activism, although it was still early in the life of the revolution in Cuba, and two catalytic events of 1961 for Moore (the assassination of Patrice Lumumba in January and the Bay of Pigs invasion in April) had not yet occurred.[1] However, they provided the condition for the tutoring that Moore was to receive in Angelou's circle. He learned, that day, that many Black American artists had to forge their identities to get work, that for "a black artist to achieve anything here in music and theater, you must be from somewhere else" (Moore 2008, 111). Born Marguerite Annie Johnson, Angelou took the name she became famous for (her nickname and married name) in 1954 on the advice of her managers in San Francisco, who felt it would serve her well as a professional artist.

In the course of that visit, Angelou posed a delicate question to Moore: "Little brother," she asked, "don't you like *black* women?" The question had been waiting to be asked since the disastrous incident at the jazz club with Moore and his white girlfriend. It made him uncomfortable, and the more vehement his protests, the more insistent Angelou became in asking the question, with gentle variations intended to keep him on the spot. The aim was less to deflate his ego than to create for him an opening for self-examination. A Black boy with straightened hair, bleached skin, fond of blonde white women. Though far from easy on Moore's confidence, the visit was enough to score yet another invitation to the jazz club. There he met Laura, a Black woman and lover of poetry (she worked in a bookstore) who was to be his girlfriend for a few months. When the affair ended, it was at her instance. She felt that Moore had not yet found himself. He and Angelou were involved in several political events in the months that followed, until his departure for Cuba in mid-1961, but his assessment of the relationship with Laura was that for the Black women who moved with Angelou there was more at stake than sexual dalliance. Moore writes that "in retrospect I realize that at twenty-four Laura was in every way a mature woman. It was enough for me to be appreciated as a good lover. She had wanted not a sexual fling but a meeting of equals. She had tried to get me to look inward, but I had resisted" (Moore 2008, 125).

Even with the benefit of gentle rebuke from Angelou, Moore had envisioned his relationship with Laura in much the same way he had dealt with female comrades who were white. "I wanted to go to bed immediately," he confesses as he recalls their first time together, "but Laura wanted to talk. I did not see what there was to *talk* about; I was used to the wham-bam-thank-you-ma'am style of Greenwich Village. She sat me down in her tiny kitchen and made us sandwiches while talking about her family and where she was born" (Moore 2008, 121).

Moore's recollections about his years in New York are heartfelt, detailed, and carefully observed. They are *reconstructions*, stories recalled in hindsight, with the intention of marking the evolution of a personal political worldview. They are not embellished. There is convincing evidence of his activism even in those days when he made a clean break with formal education and turned his full attention to political agitation, first in the United States and then in Cuba, to the displeasure of Castro's people. Stylistically the details are not innocuous, because they are recalled to shape a narrative of political awakening. A young man who makes an instinctive common cause with progressive politics is paradoxically bereft of racial consciousness. While in New York he saw himself as "an internationalist," "a humanist" who did not see color in love. However, upon his return to Cuba, he fell out with the communist regime over its nonracial policy, seeing its internationalism as insufficient excuse for perpetuating the marginalization of Black people in the country.

Conditional Love

"I was born on the 11th of May 1961, in Yaba, Lagos, Nigeria. By a Ghanaian mother and a Cameroonian father, the late Ernest Ouandié." Those words begin the narrative of *Leaf in the Wind*, a documentary film by the Cameroonian filmmaker Jean-Marie Teno (2013b), released in 2013. The speaker is Ernestine, the daughter born to Ouandié while he lived underground as an activist, hiding from the security forces of his country. Following the screening of this film during a conference at Indiana University in October 2013, Teno revealed his primary motivation for undertaking the project:

> When you have a hero, see a hero from a distance who dedicates his life to a great cause, you wonder, Does he have a family? What about his relatives? So, for me, it was a way of knowing what she thought about her father, just out of curiosity. (Teno 2013a, 6:45–7:04)

Teno first taped Ernestine in 2004, touched by her story and hopeful for a full-length treatment at a later date. "This for me was like research material because I had no sound recording and I said I would just record the sound on camera. And that was the only image of her that I had" (Teno 2013a, 5:11–5:27). Even in its final, premeditated form, the film remains a troubling record of a failed love's encounter with a failing revolution. Ernestine's gentle passion redeems some of the tragedy; her voice offers the testimony that the encounter is not without a trace.

The story of Ouandié's arrest, trial, and execution in January 1971 has been told in several forms and by several people, including in *Prisoner Without a Crime*, a memoir by Albert Mukong (1989), who had been in detention with the revolutionary leader. In a gleeful *New York Times* report published later that month, Ouandié's arrest was described as sealing "the fate of the guerrilla movement, which already had degenerated into banditry and indiscriminate murder" (*New York Times* 1971). As one of the vice presidents (with Abel Kingué) of the radical Union des Populations du Cameroun (UPC), Ouandié played a central role in the anti-colonial guerrilla activities in the years leading up to transfer of power in 1960.

Under pressure from the French government, the British authorities in western Cameroon deported Ouandié and other leaders of the UPC to Khartoum, Sudan, in July 1957, nine years after the party was formed. Before that, he had lived in a hideout in Kumba, Cameroon, for up to a year. From Khartoum, he moved successively to Cairo, Egypt; Conakry, Guinea; and finally Accra, Ghana. During this time, the leadership of UPC suffered a series of devastating setbacks. Ruben Um Nyombé, the union's secretary-general and most inspirational leader, was killed in a Cameroonian forest in 1958. Félix Moumié, the president, was poisoned in Geneva by agents reportedly working for the French secret service. In 1960, the year Cameroon became independent, Ouandié and other remaining UPC leaders were quite desperate, with places for refuge shrinking. Already living underground and in exile, they were further isolated by the change in the political climate. On May Day 1961, a military tribunal in Yaoundé again condemned him and Kingué to deportation in absentia, a declaration that they were of no standing in the country.

Stories of the prelude to Ouandié's tragic ending are not so well known. The details of his group's exactions for nearly a decade in the forest and, before that, of his life underground across West Africa, between 1959 and his departure for Cameroon in mid-1961, may still emerge, free of distortion by vested interests. Of his time in the forest, a surviving member of the guerrilla force said that they did not do much fighting in the final years, except in the kitchen. The total isolation of the fighters cut them off from food supplies, and the proposed struggle "to work towards the overthrow of the Ahidjo regime" disintegrated into a daily struggle for bare living. In *Radical Nationalism in Cameroun*, perhaps the most comprehensive account of the nationalist party, Richard Joseph mentions Ouandié's execution in the closing chapter in light of the exhaustion of what began as one of continental Africa's earliest instances of anti-colonial armed struggle. This treatment reinforces the observation in the introduction that "in Cameroon those who fought and died for independence are only mentioned to be execrated" (Joseph 1977, 2).

Details of Ouandié's life underground, when accessible, are even sketchier. There is an undated interview with him by a French television journalist. It focuses on the circumstances of Moumié's murder, so it must have been in late 1960 or early 1961. The interview also features Moumié's widow. As it happens, the most resonant, and historically most memorable, episode of that period is Ouandié's secret affair with a Ghanaian woman. On May 11, days after the tribunal's pronouncement on Ouandié and Kingué, a child was born in Lagos from Ouandié's affair with the Ghanaian woman. This child, a girl, was named Ernestine. That month, maybe a few weeks after the birth, maybe a few months, Ouandié returned secretly to Cameroon to restoke the waning embers of the revolutionary fight. He and his comrades carried on with the fight for the next nine years or so. In the parlance of the time, when the logic of the Cold War crudely presented politics in most African countries in terms of a struggle between "Muslim North" and "Christianized southern tribes," the UPC was viewed (by the *New York Times*, for one) as a group of "pro-Communist rebels [whose support had] been limited to the Bamileke, a highly educated and commercially successful group that has extended its influence throughout the country" (*New York Times* 1971).

But how did Ouandié meet the woman simply known as Regina Kwedu? What was their time like together? Did they share a dream of a future? What was that dream? Did he let her know of his other wife, the family he left behind as he was forced to go underground in 1956? We know, we think we know, why he had to return to Cameroon in the year Ernestine was born. But what did the woman, the young mother he left behind, feel? Fear? Apprehension? Betrayal? A mixture of hope and desire? Dis she feel abandoned? Did she imagine him going to make arrangements to take her to a place where she could raise the child? Did she share his political ideals and wish to be part of his life of struggle? How much did the daughter know of this sometimes legendary, sometimes mythical, father?

> All I can show to my children is a picture of a grandfather in a handcuff. . . . Not so far ago, not so long ago, my first son asked me, "Why is grandfather in a handcuff?" What do I give him as explanation? (Teno 2013b, 48:17–48:28, 48:42–49:02)

With Ouandié out of the picture, the story that his daughter tells boils down to one of tension between two women—she and her biological mother. As a child, she was taken to her aunt in Accra and left there, and for much of her childhood Ernestine's life revolved around four relations: the aunt, two others in the city, and a distant grandfather. The tales of her upbringing in these circumstances are ear stopping, literally; she developed hearing problems from being slapped regularly by the aunt.

To speculate on the romantic encounter that brought Ernestine into the world, Teno fills the silence-heavy spaces of her narration with newsreels from the archive of French colonial propaganda, hand-drawn images of lovers in imaginary embrace, over which E. T. Mensah's highlife song, "Day by Day" soars, plaintively. Occasionally, silent headshots of the revolutionary appear, ripped out of the interview he gave after his comrade Moumié's death. There are no indications of what Kwedu looked like. Ernestine was either not asked or she chose to prioritize the narrative of her hurt. These formal devices are common to Teno's unique documentary style. One of the most storied African directors in that genre, he has perfected the art of working with very little. Starting from the unforgettable *Afrique, Je te Plumerai* (1993), he has regularly opted for neglected topics, stories that seem strange, until the viewer, looking and listening closely, is convinced of being in the presence of the most routine incident, but so conveniently ignored that its presentation now acquires a magical quality, on film. Sometimes, the presence of talking heads shows Teno moving slightly toward standard-practice documentary style, as he does in *The Colonial Misunderstanding* (2005) and *Sacred Places* (2009). His aesthetic preference, however, is today definitively for the conceptual treatment of a subject carefully or sloppily hidden, and that conceptual approach is evident from the given script. The narrator's voice, Teno's, interjects in sententious French, its perspective a cross between journalism and essay. It is a strong style. In *Leaf in the Wind*, Teno listens at length, although his approving "uh-huh" occasionally comes through the flow of Ernestine's recollections.

Years after Ernestine's biological mother abandoned her at her sister's place, she appeared suddenly with a suitcase of underwear. The daughter was now old enough to menstruate and had written to her that she had no way of keeping her dignity in this private station. Months, perhaps years, elapsed. At the point in the story when Mensah's music is first heard, one of Ernestine's cousins has just taken her to her mother, after a final falling-out with the abusive aunt. If the daughter imagined this as a rapprochement, her illusions disappeared quickly. Ernestine recalls:

> The worst I should hear is that I should call her sister and not mother. . . . Then she gave an answer. That I was too old to call her mother, and so I should call her sister and that would make her look younger. Or feel younger. (Teno 2013b, 22:02–22:34)

Are there indications of the mother's view of things in this declaration? Is the knowledge of the child's existence a traumatic reminder of the failed love? If this woman was young enough to imagine her daughter as a sister, did she also judge Ouandié as having walked away from her? Did she, in turn, abandon the child to make a new life for herself? Ernestine wastes no time second-guessing her biological mother. The most she can deduce about her mother is that "the hatred she had . . . for me came from the fact that her dream for my father fell apart before it could begin" (Teno 2013b, 43:35–43:50). It was only a matter of time before the brittle mother-daughter relationship collapsed, and Ernestine ended up living on the street. From there, she was rescued by the Cameroonian community in Accra, and then Ouandié's first wife, Martha, took her to Lomé where the United Nations Refugee Agency registered her as the child of a political refugee. That opened for her a path to secondary-school education. In 1986, at twenty-five, she obtained a diploma from the Ghana Institute of Journalism.

Teno's camera shifts focus to Cameroon and Ouandié. Fragmented stories of Ouandié's arrest and trial are punctuated with the black-and-white image of the prisoner, possibly awaiting trial, followed by diegetic sounds of gunshots and scattered leaves flying in the wind. Ernest Ouandié was arrested in August 1970 and executed in January 1971, despite international protests from figures such as Noam Chomsky and Paul Ricoeur. There is another image: a group of military officers posing behind human heads.

We also return to the present time of the filming, since Ernestine has since relocated to Cameroon and settled into family life, after having tried to connect with the last sibling of her late father. This is where she articulates her pan-African ideas most passionately. It is stunning to hear someone who has had such a traumatic life speak with that kind of conviction about African unity, evoking the memory of Kwame Nkrumah and linking it to what her father and others in the UPC struggled for. Finally, over the rising tempo of what sounds like a Hindi film score, Teno's voice returns: "One October morning in 2009, before daybreak, Ernestine left the family home wearing a cloth and a pair of sandals. Her car was found near a bridge, and her body a few days later" (Teno 2013b, 53:43–54:03).

Staring at the Sun

Different though these stories may be, it is significant that they occurred between men and women, and that love, romantic and otherwise, played a role in how they have come down to us. There is added significance in their occurring during perhaps the most volatile revolutionary decade in the modern history of global Blackness. There are ways to put them in focus, the better to speculate on futures once imagined by the utopian efforts out of which they originated. Our present was once part of those futures; admittedly, some arrived too quickly as nightmares, crashing even before they got off the ground. The fate of the Cameroonian revolutionary struggle was one case in point, that of Lumumba's Congo was yet another. But it is in the nature of the future to be permanently ahead. Hope springing eternally.

Moore and Angelou sat in the latter's New York apartment circa 1960 and she taught him about Black life and Black women. Fẹlá and Sandra spent much of 1969 finding their way toward a common political and artistic understanding that would prove transformative of Black musical tradition. Ouandié fought an increasingly attritional war against the Cameroonian state until his death. His execution on January 15, 1971, two days before the tenth anniversary of Lumumba's assassination, occurred out of the earshot of most Black political activists: it coincided with Sandra's time in Nigeria, a guest of Fẹlá and a refugee from Nigerian immigration bureaucrats.

These three stories are made real by the sheer effort of aesthetic awareness, the creative hunch that gathers disparate anecdotes into a coherent object of sensibility. By going beyond the rumors of the existence of an Ouandié love child, Teno manages, first accidentally and then belatedly, to reanimate a traumatic childhood and rekindle the fire of a revolution long discarded. Getting a narrative, an art, a story, out of unseemly data is an aesthetic daring that holds considerable promise for black hosts. Ernestine's childhood memories included throwing stones at the decapitated statue of Nkrumah, lately overthrown in a military coup. In the film, however, her Pan-African views were on full display.

The power of speculation propels the writer gathering these fragments of intense experience into a narrative to imagine a reckoning beyond sensual gratification. How to reimagine political solidarity in the face of actual, human travails? What if, during a passionate affair, one discovers one's lover to be suffering from a terminal illness, like cancer? Body beloved as disabled body. What becomes of a lover who turns out to be undocumented and faces the threat of deportation, victim of a rallying cry of hate? How does the young lover of a man caught up in the war in Yemen keep hope alive? What is love to a citizen of Iraq, a country that has hardly known peace for nearly two generations? What is the value of love caught in the teeth of a scary beast, the manufactured risk of being an abettor of terrorists?

"Love don't pay," says Marlene, a character in the director Haile Gerima's film *Bush Mama*, another story of unforgettable Black love. Maybe so. Maybe it is hate that is getting cured of its ailment, which for the most part is the absence of vigilance.

NOTES

Acknowledgments: My sincere gratitude to Jahman Aníkúlápó for his help with finding some of Fẹlá's earliest recordings.

1. Moore erroneously records February as the month of Lumumba's assassination.

WORKS CITED

Blyden, Edward. 1994. *Christianity, Islam and the Negro Race*. Baltimore: Black Classics Press.

Gerima, Haile, dir. 1979. *Bush Mama*. Washington, DC: Mypheduh Films.

Hall, Stuart. 1996. "A Conversation with C.L.R. James." In *Rethinking C.L.R. James*, edited by Grant Farred, 15–44. Cambridge, MA: Blackwell.

Joseph, Richard. 1977. *Radical Nationalism in Cameroun*. Oxford: Clarendon Press.

Kates, Nancy, and Bennett Singer, dirs. 2003. *Brother Outsider: The Life of Bayard Rustin*. New York: Question Why Films.

Kuti, Fẹlá. 1976. "Upside Down." Track 1 on *Upside Down*. Decca Afrodisia DWAPS2005.

Moore, Carlos. 2008. *Pichón: A Memoir*. Chicago: Lawrence Hill.

———. 2009. *Fela: This Bitch of a Life*. Chicago: Lawrence Hill.

Mukong, Albert. 1989. *Prisoner Without a Crime*. Paris: Editions Nubia/Nubia Press.

New York Times. 1971. "Rebellion in Cameroon Reported Virtually Crushed." January 24, 1971. https://www.nytimes.com/1971/01/24/archives/rebellion-in-cameroon -reported-virtually-crushed.html.

Ọláníyan, Tẹjúmọlá. 2004. *Arrest the Music! Fela and His Rebel Art and Politics*. Bloomington: Indiana University Press.

Teno, Jean-Marie. 2013a. "Discussion with Jean Marie Teno." October 18, 2013. Indiana University Bloomington. https://media.dlib.indiana.edu/media_objects/9s1616317.

———, dir. 2013b. *Leaf in the Wind*. Metz, France: Films du Raphia.

TheNews (Lagos: Nigeria). 2020. "Throwback: Fela's Prison Interview with *TheNews* in 1993." April 24, 2020. https://thenewsnigeria.com.ng/2020/04/24/throwback-felas -prison-interview-with-thenews-in-1993-2/.

Veal, Michael. 2000. *Fela: The Life and Times of an African Musical Icon*. Philadelphia: Temple University Press.

8

Seeing, Hearing, Breathing, *and* Witnessing from the Africana Center at Cornell

An Afterword

PIERRE-PHILIPPE FRAITURE

Anniversaries are useful for they help us return to a specific moment, such as the creation of the Africana Studies and Research Center at Cornell University in 1969. The temporal framing offered by anniversaries is often a pretext to take stock of a particular sequence of events; anniversaries are subterfuges to remember, commemorate, and pay tribute but also disinter cumbersome corpses. Anniversaries test our vigilance and ability to submit these corpses to renewed autopsies. The term "Africana" reflects the worlding of Africa and the re- and translocation of its objects, subjects, and discourses within a diasporic network of relations (Hallen 2009, 8n2). From African to Africana studies, one can therefore identify a definitional and heuristic shift: like their postcolonial and decolonial counterparts, Africana scholars are engaged in the dismantling of (neo)colonial cartographies and in the creation of what Pheng Cheah calls "*a* world"— that is, a creative and discursive entity and realm of possibilities that are not reducible to the "epistemic violence" of "canonical literature" and the other "processes" shaping "how colonized subjects see themselves" and continue to see themselves "after decolonization" (2016, 19). Africana studies are concerned with Africa but also with the many cultural entanglements generated by African displacements and reterritorializations before and, above all, *after* the Middle Passage. Africana studies, then, provide the basis for analyzing African pasts and presents in Africa and beyond and anticipating future possibilities.

This volume contributes to this world-making endeavor. Its sheer diversity is a sure sign of its authors' belief that the world is "not governed by a single unifying principle but is instead the effect of overlapping and frequently conflictual processes of world-making that issue from different local, national and regional sites" (Cheah 2016, 59). The Africana scholars summoned here by Grant Farred invite us to participate in a transatlantic, transgenerational, and intermedial debate. This debate takes place in Africa (Kenya, Nigeria, Cameroon, Ghana, Senegal, and the Democratic Republic of the Congo), in the Caribbean (Cuba and Martinique), but also in the United States. Among others, it includes literary pioneers (Phillis Wheatley), African American key thinkers (W.E.B. Du Bois), civil rights movement activists (Zora Neale Hurston, Sandra Smith), anti-racism figures (Frantz Fanon, Aimé Césaire, Carlos Moore), proponents (and critics) of African philosophy (Fabien Eboussi Boulaga, Paulin Hountondji), poets (Édouard Glissant, Maya Angelou, Paul Laurence Dunbar), novelists (Patrick Chamoiseau, Ralph Ellison, Fiston Mwanza Mujila, Sinzo Aanza), musicians (Fẹlá Kuti, Janelle Monáe), filmmakers (Jean-Marie Teno), political meteorites (Patrice Lumumba, Ernest Ouandié, Ruben Um Nyobé, Félix Moumié), and religious leaders (Simon Kimbangu, Kimpa Vita). But also— and this brings us to the core of this volume, race—the biblical characters Noah and Ham.

Seeing

When did the *invention* of blackness take place? To this question, only conjectural answers can be provided. In their premodern and modern iterations, racial constructions were suffused with scopic annotations. The ancients drew on their imagination to fill the unknown parts of the world with vivid images of teratological Others as famously exemplified by Herodotus's *History* and medieval anthropology (Eze 2008, 163–164). The Renaissance inaugurated a new age of discovery and exploration. Interestingly, it has been argued that the noun "exploration" might originate from a verb first coined in 1546 and used among hunters who, while engaged in their reconnaissance activities, had to "observe" and "examine" hitherto untrodden spaces (Rey 1998, 1:1371). Renaissance explorers *saw* Africa with their own eyes. Their undertakings significantly contributed to the anointment of one of the most ubiquitous figures of our modernity: the eyewitness qua data gatherer. Scientific racialism, as is well known, slowly emerged from their predatory observations and fed the taxonomies later developed by Johann F. Blumenbach, Georges L. Cuvier, Arthur de Gobineau, George Combe, Carl von Linné, and many others (Eze 1997; Hall 2019). Despite their repeated refutations in the court chambers of Nurnberg, The Hague, and Kigali, these taxonomies have continued to hold sway:

> Archaic as some of the ancient and classical categories may sound, it is . . . the Hippocratic-Galenic and Linnean taxonomy that, residually, informs today's most influential biological thinking in the areas of racial science. . . . In the United States today, citizens are every day asked to choose self-identification by racial classificatory systems whose biological outlines are so obviously Linnaean. (Eze 2008, 166)

Slavery and colonialism also established the era of an eyewitness of a particular kind—the eyewitness qua overseer—who would, through the power of seeing, recast the very notion of human freedom and lock up black bodies in a system premised on the distinction between those "worthy of self-rule" and those expected "to be ruled" (James 2003, 250). This distinction has continued to haunt modern democracies like the United States—particularly there and where state terror and tyranny still operate. Of course, the paradox is that tyranny is the opposite of democracy. However, the residual power of "classical and ancient" taxonomies has maintained tyranny in place: "The tyranny of a racialized democracy resides in its ability to use violence and domination much more freely against marginalized sectors, whether Native Americans on reservations . . . [or] Palestinians in occupied territories" (James 2003, 257) or African Americans or Afro descendants in, say, France, the United Kingdom, or the Netherlands. This goes a long way to explain why the African transplantation of the "Westphalian nation-state model" failed after the demise of colonialism, for at its core, this model has always been a vehicle to promote the sacrosanct legitimacy of the national "imagined political community" (see Radwa Saad's Chapter 3). And this legitimacy—whether in Algeria, Burundi, Cameroon, Nigeria, or Rwanda—has invariably been implemented at the expense of ethnic, and sometimes *visible*, minorities.

Colonial systems and the plantocracies established in the wake of the Middle Passage relied on the visibility of the colonized (see Gregory Pardlo's Chapter 5) and on the rise of the "Beobachtende Vernunft" (observing reason; Fabian 2002, 122). Hitherto representations of the American and African Others had remained under-racialized, perhaps in the name of the Christian monogenesis, as suggested by Hans-Joachim Kunst (1967, 8–10). On American (French, British, Spanish, and Dutch) plantations, however, economic efficiency crucially depended on the overseer's ability to radicalize visibility and call on external—racial—markers to exercise his authority and contribute to the development of usable taxonomies as illustrated by Jean-Baptiste Labat's "remarkable" (Toczyski 2007, 1) but chilling eighteenth-century classic *Nouveau Voyage aux isles de l'Amérique*. Plantations were tabularized and "visualist" (Fabian 2002, 118–123) spaces, and to function each member of their workforce had to be allocated an identifiable and readily visible slot. This point, and the utter visibility of the slave, seen and used as a mere instrument, is aptly captured by Patrick Chamoiseau's historical novella *The Old Slave and the Mastiff*. In the following extract, the slave reassuringly remains in his master's field of vision:

> In the gleam of the boilers, [the slave's] skin takes on the texture of the cast-iron buckets or rusty pipes, and at times even the coppery yellow of crystallizing sugar. His sweat dots him with the varnish of old windmill beams. . . . Sometimes, even, the Master's attentive gaze does not distinguish him from the mass of machines; they seem to keep going on their own, but the Master goes off again with the feeling that he is there. (Chamoiseau 2018, 8)[1]

The emergence of "visualism"—which Léopold Senghor dismissed as "reason-eye" (see Diagne 2019, 27)—coincided with the development of ethnographic, colonial, and literary modernity. Albert Camus's remarkable (and chilling) *L'Étranger* offers an intriguing manifestation of visualism. First, it allows the French novelist to rely on his readers' visual memory and their internalization of centuries of anthropological ocularcentrism. One of the most noteworthy aspects of this book is that Camus's first-person narrator, Meursault, provides very little information about the physical appearance of "the Arab," his faceless victim. As widely discussed, particularly at the time of the publication of Kamel Daoud's *Meursault, contre-enquête* (Schatz 2015), Meursault seemed to assume that the Arab—being *the* Arab—physically, ethnically, visually, *and* ontologically—does not need any introduction. Interestingly, the unnamed Algerian victim is said to be wearing work overalls ("bleu de chauffe"), and this visual annotation serves to confirm the distance between the Frenchman and the colonized because, like Chamoiseau's slave, he is reduced to his subservient position within the colonizer's field of vision. This classical dialectic between the seer and the seen is a clear sign that Camus remained tethered to the visualist imaginary underpinning French colonialism. This point—the underlying coloniality of the novel—escaped early commentators, Jean-Paul Sartre (1947), famously. During the Algerian war, however, it was argued "that the scene of homicide in the novel gave expression to the unconscious desire of the settler to be rid of the colonized" (Hughes 2015, 72).[2] This murder also signals Meursault's inability to exercise his authority and contain the colonized within the epistemological parameters of an imperial field of vision. The Arab's assassination occurs when Meursault loses sight of him, and thus, Meursault's temporary blindness marks the end of a certain mode of knowing. Suddenly, he realizes that the colonized is no longer knowable and that his act has irretrievably ruined "l'équilibre du jour" (the balance of the day) (Camus 1962, 1166).

Hearing

The wide-ranging phenomenology-inspired discussions conducted in the immediate post–World War II era on the (white) gaze—by Sartre and Maurice Merleau-Ponty but also Richard Wright and, of course, Frantz Fanon—was accompanied by a reflection on language (see John Drabinski's Chapter 1). Seen and trapped in the purported ontological fixity of their race, the colonized were also dependent on the colonizers' languages. In his *Cahier d'un retour au pays natal*, Césaire (1947) famously deplored the silence and inertia of Fort-de-France, in the age of the craniometer. Although this poem inventively reterritorializes the French language, there is no doubt that this period continued to be subjected to a process of imperial glottophagy (Calvet 1974). Despite some genuine attempts on the part of thinkers like Cheikh Anta Diop (see *Nations nègres et culture*, 1955) to decolonize knowledge through non-Western languages, part of the twentieth century was still residually characterized by pseudoscientific linguistic classifications (Ricard 2004), and in this context, it remained arduous for local intellectuals to be published and *heard* in their vernaculars. This attempt on part of the colonizers to impose Europhone languages, however, was not entirely successful. Indeed, colonial language policies remained "heterogeneous, uneven, and often self-contradictory" (Barber 1995, 13), and the colonial process of linguistic homogenization did not prevent Indian Ocean and Caribbean Creoles and African languages—Yoruba, Shona, Kiswahili, Lingala, Wolof, and many others—from becoming powerful vectors of ethnic and cultural identities (Barber 2007, 160–161).

Eye- and earwitnesses from the peripheries must rely on audible languages because, however crucial their message might be, they will need audiences and a stage where they will be expected to connect and relate (Glissant 1990)—the "petit contexte" to the "grand contexte" (Chamoiseau and Larcher 2007, 125–126). National languages are often ill equipped to achieve this transcending objective because they invariably are the vehicles of atavistic mythologies. Patrick Chamoiseau and Silyane Larcher argue nonetheless that literature's ultimate "mission" is the exploration of literature itself (123). Like Jean-Luc Nancy, then, they contend that literature, unlike myth, does not serve the immanent community. If "myth is the opening of the mouth immediately adequate to the closure of a universe" (Nancy 1991, 50), literature or writing has the ability to interrupt the communion of the immanent community.

Building on the tension between these terms, "myth" and "literature" or "writing," it would be interesting—as some of the contributors to this volume have done (see Akin Adeṣọkan's Chapter 7 and Sarah Then Bergh's Chapter 6)—to ascertain the role of music in the long decolonial process to which Africana scholars at Cornell, and beyond, have borne witness. Does African, African American, and Afro-Caribbean music have a mission, and if so, how does it manifest itself and how can we *hear* it? Does it contribute to the mythical wholeness (to the organic homogeneity) of *the* black community, or is it a more diffuse entity ("being in common") whose plurality of meanings is shared and perpetually deferred (Nancy 1991)? The type of communication produced by this sharing is no longer communion—indeed, Nancy contends that it "does not commune" (78)—but is what he calls "literary communism": "something that would be the sharing of community in and by its writing, its literature" (26).

Music could play here a compensatory function because it permits bypassing national languages and their inherent atavistic trappings and classificatory parameters. It has been argued that the "enhanced mode of communication" generated by music occurs "beyond the petty power of words—spoken or written" (Gilroy 1993, 76). Daniel Maximin, the Guadeloupean poet, Césaire scholar, and novelist, seems to endorse this conception of music seen as a language that, while transcending national boundaries, reveals intellectual achievements from another viewpoint. Maximin's novelistic trilogy *L'Isolé soleil*, *Soufrières*, and *L'Île et une nuit*, constitutes one of the most accomplished (and opaque in Glissant's understanding of this adjective) depictions of French Caribbean history over several generations. Maximin's novels are also concerned with the exploration of literature itself. His complex and at times elliptical narrative detours, and syncopated annotations are strategic—and *poetic*—ploys to engage with Caribbean "non-histoire" (Glissant 1981, 222–231). His focus on music—from Guadeloupe, Cuba, and the American continents (north, central, and south)—provides a more temporally diffuse and less spatially rooted type of cultural excavation (Britton 2008, 111–130). There is here no attempt to identify a strict point of origin, a biblical sin, and a mythical premise. Music, however, is shown to have triggered (and have been triggered by) a deep sentiment of transatlantic deracination. Alongside a rich network of intertextual references to painting (Wilfredo Lam) and poetry (Saint-John Perse and Césaire), music is summoned to resurrect what was obfuscated by centuries of bondage. Like Glissant, Maximin seems to favor "a remembrance evoked from the senses and the imagination over the memories contained in facts, dates and incontrovertible truths" (Munro 2007, 396). The fifth chapter of *L'Île et une nuit* is characterized by a shift from seeing to hearing. One of the narrators announces a "trêve de l'œil" (truce of the eye) and invites another narrator to make use of her "oreilles" (ears) (Maximin 1995, 97). It is an invitation to listen to the intercontinental connections—and the "étranges fruits" (strange fruit) (103)—generated by musical encounters and displacement in the black diaspora. If facts fail to render the Afro-Caribbean past, Maximin seems to suggest that the traces of this past are everywhere to be seen and *heard*: in the *biguine* and *léwoz* from Martinique, the performances by Guadeloupean *Ka* drummers, salsa musicians from Cuba, gospels from New Orleans, jazz and blues from Chicago and New York City, popular music from Haiti, and Afro-jazz from South Africa. The "brotherhoods" and "sisterhoods" (97–125) elicited by this process of musical dissemination are postnational. This process indicates the existence of a community of sorts, and it also suggests that this community does not quite fall into the immanent category. The musical genres evoked in these texts "unwork" the myth underpinning the "immanent community" (Nancy 1991) and conjure an "open-ended, mobile, [and] 'spaced-out' community" (Britton 2008, 126).

Breathing

This idea of the community is also the focus of Fiston Mwanza Mujila's *Tram 83* (see Kasereka Kavwahirehi's Chapter 4). Tram 83 is a bar, a jazz club, and a brothel in Lubumbashi, Democratic Republic of the Congo. In this dystopian tale, the Congolese city has become a dictatorial city-state and has fallen prey to international entrepreneurs (from Europe, the United States, China, and Africa) interested in appropriating Katangese mining resources. These industrialists cum gangsters regularly visit Tram 83, where they interact—argue, converse, fight, and pay for sex—with a wide range of characters including locals, petty criminals, prostitutes, journalists, publishers, and artists. Tram 83 is a place where deals are struck, ideas are exchanged, and where, crucially, jazz is listened to by transient and interloping characters. It is a community but it "does not commune" and jazz—free, improvised, and subjected to procedures of perpetual reinvention (Herbeck 2005)—interrupts the coming of *the* community while also being the very symptom of a globalized cultural commodification process in which jazz has "become a mere product like any other" (Higginson 2017, 155). Thus, Tram 83 presents itself as the interrupted community—what Nancy (1991, 71) also calls "community without community." For Nancy, however, this interruption offers a model of resistance: "It is to *come*, in the sense that it is always *coming*, endlessly, at the heart of every collectivity [and] it ceaselessly resists collectivity itself" (71). Interestingly, the interruption elicited by jazz in Fiston Mwanza Mujila's novel delivers only partial resistance because it remains torn between "the forces of neocolonial exploitation and abuse" and those of "*marronage* and liberation" (Higginson 2017, 155).

Jazz, blues, and the other musical genres alluded to by Maximin and Fiston Mwanza Mujila, precisely because they are the "jewels brought from bondage," can be (and have been) used to enact "politics of authenticity" (Gilroy 1993, 72–110) and assert "metaphysics of difference" (see Zeyad el Nabolsy's Chapter 2).

In *Black Skin, White Masks*, Fanon argues that African rhythm, as this notion had been understood, romanticized by Senghor (1939) but also by Césaire (1947) in *Cahier*, was yet another tool to maintain blacks from the diaspora in a fixed ontology and in "the materialized Tower of the Past" (Fanon 2008, 176). His appraisal of jazz and other (then) black musical expressions is equally critical and aimed at those, Senghor among others, who had "promoted jazz as a kind of antidote to machine-age modernity" (Lane 2013, 94). Fanon's examination of endogenous culture—the same applies to his quick dismissal of Creole in *Black Skin*—is paradoxical because he deplores the annihilating effects of slavery and colonialism on black cultures while remaining convinced that these cultures will be superseded by the universal. Adopting Sartre's Hegelian model in "Black Orpheus," Fanon also contends that the examination of African cultures should not be an end in itself but remain a transitory stage of the dialectic. The black Martinicans on whom Fanon focuses in *Black Skin* find themselves in an impossible predicament: they are bereft of their original cultures but advised not to indulge (for too long) in the resurrection of these cultures; at the same time, they are warned of the alienating effects of French assimilation.

In her ascent, (a presumably black) Eurydice dies—stops breathing—after being gazed at by a black Orpheus. Similarly, Fanon argues that, as a result of having to assimilate an objectively constraining language—"To speak means . . . to assume a culture, to support the weight of a civilization" (Fanon 2008, 8)—alienated Martinicans "literally cannot breathe" (Fanon 2008, 17). This cultural suffocation is constitutive of French educational practices in the Antilles, and Fanon provides the telling example of Martinican schoolchildren being asked to write a composition on "My Feelings before I Went on Vacation." The outcome, Fanon argues, is worryingly mimetic: "They reacted like real little Parisians and produced such things as, 'I like vacation because then I can run through the fields, breathe fresh air, and come home with *rosy* cheeks'" (Fanon 2008, 125). This imaginary breath of "fresh air" is but an effect of the epistemic conditions generated by the imposed adoption of the white mask, and thus, it does not engender any homecoming. It stands in stark contrast to Césaire's own miasmic homesickness when depicting the island's "stagnant air undisturbed by the bright flight of a bird" and its "sun that keeps coughing and spitting out its lungs" (Césaire 1995, 82, 95). Like Césaire in his *Cahier*, Fanon, then, recurrently equates colonial violence and occupation with breathlessness. In this context, fighting colonialism is the only *vital* (and existential) option, and the exploited black Martinican "will embark on this struggle . . . not as the result of a Marxist or idealistic analysis but quite simply because he cannot conceive of *life* otherwise than in the form of a battle against exploitation, misery, and hunger" (Fanon 2008, 174; my emphasis). By means of a quick reference to Indochina, he explains that fighting colonialism is a matter of life and death: the Vietminh goes into war "because 'quite simply' it was, in more than one way, becoming impossible for him to breathe" (176). In "Algeria Unveiled," Fanon returned to this breathing metaphor:

> There is not occupation of territory, on the one hand, and independence of persons on the other. It is the country as a whole, its history, its daily pulsation that are contested, disfigured, in the hope of a final destruction. Under these conditions, the individual's breathing is an observed, an occupied breathing. It is a combat breathing. (Fanon 1965, 65)

This metaphor is powerful, and it suggests that by converting "observed" and "occupied breathing" into "combat breathing," the colonized will contribute to the emergence of this new decolonized human dreamed of by Fanon, Sartre, Amílcar Cabral, Che Guevara, and (as already mentioned) Césaire himself:

> And suddenly, strength and life charge me like a bull and the tide of life surrounds the taste bud of the morne, and all the veins and veinlets busy themselves with new blood, and the enormous lung of the cyclones breathes and the hoarded fire of volcanoes and the gigantic seismic pulse now beats the measure of a body alive in my firm blazing. (Césaire 1995, 125)

Fanon did not always agree with Césaire and, as is well known, gently lampooned in *Black Skin* the essentializing aspects of *Cahier d'un retour*, a poem that nonetheless greatly influenced his own "seismic" posture as an essayist. Indeed, this passage foreshadows Fanon's focus on the body as a site of colonialism (tabularized by Blumenbach, Linné, and Francis Galton) *and* decolonization. The accumulation of biological details anticipates Fanon's own approach as a psychiatrist (and hence physician). For Fanon, who in Martinique and Algeria realized that medicine had been "an integral part of an oppressive system" (Macey 2012, 215), this focus on health, hygiene, and "life" is the premise of a decolonial future. The assassination of George Floyd in May 2020 has shown that breathing cannot be metaphorized and that, indeed, it would be ethically irresponsible to metaphorize it. But Fanon's own take on breathing was far more than a poetic stance. It was, as argued by Pheng Cheah, the product of Fanon's organicist approach:

> Fanon figures the temporal project of decolonization as the creation of a world in which one can "breathe" in a metaphorical sense. But one can very easily conflate this with the literal breathing of air as basic necessity of animal life for two reasons. First, temporalization, which is the ground of human existence, is generally apprehended as biological life because our loss of life and loss of time coincide. As individuals, we run out of time when we die. Second, there is an entire Western philosophical tradition that uses the vitality of organic life as a metaphorical template for understanding freedom. (Cheah 2016, 195)

In its fifty years of existence, the Africana Studies and Research Center at Cornell University has borne witness to decolonization and has registered the many manifestations of this process in the United States, the Caribbean, and Africa and where African diasporas, in the West and beyond, have engaged with the world and displayed their commitment for the emergence of a more equitable world. The contributors to this volume demonstrate that this task is all-encompassing and all-consuming. And still ongoing. Once burned down by white supremacists, the Africana Center has recovered and has continued to see, hear, and breathe. The context in which this fiftieth anniversary took place is, however, strangely reminiscent of the climate of racial violence that led to the criminal "pre-dawn fire" at 320 Wait Avenue in April 1970 (*Cornell Chronicle* 1970a). In an interview for the *Cornell Chronicle*, the then Africana Center director James E. Turner commented on this tragic incident and linked it to "the systematic cultural and political response of the white nation toward those black people oppressed in this country" (*Cornell Chronicle* 1970b). The depressing point is that these words could have been uttered today. Now rehoused at its former address, the center's task is gigantic. But where to start? "Start what? The only thing in the world worth starting: The End of the world, for Heaven's sake." (Césaire 1995, 99).

NOTES

1. I thank Maeve McCusker for providing me, at a time (January 2021) when access to libraries was very limited, with the page reference of this quote from the English-

language version of Chamoiseau's novella. Unless otherwise noted, translations are mine.

2. Hughes shows here that Jacques Derrida developed this argument in a letter addressed to Pierre Nora in 1961.

WORKS CITED

Barber, Karin. 1995. "African Language Literature and Postcolonial Criticism." *Research in African Literatures* 26 (4): 3–33.

———. 2007. *The Anthropology of Texts, Persons and Publics: Oral and Written Culture in Africa and Beyond.* Cambridge: Cambridge University Press.

Britton, Celia. 2008. *The Sense of Community in French Caribbean Fiction.* Liverpool: Liverpool University Press.

Calvet, Louis-Jean. 1974. *Linguistique et colonialisme: Petit traité de glottophagie.* Paris: Payot.

Camus, Albert. 1962. *L'Étranger.* In *Théâtre, récits, nouvelles.* Edited by Roger Quilliot. Paris: Gallimard.

Césaire, Aimé. 1947. *Cahier d'un retour au pays natal.* Paris: Bordas.

———. 1995. *Notebook of a Return to My Native Land / Cahier d'un retour au pays natal.* Translated by Mireille Rosello with Annie Pritchard. Newcastle upon Tyne, UK: Bloodaxe Books.

Chamoiseau, Patrick. 2018. *The Old Slave and the Mastiff.* Translated by Linda Coverdale. London: Dialogue Books.

Chamoiseau, Patrick, and Silyane Larcher. 2007. "Les Identités dans la totalité-Monde." *Cité* 29 (1): 121–134.

Cheah, Pheng. 2016. *What Is a World? On Postcolonial Literature as World Literature.* Durham, NC: Duke University Press.

Cornell Chronicle. 1970a. "Pre-Dawn Fire Destroys Africana Studies Center," April 5, 1970, p. 1.

———. 1970b. "Turner Issues Fire Statement," April 5, 1970, p. 2.

Diagne, Souleymane Bachir. 2019. *Postcolonial Bergson.* Translated by Lindsay Turner. New York: Fordham University Press.

Diop, Cheikh Anta. 1955. *Nations nègres et culture: De l'antiquité nègre égyptienne aux problèmes culturels de l'Afrique noire aujourd'hui.* Paris: Présence Africaine.

Eze, Emmanuel Chukwudi, ed. 1997. *Race and the Enlightenment: A Reader.* Malden, MA: Blackwell.

———. 2008. *On Reason: Rationality in a World of Cultural Conflict and Racism.* Durham, NC: Duke University Press.

Fabian, Johannes. 2002. *Time and Its Other: How Anthropology Makes Its Objects.* New York: Columbia University Press.

Fanon, Frantz. 1965. *A Dying Colonialism.* Translated by Haakon Chevalier. New York: Grove Press.

———. 2008. *Black Skin, White Masks.* Translated by Charles Lam Markmann. London: Pluto Press.

Gilroy, Paul. 1993. *The Black Atlantic: Modernity and Double Consciousness.* London: Verso.

Glissant, Édouard. 1981. *Le Discours antillais.* Paris: Seuil.

———. 1990. *Poétique de la relation.* Paris: Gallimard.

Hall, Stuart. 2019. "The West and the Rest: Discourse and Power." In *Essential Essays*, edited by David Morley, 2:141–184. Durham, NC: Duke University Press.

Hallen, Barry. 2009. *A Short History of African Philosophy*. 2nd ed. Bloomington: Indiana University Press.

Herbeck, Jason. 2005. "'Jusqu'aux limites de l'improvisation': Caribbean Identity and Jazz in Daniel Maximin's *L'Isolé soleil*." *Dalhousie French Studies* 71:161–175.

Higginson, Pim. 2017. *Scoring Race: Jazz, Fiction, and Francophone Africa*. Woodbridge, UK: James Currey.

Hughes, Edward J. 2015. *Albert Camus*. London: Reaktion Books.

James, Joy. 2003. "All Power to the People! Hannah Arendt's Theory of Communicative Power in a Racialized Democracy." In *Race and Racism in Continental Philosophy*, edited by Robert Bernasconi with Sybol Cook, 249–267. Bloomington: Indiana University Press.

Kunst, Hans-Joachim. 1967. *L'Africain dans l'art européen*. Bad Godesberg, Bonn, Germany: Inter Nationes.

Labat, Jean-Baptiste. 1724. *Nouveau Voyage aux isles de l'Amérique*. The Hague.

Lane, Jeremy. 2013. *Jazz and Machine-Age Imperialism: Music, "Race," and Intellectuals in France, 1918–1945*. Ann Arbor: University of Michigan Press.

Macey, David. 2012. *Frantz Fanon: A Biography*. 2nd ed. London: Verso.

Maximin. Daniel. 1981. *L'Isolé soleil*. Paris: Seuil.

———. 1987. *Soufrières*. Paris: Seuil.

———. 1995. *L'Île et une nuit*. Paris: Seuil.

Munro, Martin. 2007. "Listening to Caribbean History: Music and Rhythm in Daniel Maximin's *L'Isolé soleil*." *International Journal of Francophone Studies* 10 (3): 393–405.

Nancy, Jean-Luc. 1991. *The Inoperative Community*. Edited by Peter Connor; translated by Peter Connor, Lisa Garbus, Michael Holland, and Simona Sawhney. Minneapolis: University of Minnesota Press.

Rey, Alain, ed. 1998. *Le Robert. Dictionnaire historique de la langue française*. 3 vols. Paris: Le Robert.

Ricard, Alain. 2004. *The Languages and Literatures of Africa*. Oxford: James Currey.

Sartre, Jean-Paul. 1947. "Explication de *L'Étranger*." In *Critiques littéraires: Situations I*. Paris: Gallimard.

Schatz, Adam. 2015. "Stanger Still." *New York Times*, April 1, 2015.

Senghor, Léopold Sédar. 1939. "Ce que le noir apporte." In *L'Homme de couleur*, edited by Jean Verdier et al., 292–314. Paris: plon.

Toczyski, Suzanne C. 2007. "Navigating the Sea of Alterity: Jean-Baptiste Labat's *Nouveau voyage aux îles*." *Papers on French Seventeenth Century Literature* 34 (67): 1–25.

Contributors

AKIN ADEṢỌKAN is an associate professor of comparative literature at Indiana University Bloomington. He is the author of *Postcolonial Artists and Global Aesthetics* (Indiana University Press, 2011) and *Roots in the Sky, A Novel* (Festac, 2004).

JOHN E. DRABINSKI is Professor of African American Studies and Comparative Literature at University of Maryland. He is the author of *Sensibility and Singularity* (SUNY, 2001), *Godard between Identity and Difference* (Continuum, 2008), *Levinas and the Postcolonial: Race, Nation, Other* (Edinburgh University Press, 2011), and *Glissant and the Middle Passage: Philosophy, Beginning, Abyss* (University of Minnesota Press, 2019). He is coeditor of the *Journal of French and Francophone Philosophy.*

ZEYAD EL NABOLSY is a doctoral student at Cornell University's Africana Studies and Research Center. His work has been published in the *Journal of African Cultural Studies* and *Science and Society.*

GRANT FARRED is the author of *Long Distance Love: A Passion for Football* and *The Burden of Over-representation: Race, Sport, and Philosophy* (both Temple University Press, 2007 and 2018, respectively).

PIERRE-PHILIPPE FRAITURE is a professor of French studies at the University of Warwick. He is the author of *V. Y. Mudimbe: Undisciplined Africanism* (Liverpool University Press, 2013), *La Mesure de l'Autre: Afrique Subsaharienne et Roman Ethnographique de Belgique et de France (1918–1940)* (Editions Honoré Champion, 2007), and *Le Congo Belge et Son Récit à la Veille des Indépendances: Sous l'Empire du Royaume* (Editions L'Harmattan, 2003) and the editor of several volumes, including *The Mudimbe Reader* (University of Virginia Press, 2016).

Kasereka Kavwahirehi is a professor of francophone literature at the University of Ottawa. He is the author of *Politiques de la critique: Essai sur les limites et la réinvention de la critique francophone* (Éditions Hermann, 2021), *Y'en a marre! Philosophie et espoir social en Afrique* (Éditions Karthala, 2018), *Le prix de l'impasse. Christianisme africain et imaginaires politiques* (Peter Lang, 2013), and *V. Y. Mudimbe et la réinvention de l'Afrique: Poétique et politique de décolonisation des sciences humaines* (Brill, 2006).

Gregory Pardlo is a Pulitzer Prize–winning poet and the author of *Totem* (Copper Canyon, 2007), *Digest* (Four Way Books, 2014), and *Air Traffic: A Memoir of Ambition and Manhood in America* (Knopf, 2018). He is director of the master of fine arts program at Rutgers University–Camden.

Radwa Saad is a doctoral student at Cornell University's Africana Studies and Research Center.

Sarah Then Bergh is a doctoral candidate at Cornell University's Africana Studies and Research Center. She earned a bachelor of science in economics and a master of international relations at Aberystwyth University (Wales), and she was awarded the Alfred Zimmern Prize for her master's thesis. Her current research interests combine Africana philosophy, political and international relations theory, and musicology.

Index

www.ingramcontent.com/pod-product-compliance
Lightning Source LLC
Chambersburg PA
CBHW020354270326
41926CB00007B/425